# ALPHA BRA
## GUIDE TO

# STEALTH
# WARFARE

## DAVID ALEXANDER

**ALPHA**

A member of Penguin Group (USA) Inc.

*This book is dedicated to my niece, Miranda.*

International Standard Book Number: 1-59257-178-6
Library of Congress Catalog Card Number: 2004101837

06  05  04    8  7  6  5  4  3  2  1

Interpretation of the printing code: The rightmost number of the first series of numbers is the year of the book's printing; the rightmost number of the second series of numbers is the number of the book's printing. For example, a printing code of 04-1 shows that the first printing occurred in 2004.

*Printed in the United States of America*

# CONTENTS

# FOREWORD

*Stealth* is defined as secret, clandestine, or surreptitious. Since the beginning of recorded warfare, armies have sought an advantage by the use of secret, clandestine, or surreptitious means. Rarely have stealth means been the decisive event leading to victory in battle, but they have been a major supporting attribute that helps shape the decisive strategy for military campaigns.

David Alexander has framed the essence of stealth warfare from the mythological beginning with the Trojan Horse to the modern technological marvels of stealth aircraft, submarines, and satellites. *Alpha Bravo Delta Guide to Stealth Warfare* is the most comprehensive open source reference to this field of military endeavor you will find. It is an excellent reference for the military professional as well as historians or the casual reader.

Stealth warfare is characterized by speed, surprise, and lethality. One or more of these attributes must be present for the stealth operation, item of equipment, or intelligence capability that embodies secret, clandestine, or surreptitious means to be effective. The United States has not always been comfortable with this type of warfare but has throughout its national history embraced stealth as an economy of force measure, political means, or as an operational necessity. Aspects of stealth warfare go against the "grain" for policymakers and some conventional military thinkers. This was aptly demonstrated between the world wars by Secretary of State Herbert Stimson's remark when the U.S. Army's "Black Chamber" decoding operation was discovered and the remark "Gentlemen, do not read another person's mail" was attributed to him. In the early and mid-1970s the Church Committee Investigations, subsequent legislation and presidential directives virtually incapacitated traditional human intelligence operations conducted by the CIA and the military services. Even with serious dissent and debate over the utility, efficiency, or legitimacy, when winning or losing and national security is the cost, the U.S. military goes all the way. Examples of this American phenomenon are the joint Ultra operations with the British, which was a war difference maker during World War II, and the current effort to revitalize the human intelligence programs to combat an asymmetrical enemy by removing the restrictions of the 1970s on this age-old form of stealth warfare.

David Alexander has skillfully outlined the history of stealth warfare, carefully weaving it into the American military genre by focusing specific warfare events, real and imagined, beginning with basic soldiering and ending with the modern stealth aircraft, submarines, missiles, mines, drones, robots, and the individual soldiers' combat equipment. The most striking aspect of this guide is the technical realities that are vividly described from the beginning of the high reconnaissance programs (U-2 and SR 71) as well as the overhead satellite (Corona) program. The understanding gained from the tactical histories and operational capabilities of the F-117A Nighthawk and the B2 provides an understanding of the vast superiority the United States has in the air in regard to stealth technology. This is equally true on and below the seas as well as on the ground. Conversely, also described are the vulnerabilities of our stealth programs to lesser or outdated technological inferior systems. Highlighted is the not fully explained downing of an F-117 Nighthawk in Kosovo by a possible antiquated SA-3 missile SAM system.

In conclusion, the vastness of the stealth requirement for the U.S. military is underscored by the threats of the twenty-first century. If America is to successfully combat the complete spectrum of warfare from the conventional through the nuclear, biological, and chemical weapons of mass destruction (WMD) to the asymmetrical forces throughout the world, the stealth concepts from the individual soldier all the way to space must be exploited. Although not an end within itself, modern warfare today cannot be successfully concluded without a significant stealth advantage. Speed, surprise, and lethality will continue to be the *sine qua non* of these very special capabilities.

Col. John G. Lackey (Ret.), U.S. Army
Colonel Lackey is currently the Deputy Commandant of Cadets at The Citadel in Charleston, South Carolina, and former director of intelligence of the Joint Special Operations Command during Desert Storm.

# INTRODUCTION

Warfare is the art of deceit.

—Sun-tzu

There is an ancient Hindu myth that tells of how Shiva, the all-seeing, illuminated the universe by the beams of brilliance that shot forth from his eyes. The light was a form of super-radar that permeated every corner of the universe. No crevice of the cosmos was free from it. No danger was hidden from Shiva's sight. All was well in the universe.

Then came Parvati, Shiva's wife. One day Parvati stole up behind Shiva and playfully covered his eyes. Parvati didn't even have a chance to ask "Guess who?" In that instant the cosmos went darker than a black cat in a coal scuttle at midnight.

With the all-seeing light of Shiva suddenly extinguished, the enemies of mankind erupted from the Underworld where they had waited for their chance to strike. In this total darkness the evil ones subjected humankind to an orgy of destruction. It was a war fought in total darkness in which the beasts from the pit held all the cards.

Before it was too late Shiva performed a miracle. He opened a third eye in the center of his forehead. The inner light of Shiva's godlike being had been concentrated within him, building up like a charge of electricity inside a dynamo. When the third eye opened, this beam of light issued forth with incredible power. The light scattered the darkness. The evil ones shriveled as if struck with a laser. Forever after, say the Hindus, the third eye of Shiva has shone on the universe, revealing all.

In this myth of Shiva is found one of the oldest known parables of stealth warfare. There are probably older ones still. The quest for stealth is as old as human conflict and as basic as the quest for fire.

In fact it is in many respects the direct opposite of the quest for fire, whose heat and light promise security and defense against attack. In darkness there is vulnerability to all the perils that lurk unseen on the periphery. Because the visual sense is the most highly developed and essential of the five senses, to impair it is to emasculate, to take it away is to strip away the warrior's shield.

Shiva's power to defend was rooted in the power of his eyes. In the Bible story Samson was deprived of his strength when he was blinded by Delilah, and vision—physically and metaphorically—has always been closely linked with power. In modern warfare, one of a commander's first axioms is "you can't kill what you can't see," and preparing a strike to decimate the enemy is sometimes referred to a strategy of "emasculation."

Even older—by millions of years—are nature's experiments in stealth warfare. What might be considered the oldest radar system ever developed (and still in use today) is the biological ultrasonic sensor system of the common garden variety bat—bat-radar.

As Cooper Man—the only living person known to have flunked the Army I.Q. test—found out to his chagrin while night manager of a decrepit Borscht Belt hotel I worked at one long-ago summer, bats are pretty good at finding their way around in the dark and avoiding being swatted.

As bats fly around they send out ultrasonic chirps through their noses. These pulses of ultrasonic energy bounce off objects and the echoes are received by the bat's shell-like ears, the equivalent of radar dishes. The workings of bats' ears is virtually identical to that of pulse-Doppler radar, except for the fact that sonic rather than electromagnetic radiation is used to "illuminate" the targets. But the rest is pretty much the same: pulse-Doppler target tracking, terrain avoidance, and fine-angle measurement based on a monopulse principle.

So okay, you probably knew all this stuff already. But you didn't even begin to think about Mother Nature's countermeasures to the bat's radar, now did you? And this is the whole point of the story illustrating stealth warfare. For our bat of the Borscht Belt isn't just interested in not bumping into Cooper Man in the lobby of the decrepit hotel. Borschtie the bat wants something to eat. Which brings us to consideration of the fact that what Borschtie wants to devour doesn't want to end up in Borschtie's stomach. And so, Mother Nature in her wisdom has equipped some of bats' prey with countermeasures to the bat's biological radar system.

Take Timmy the tiger moth, for example. Built into Timmy's neurological circuitry is a biological detector-jammer that is precisely tuned to the specific frequency of Borschtie's ultrasonic chirps. When Borschtie's bat radar homes in on Timmy, our plucky moth sends out chirp pulses that cancel out those from Borschtie's nasal emitter.

At the same time Timmy wisely takes evasive action. The result: Timmy lives to fly on another night while Borschtie has to go suck a mosquito or, worse yet, contend with Cooper Man, who hated bats in his lobby.

The stories about Shiva and our little Aesopian fable of the bat and the moth illustrate a basic principle of stealth warfare, but by no means is this all there is to the subject. Thinking about stealth warfare in these terms may be familiar to us because of radar and planes, but it is somewhat misleading. Stealth warfare encompasses considerably more than electronic ranging and detection, countermeasures, and counter-countermeasures. Stealth warfare includes within its purview camouflage and deception (which in the pages to follow will often be referred to by the Russian term *maskirovka*), ciphers and crypts, and even more exotic things such as nanoweaponry and psychic warfare.

Stealth has been a quality of warfare since time immemorial. Mankind has sought after its magical properties since the days of the cave. Warriors, commanders of troops in the field, kings, potentates, and mercenaries throughout history have sought to make themselves stealthy and at the same time defeat the stealthy stratagems of their enemies in order to prevail. The "cloak" has always opposed the "dagger" in a never-ending cycle of move and countermove.

In mankind's long history of warfare it is not only the gods who have availed themselves of stealth. The Japanese martial art of Ninjutsu literally means the fighting art of stealth, and the ninja warrior's mastery of his discipline is intended to enable him to move like a shadow and strike the enemy unseen. The ancient Chinese military strategist Sun-tzu, who is these days quoted by Western generals as often as they once quoted Clausewitz, also devoted considerable philosophical bandwidth to discussing stealth warfare.

The Romans were not prone to using stealth in warfare and suffered near-defeat at the hands of Hannibal, who was a master of deception and evasion strategy. Napoleon Bonaparte's crossing of the Alps to invade Austria in 1800 reenacted Hannibal's earlier crossing some two thousand years before, in 218 B.C.E.

Early commandos in the French and Indian Wars, Rogers's Rangers, used stealth, and Rogers's rules of irregular warfare laid down techniques of surprise and stealth in attack. Deception strategies were used by beleaguered colonial forces during the American Revolution. General U. S. Grant was also a stealthy strategist, and Union forces were able to surprise Confederate troops where and when they least expected it throughout the Civil War. Grant, who had attended West Point with Lee and other generals of the opposition, was said to be able to know what his opponents were thinking practically before they themselves even knew it.

Of course there's also the most famous illustration of stealth warfare in history—the Trojan Horse. I left it for last because it's undoubtedly semi-mythical, but if it happened it sure helped the invaders make Greek salad out of the Trojans.

Modern examples of stealth warfare are too numerous to mention, but the Second World War is notable because it not only marks the birth of stealth aircraft technology but also because it was largely won by deception and in fact represents the first wide-ranging military deception campaign in history. In the days of World War II, the modern definition of stealth warfare became crystallized into what we know it to be today. The military art of strategic deception was practiced by both sides, and affected the outcome of the war.

In fact, a strong case could be made for the Allied side winning because of this campaign due to their having had a form of military intelligence code-named Ultra. This stood for intercepts of German (and later Japanese) coded messages encrypted on the Enigma cipher machine.

Enigma had been developed in Germany in the early years of the Nazi regime and was intended to be an absolutely secure encipherment system. The Nazis believed that it was impenetrable right to the end. It might have been all the Germans thought it to be, had the British not acquired an Enigma through covert channels a few years before war was declared.

After Germany's invasion of Poland in 1939 and the subsequent British declaration of war, and after U.S. entry into the fight following Pearl Harbor, the existence of Ultra intercepts meant that the Allies had a window on the inner councils of the *Oberkommando Wehrmacht* or OKW (the Nazi high command), on commanders in the field, on Third Reich insiders such as Göring and Himmler, and even on Hitler himself. Even so, winning the war was a near-done thing.

Today this "fifth dimension of warfare," as vision statements by the three U.S. service arms refer to those intangibles such as operations in the electromagnetic realm, is critical to the prosecution of war. Tomorrow, where target acquisition by remote sensors will doubtless prove as good as having made a missile kill, the issue will not be about firepower per se but about which weapon gains the critical edge of detection before the other. At the same time, the size of many fielded military forces will shrink, as it already has begun to do, and these will become more agile, mobile and lethal. Stealth will be a force-multiplier and combat-enabler for military systems of all kinds as twenty-first–century warfare develops.

Not only will aircraft benefit from stealthy technology applications. Main battle tanks and armored personnel carriers will also need to be con- structed along stealthier lines to avoid detection by radar and thermal imaging, and tomorrow's stealth technologies and tactics will also have to contend with new methods of detection, such as passive radars and laser radars (or ladars), and other invisible threats to friendly forces.

In order to meet the challenges ahead, stealth will have to evolve beyond even its most ambitious and exotic applications today. Tomorrow, stealth may not just mean invisibility to radar, but invisibility to the naked eye. Planes, tanks, ships—anything on the battlefield—may be equipped to vanish from the view of the enemy, to pop out of existence not merely on radar screens but out of human sight as well. These systems are already being tested; the technology exists to make them realities before too long.

More ancient forms of stealth warfare may also find new realizations in the battlespace of the twenty-first century. Indian researchers, in a project being undertaken by the Defense Research and Development Organi- zation in association with the University of Pune, are studying an ancient

Vedic text for methods that can be used to make modern soldiers not only more stealthy but better fighting machines.

*The Arthashastra*, a textbook for the warrior, was written by Kautilya, a prime minister under Emperor Chandragupta Maurya. Kautilya, who claimed that a ruler should use any means to win and that his actions required no moral sanction, wrote about how troops could become invisible, endow themselves with night vision by special dietary and yogic practices, and fight without eating for an entire month.

"All of us are excited about the possibilities and do not for a moment think the idea is crazy," said Professor S. V. Bhavasar, who has spent the last decade delving into *The Arthashastra*'s secrets.

Whether or not this ambitious experimental Indian program succeeds, one thing is sure: Stealth warfare is at a threshold today. It will ultimately, and very soon, change warfare on every level in the twenty-first century. It will become the dominant enabler of weapon systems. It will permeate all aspects of the art of war, from robotic weaponry to the soldier on the battlefield. The age of stealth warfare will then finally be upon us. Stealth will redefine warfare. It will change the concept of peace.

This is its story.

## Special Thanks to the Technical Reviewer

*Alpha Bravo Delta Guide to Stealth Warfare* was reviewed by an expert who double-checked the accuracy of what is presented here, to help us ensure that this book gives you everything you need to know about stealth warfare. Special thanks are extended to Lt. Col. George A. Larson, (Ret.) USAF.

# PART 1

# THE PRECURSORS OF MODERN STEALTH

We've talked a little in the introduction about ancient stealth in warfare, the precursors of the modern systems and combat doctrines that have preceded stealth warfare as we know it today.

Obviously stealth has been around awhile. Ancient man wasn't less intelligent than us, after all; he just lacked the technological means to realize many of his ideas. But to whatever extent it could, humankind used stealth tactics and technologies in warfare to achieve combat ends.

Before discussing contemporary stealth, we must ground ourselves in the stealth of the ancients and early moderns.

# CHAPTER 1

# STEALTH WARFARE IN HISTORY

The war went on for ten long, bloody years. The supreme military power of the age launched wave after wave of assaults on the distant target and was thrown back each time.

The city still stood. Safe behind the protection of its impenetrable defenses its leader mocked his adversaries and their reliance on technological gimmicks to win the war. He rallied his people to hurl the invaders into the sea from which they had come. He promised the enemy would never succeed, no matter how hard they tried.

It was the twelfth century B.C.E. The city was Troy. The leader, named Priam, was referring to the Achaeans who came from Greece, a nation of many islands scattered across the Aegean and Ionian seas. Troy, located on the coast of what is today Turkey, had challenged the military superpower of the age and so far had emerged unbeaten if not victorious. Priam surmised that the Achaeans would, to use one of Colin Powell's favorite phrases, "declare victory and go home" if only Troy could hold out a little longer.

Priam wasn't wrong. The Greeks decided to do just this. They all but wrote off the battle to seize Troy as a failure. From the ramparts of their stout walls, Trojan spies detected enemy movements that seemed to indicate that the Achaean fleet was about to set sail for home.

The Achaeans were in the final stages of preparation to leave the shores of Turkey when one of their number named Epeus suggested a bold stratagem that might snatch victory from the jaws of defeat. If Troy could not be taken by force of arms, it might be vanquished by deception, stealth, and guile. Epeus proposed that the Achaeans build a gigantic horse of wood. The enormous wooden statue would be hollow inside. Within its interior a company of Greek warriors could easily be concealed.

The preparations for departure of the fleet continued without interruption, but behind the scenes the giant statue envisioned by Epeus was being hastily built. Greek warriors vied with one another for the honor of being selected to be part of the plan. The contingent that was finally picked was composed of the finest of the Greek fighting force. While the horse was being prepared, the Greeks secretly practiced the fighting techniques that they would need to master to pull off the operation.

In nightly councils before the campfire, the tight-knit group and its commanders discussed the practice drills of the previous day. The commanders determined that the operation could succeed if brought off with clockwork precision and flawless teamwork. They decided to divide the small force into three squads. The smallest team would unlock the city gates. The other two would take care of any guards. They would need to be able to practice fighting in darkness, because their emergence from the horse was planned as a night operation.

When the warriors finished their mission analysis, they fell into excited talk of what coming battle betokened. As first to enter the city they would be first to plunder the treasures of Troy. In the custom of war this booty would include license to rape and slaughter.

As they drank the dark Thracian wine that came from huge amphorae in the holds of their black ships, the Achaean commandos' talk grew more brazen. Each strove to outdo his companions in boasting of how he would rape and plunder and kill, each vying with the other to top the last boast with a fresh and even bolder one.

The day of the operation soon arrived. The enormous horse was ready and the platoon of elite fighters took its place on benches built into the sides of the statue's interior. The cunningly constructed hatch, made to appear invisible from the outside, was closed. The men sat silently in darkness, cradling their swords, spears, and long archers' bows, patiently waiting for the moment to strike, as they had been trained to do.

The Trojans were as relieved as they were puzzled when they saw a crew of Greeks drag the immense statue to the city gate, and then hasten back to shore to join the throng boarding the black ships, many of which had already departed. Before the day was out the last of the invaders' vessels was under sail.

Rejoicing in their victory the Trojans made a fatal error. Instead of suspecting a trap and setting fire to the horse, they let their guard down and poured from the city gates to inspect this strange object left behind by their enemies. They were sealing their fates and falling into the Greeks' plans. As they scrambled around the horse the black ships hove to just over the horizon. They would wait there till after darkness, when a fiery arrow would signal the mission's success. Then they would return and capture the prize that had eluded them for so many years.

Meanwhile a lone Greek in rags staggered onto the scene. His name was Sinon and he posed as a deserter from the main force. Sinon begged for asylum. The Trojans offered it to him if he could explain the meaning of the horse. Already knowing the part he was to play, Sinon glibly recited the story he'd memorized as part of the invasion plan. The horse, he said, was an offering to the Greeks' war goddess, Athena. He also added, with apparent guilelessness, that should the Trojans take the horse inside the city gates Athena would bring destruction upon the Achaean fleet before it could return home.

Hearing this, some of the Trojans, already besotted by drink, formed a squad to drag the horse inside Troy. The others cheered them on. Before they could carry this out the high priest Laocoön stepped forward. Using his staff he bloodied the head of the first man who touched the horse. The priest shouted at his jubilant people in warning. This Greek Sinon was obviously a traitor and a spy in their midst. Destroy this horse at once, he commanded.

It was not to be.

At that moment two immense sea serpents appeared from the shore, slithering their way toward the city gates. Before Laocoön could finish his exhortations to the crowd, they twined themselves around him and began to squeeze the life out of him. When Laocoön's two sons intervened, they too fell prey to the serpents. The crowd believed that Sinon was telling the truth as these apparitions dragged the three limp corpses back into the sea and disappeared. Solaced by this portent, they dragged the horse inside the gates of Troy.

The rest, as they say, is history. That night, as the Trojans slept soundly, aided by the stupefying power of the wine they had freely indulged in throughout the day of celebration, Sinon unfastened the secret door in the side of the horse. The warriors within sprang from the interior in which they had hidden and went to work. Sinon joined them in drawing first blood with a sword they had thrown him, which he thrust into the heart of one of the guards posted inside the city gate. As one of the soldiers shot a fiery arrow into the sky, the black ships made haste to return to the Trojan shore. Before the Trojans could react, the Greeks poured in through the wide-open gates, winning by stealth in one bold, decisive stroke what they had been unable to win through ten long years of conventional war.

Despite the embellishments of this myth, to which I admit to having freely added in the course of my narrative, there is probably more than a little basis in fact. History teaches that while stealth warfare was practiced more in the breach than in the act in ancient military campaigns, it was a recognized part of strategy and tactics that was used by wise and cunning commanders.

Stealth warfare could not have more than a niche application in ancient forms of warfare because of the primitive stage of technology, but where possible it was often used to defeat the enemy, and certain commanders, known for relying on stealth and deception in warfare, have earned perpetual fame thereby to this day.

## GIDEON VERSUS THE MIDIANITES

Although we don't know the name of the commander who okayed Epeus's plan to build the Trojan horse, we do know the name of another early commander who did use stealth warfare. This was Gideon, who in the thirteenth century B.C.E., according to the Bible, used stealth warfare to outwit and destroy Israel's ancient foe, the Midianites. According to the Book of Judges in the Old Testament, Gideon ordered his troops to use a tactic that would be repeated by Gen. Patton in World War II; he ordered a deception campaign to convince the enemy that he had an extra army waiting in the wings, ready to stage a flank attack when his main forces had engaged.

Patton's bogus First United States Army Group in England relied on radio transmissions, dummy barracks, and flipped double agents to give it the semblance of reality, but Gideon was able to bring off his deception strategy merely by having a handful of his troops duplicate the sounds of an army preparing to move. Spears clashed, trumpets sounded, earthen vessels clattered, chains clanked, hammers pounded, voices cried out lustily on the desert winds.

The ploy had its intended result; the Midianites broke and ran in the opposite direction, right into an ambush by Gideon's real force. The result—well, you can eat a nice knish in Tel Aviv but just try to find a good Midianite restaurant anywhere these days.

# HANNIBAL OF CARTHAGE

Another great military commander who is notorious for having used stealth warfare to bring his opponents to their knees was Hannibal of Carthage. Many military historians consider Hannibal to be the founding father of stealth warfare, in fact. In the third century B.C.E. Hannibal effectively used deception tactics to shred a much larger and far better equipped Roman army at a decisive battle at Lake Trasimenus.

By hiding his forces and waiting until darkness, when he knew a dense mist from the lake would descend on the battlefield, he was able to achieve devastating tactical surprise against his enemies. The result was total slaughter, a defeat of the mighty and heretofore unvanquished Roman legions such as had never before been witnessed. Said the Greek historian Polybius of the battle (unknowingly summing up the main strategy of stealth warfare in the bargain), "While they [the Romans] tried to think what to do, they were slain without realizing how."

Later, at the battle of Cannae, Hannibal again used deception to trick an even larger Roman army into marching into a deadly ambush that was to result in over 50,000 Romans killed, a body count that was ten to one in favor of Hannibal's losses.

Hannibal went about his strategy this way: While encamped before battle, the Romans began receiving a steadily increasing number of deserters from the Carthaginian camp. The deserters began appearing in groups, pledging to join the Roman forces and telling convincing stories of how Hannibal could be defeated.

While the Romans were busy deciding what to do with this unexpected windfall, the large force of "deserters" that had assembled within the Roman ranks drew their swords and began to take out targets of opportunity. While this bloody and sneaky diversion was being staged, Hannibal launched raids by larger forces, always retreating again to strike from a different direction the next time. By means of these tactics he was able to whittle the Romans down to the butt end, and stage an all-out attack to slaughter the hollow force that was left.

The Romans, hidebound military strategists who did not favor stealth, fell for tactics such as these time and again, until there was virtually nothing left to oppose Hannibal's invasion of Italy itself. Only when the Carthaginians were almost at the gates of Rome was Cornelius Scipio given command. Unlike his predecessors, Scipio realized the value of stealth warfare and developed strategies that turned the game around on Hannibal. In the end the Romans proved not only to have outmastered Hannibal in deception but to have outdone him at the game. Promising to spare Carthage should Hannibal surrender, Caesar went back on Rome's pledge and ordered the city razed, and then the land was to be sown with salt so that nothing would ever grow there.

It's worth noting that the word "Punic," when used as an adjective, has long been synonymous with treachery. The word Punic is synonymous with Carthage and is the reason why the wars between ancient Rome and Carthage are collectively known as the Punic Wars. Because it's the winners of wars who usually write the histories, the strategic deception used by Hannibal that caused the Romans so much grief has tinged the very name of Carthage with the aura of treachery forever.

Carthage is still a desert today. Muammar Qaddafi runs what's left of it. I'm told he's interested in bringing in American tourists to visit Carthaginian ruins.

## BATTLE OF LEPANTO, 1571

On the high seas, stealth warfare played a key role in the strategy of Uluch Ali, commander of the Turks at the Battle of Lepanto. It was 1571 and the Turks were about to stage a long-awaited invasion of Europe. By a series of clever tactical feints, Ali gulled Genoese admiral Andria Doria into leaving unprotected gaps in the center of his skirmish line through which the nimbler Turkish vessels were able to maneuver in close. The fact that an oceanliner by the same name sank off the coast of New York City in the 1950s testifies to the fact that the European forces prevailed, if only by the slimmest of margins.

## AMERICAN WAR OF INDEPENDENCE

Closer to home (and as already mentioned), deception strategies were used by beleaguered colonial forces to combat the British in the War of Independence. By December 1776, Gen. George Washington was facing the bitter prospect of defeat. Both Fort Washington and Fort Lee had fallen to the Redcoats, his troops were cold, hungry, and dispirited, and his reserves of ammunition low.

Washington saw no choice but to withdraw his force of approximately 5,000 battle-weary troops across the Delaware River into eastern Pennsylvania to rest at a place called Valley Forge. It was one of the coldest winters on record and the populace gave the rebels little help. Washington's troops were starving. Their morale was at its lowest ebb. The British could sense the nearness of victory. Lord Sir William Howe, commander of Crown forces, instructed the theater commander, Maj. Gen. Charles Lord Cornwallis, to return to England. There he was to report to Parliament that the rebellion was on the verge of being stamped out.

Seeing that the nearest outpost of the Crown to the rebel encampment was Trenton, New Jersey, Howe assigned Gen. Johan Rahl, the commander of the Hessian mercenaries employed by the Crown, to detach a small force of 1,200 Hessian troops to garrison the town. Rahl, who mocked Washington's troops as "country clowns," took few precautions. The German held the Americans in such contempt that he didn't even bother building earthworks around Trenton—a basic defensive measure of the era.

Bored with this schwarmerei, the Hessians proceeded to get drunk on Trenton's home brew, parade around to something resembling oompah music, and generally raise a lot of hell instead of soldiering. Unknown to them, Washington had a spy in Trenton, a butcher named John Honeyman. On Washington's orders he became an espionage mole in the Hessians' midst.

Honeyman claimed that he was a deserter who had been captured by American rangers and sentenced to death at a court martial, and then escaped during a fire in the guard house. Washington had ordered some of these events deliberately staged where known British spies could witness them to bolster Honeyman's "legend," and so Rahl bought the scam hook, line, and sinker.

Now burrowed deep into the Hessian ranks, Honeyman regularly made secret intelligence reports that went straight to Washington. Aware that the Hessians were dipping their wicks when they should have been on guard duty, Washington secretly moved his rebel army back across Delaware and divided his forces to envelop the town. At the same time he used a detachment of Continental Marines as an added deception maneuver. The Marines were ordered to fan out in directions other than Trenton so that enemy intelligence would assume that Washington intended to strike elsewhere than his intended target—shades of Schwarzkopf's Hail Mary play in 1991.

The layered deception campaign worked and Washington's force was able to achieve complete tactical surprise when it attacked Trenton. The battle was over in just under two hours. In its aftermath Rahl and 21 other Hessians lay dead and 200 managed to escape. Almost 900 surrendered to the Americans, drunk, half-asleep, and trying to shove their weenies back into their tights. Washington had won the day.

Howe, back in New York, had second thoughts about what he'd told Cornwallis to say to Parliament. Canceling his sailing orders, he was instead commanded to assemble a Redcoat force 10,000 strong and take Trenton back from the upstart Americans. By the evening of January 2, 1777, Crown forces under Cornwallis were encamped along the banks of the Assunpink Creek, athwart the southern approach to Trenton near the Delaware River. This put the British perilously close to Washington's troops who were barely 150 yards away.

Washington's strategy was to use deception again to turn the tables on the Redcoats. Learning of Cornwallis's advance through his network of spies, Washington had already set the stage for the stealthy withdrawal by a variety of techniques.

The wheels of American field artillery were muffled by blankets, and so were the boots of the soldiery and the hooves of horses, draped Indian-style in cloth. Thousands of men with weapons and beasts of burden moved out so silently that even rebel officers billeted in farmhouses along the line of march—kept out of the loop for security reasons—were unaware of what was taking place.

The retreating force left behind a skeleton force of about 400 men. These had instructions to stage diversions behind the lines in order to cover the retreat. The stay-behinds kept scores of campfires blazing and stole a page from Gideon's campaign book by smacking shovels into the frost-hardened ground to simulate the sounds of an army digging in before combat.

Unaware that the Americans were long gone, the Redcoats marched from their positions at first light on the cold morning of January 3, 1777. They passed the dead ashes of the cold campfires that their scouts had seen blazing throughout the night. They crossed Assunpink Creek to the rebel's encampment. But they found nothing except an empty snow field awaiting them. While in the end Washington was forced to give up Trenton and Princeton again and withdraw across the Delaware River into Morristown, Pennsylvania, he had shown the British that the Americans were not pushovers, and had scored a major psychological victory that afterward was translated into improved morale and a revived will to take the fight to the enemy.

In the end the British lost the colonies, defeated by the stealth warfare tactics of the wily American general. A century and a half later, in World

War II, they would prove themselves masters of the arts of military deception and stealth, and teach their American Allies a few new tricks.

## ROBERT ROGERS'S STANDING ORDERS

During the French and Indian Wars, Captain Robert Rogers, a Massachusetts native, commanded an irregular unit made up of New Hampshire colonists known as Rogers's Rangers. Rogers composed a list of standing orders to his men that became the basic operating principles of U.S. commando operations. Though Rogers's unit was disbanded in 1763, the army named its own commando units after it when they were formed during World War II. Thereafter they would be called Rangers. Here are the stealthiest of Robert Rogers's nineteen rules of commando warfare:

3.  When you're on the march, act the way you would if you was sneaking up on a deer. See the enemy first.
5.  Don't never take a chance you don't have to.
7.  If we strike swamps, or soft ground, we spread out abreast, so it's hard to track us.
8.  When we march, we keep moving till dark, so as to give the enemy the least possible chance at us.
10.  Don't ever march home the same way. Take a different route so you won't be ambushed.
12.  No matter whether we travel in big parties or little ones, each party has to keep a scout 20 yards ahead. 20 yards on each flank and 20 yards in the rear, so the main body can't be surprised and wiped out.
15.  Don't sleep beyond dawn. Dawn's when the French and Indians attack.
17.  If somebody's trailing you, make a circle, come back onto your own tracks, and ambush the folks that aim to ambush you.
18.  Don't stand up when the enemy's coming against you. Kneel down, lie down, hide behind a tree.
19.  Let the enemy come till he's almost close enough to touch. Then let him have it and jump out and finish him up with your hatchet.

Words to live by, if I ever heard them.

# THE BIRTH OF STEALTH WARFARE

Not far from the Eiffel Tower in Paris is the French Army Museum. As soon as you enter the museum lobby you understand what combat meant for thousands of years, before the age of mechanized warfare changed everything. It's impossible to escape the realization that the nature of warfare did not change in its basic form for thousands of years. Men marched to battle in the timeless serried ranks of infantry, met on a field of battle, methodically slaughtered each other with swords and spears, and then afterward the living went forth as victors or slaves, or sometimes as neither but only to regroup to roll the dice in battle on another day.

Later, mounted cavalry came into widespread use, but the underlying principle remained unchanged: To win you had to turn, encircle, and then break the massed infantry and cavalry formations, wipe them out, or set them to rout. Good commanders tried to place their forces on high ground, with the sun in the faces of the advancing enemy; they tried to have a river or a defile at the enemy's back. A routed enemy could be driven into one of these natural obstacles and hacked to pieces, as Alexander did to his foes in the battle at the Granicus River.

This was the kind of war Rome fought, it was the way the great *condotierri* of the Renaissance, such as Giovanni de la Bandi Neri or Cesare Borgia fought, and later it was the way Napoleon's Grand Army fought at Austerlitz and after that the way the British-German coalition under Wellington fought the French to a standstill at Waterloo.

It was in the final great battle of the nineteenth century, the Franco-Prussian war of 1870, that the face of warfare began to change, although the change is more evident in hindsight than it was at the time. In that war the Prussian army adopted the new steel cannonry manufactured by Krupp, the steel miller–turned–armorer of Essen, in Germany's Ruhr Valley. Krupp's steel artillery could shoot farther, faster, more accurately, and far longer without damaging the barrel or "tube" as artillerymen call it.

The French were decimated—slaughtered might be an even more apt descriptive term—by the completely unexpected onslaught of the Prussians' superior cannonry. They shouldn't have been surprised, because Krupp had tried to sell them his advanced guns first.

Nor did the French appreciate at the time that they had the distinction of being subjected to the first legitimate example of what we today would call standoff attack. Without knowing it, the Germans were pioneering one of the basic principles of stealth combat—the ability to strike from afar, without confronting the enemy in traditional close-quarter combat. By using high-tech weaponry—the steel cannonry from the industrial Ruhr—the Prussians were able to avoid the heavy reliance upon the age-old tactic of mounted cavalry and massed infantry in battle.

Instead, it was the French, who attacked in this time-tested fashion, who saw their men and horses mowed down in windrows by high-explosive and grapeshot long before the drawn swords of the mounted cuirassiers could draw the enemy's blood.

Stealth warfare was born on that battlefield. Until that time, it had been theory; now it was fact, only nobody realized it yet. They would, before very long.

# CHAPTER 2

# STEALTH WARFARE IN WORLD WAR I

Between the Franco-Prussian War and World War I, the Western nations subsided into a comparatively long interim of peace and international trade. These were the years of the Belle Epoch, of glittering society and shipping magnates who amassed huge fortunes. The casino at Monte Carlo had just been built by Prince Albert of Monaco. The grand casino attracted the international set whose unrestricted movements mirrored the free flow of capital across the continents and seas.

It was also an era of continuing technological innovation and development in the instruments of warfare. Behind the scenes revolutionary inventions were already being perfected; these would provide warfare with the scale it needed to balloon into a global conflict before the end of the second decade of the coming century. The airplane, the tank, the submarine, wireless communications, and many other innovations were on the drawing boards or in early prototype stages.

The sensitive antennae of authors such as Jules Verne and H. G. Wells were already sketching out the ways these new weapons would be used to fight the frightening new wars of the onrushing future.

Verne, inspired by the cannonry of Krupp, wrote of an enormous cannon that could propel space travelers to the moon and of a super-submarine, the Nautilus, that cruised stealthily beneath the waters of the ocean to attack ships before vanishing back into the depths.

The captain of the Nautilus, whose very name "Nemo" bespoke the eerie insubstantiality of stealth warfare, was the archetype of the super-villain whose obsession with the technology of war presaged the totalitarian dictators to follow a generation later.

## DISPELLING THE STEREOTYPES OF WORLD WAR I

The Germans principally fought along conventional lines in World War I, but the Allies had devised a more dynamic approach to the challenges of combat. Not long after the war began, the Allies shifted from a top-down, stovepiped command structure to a more decentralized approach to operations emphasizing small mobile units that could strike and withdraw with speed and lethality. Aerial dogfights between enemy air aces is another World War I stereotype, but while these did certainly take place, they were generally fought to clear the skies of enemy air cover so that observation aircraft could fly in low over the battlefield and gather photographic reconnaissance data, another innovation that the Allies used to great advantage. Another Allied innovation largely absent or little used on the German side was the replacement of cavalry by the newly developed tank, and four-legged beasts of burden with mechanized armor in general.

## THE WAR IN THE AIR

As previously mentioned, the conflict's leading contribution to the development of stealth warfare was the introduction of the airplane to the battlefield. It was not the first time in warfare that combatants could take to the air—balloons had already been used—but it was certainly the first time that heavier-than-air flying machines were equipped for the purposes of warfare. (Balloons, too, came into new use in World War I, but more on this in a moment.)

The purposes of aircraft were threefold: first, to conduct aerial surveillance, which was necessary to obtain intelligence on the displacement of enemy strong points and artillery batteries; second, to get bomb damage assessment intelligence so that friendly forces could exploit the damage already done to opposition forces; and third to engage in bombing and aerial dogfighting missions.

Allied aerial surveillance was a deadly contest between pilot, plane, and ground troops. Surveillance planes were usually preceded by aircraft equipped for fighter-bomber missions, which skirmished with enemy aircraft and were fired at by antiaircraft guns on the ground, known in British war slang as "Archibalds."

The surveillance planes followed after the air aces had shot it out in the skies overhead. They then came sweeping over the enemy trenches at low altitude and high speed, contrasting with the dogfighters who overflew at high ceilings. The Archibalds now fell silent; their barrels were already overheated from trying to hit the high-fliers, and besides, the incoming planes were vectoring in too low to be safely hit by a German artillery shell without the shooters killing themselves with their own shrapnel.

Instead, the Germans opened up with rifle and machine-gun fire as the planes swept only a few hundred feet over the tops of the trenches, so close that the troops on the ground could see the steel plates and rivets on their underbellies, so close that the stink of the Spad's engine exhaust was almost as powerful a smell as the stench of cordite belched from the defenders' own guns.

Where the fighter planes were light and equipped with automatic guns fore and aft, the surveillance aircraft were heavily armored and equipped with surveillance cameras instead of guns. The cameras they carried could be enormous—their telescoping barrels five or six feet in length. The surveillance planes were designed to take hits and keep on flying. The head and thorax of the pilot and the gas tank were considered the only vital areas. The pilots of these planes would make pass after pass directly over the heads of the enemy. Overflying the lengths of the German positions they would expose plate after plate of film.

In the process it was not unusual for planes to return with forty or fifty bullet holes in the fuselage. When the final photographic plate the pilot carried had been exposed he would return to base. The plates would be developed and the individual photos stitched together into a continuous panorama of many miles of battle front. Intelligence analysts would then pore over the photos, making bomb damage assessments on which to base new missions, and the process of reconnaissance, attack, and then fresh reconnaissance, would begin all over again.

## DECEPTION ON THE GROUND

The ability of aircraft to accurately sight enemy positions from the air gave rise to the first modern use of stealth warfare—camouflage and deception. Observers at the front, such as civilian reporters, were struck by the lengths that were taken to disguise artillery from detection by airborne surveillance assets.

Artillery, for the first time in warfare, was being painted in camouflage colors intended to make the heavy field pieces blend in to the natural background. Elaborate measures were for the first time being taken by armies in the field to avoid detection as a standard part of combat doctrine. Camouflage was an evolutionary development in the continuing battle between the antiaircraft artillery and the warplane.

The ability to take a camera into the air and bring back photographic intelligence—known today by the acronym PHOTINT—for careful analysis was a revolution in precision warfare. After every advance there would be a pause during which the big guns would be moved closer to enemy positions and planes would be sent up and fresh aerial intelligence gathered. Then another attack on German positions would relentlessly pound them.

The kaiser's side—on which my own great-grandfather fought at the time—had no such doctrine; largely as a result German counterattacks rarely succeeded. The Germans stubbornly clung to the combat doctrine of an already bypassed era. They attacked in close order formation while their opponents broke ranks and instead preceded attacks with pinpoint artillery preparation, using surveillance data to target their rounds. As a result the Germans were forced into fighting a defensive war and were often outflanked by the more mobile and technologically superior forces of the enemy.

The introduction of the "land ironclad" was also another revolutionary milestone on the road to stealth warfare. Considered secret weapons, these tracked vehicles were originally described as "tanks" on cargo manifests to conceal the truth. Likened to monstrous steel slugs by astonished observers, the tracked, armored war wagons struck fear and awe into friend and foe alike. Heavily armed, able to surmount obstacles with ease that would have bogged down even the hardiest living beast of burden, the tank was considered invincible.

"In the old attacks you used to see the British dead lying outside the machine-gun emplacements like birds outside a butt with a good shot inside," a British Tommy told H. G. Wells on his tour of a battlefield in the Somme campaign as a reporter, "now these things walk through."

Tank warfare might seem the direct antithesis of stealth, conjuring up visions of lumbering steel leviathans cutting swathes of destruction through enemy territory, but the tank was also an instrument of early stealth warfare. As the first expression of mechanized land warfare, the tank was also used to create a moving wall of armor behind which troops could be screened from enemy attack and reconnaissance alike. Tank warfare provided infantry with a form of active camouflage in other ways, too, such as the ability to lay down screens of smoke and noise to conceal the movements of ground forces during attacks and provide diversionary cover.

## STEALTH MARITIME WARFARE

In maritime warfare, stealth played an even more active part: World War I introduced the undersea boat or U-boat as an instrument of delivering silent death on the high seas to Allied commercial and military shipping vessels.

U-boats of the era were not actual submarines as they were in the Second World War, and spent most of their time on the surface. During attacks they could submerge to a few feet below the waterline to torpedo depth. They could not remain submerged even at such shallow depths for any length of time nor could they make great speed.

This meant the kaiser's U-boat fleet was highly vulnerable to counterattack. One defensive strategy was camouflage painting of the hulls of

U-boats in a color scheme that was intended to make them hard to visually sight in the water. Allied shipping adopted the same strategy to make its own fleets harder to detect by the U-boat wolf packs that prowled the Atlantic. Germany's U-boat fleet was destined to become a feared nemesis of Allied shipping on the high seas.

## STEALTH ZEPPELIN

Possibly the least well-known development in stealth warfare during the First World War was the use of zeppelin airships to bomb England. These attacks, which became known as zeppelin raids, used dirigibles heavily laden with bombs to invade the UK in an ominous prefiguring of the attacks launched by Hitler a generation later with V-1 and V-2 missiles. The zeppelins were the perfect stealth platforms for the delivery of air-to-ground munitions—they would even be formidable today, with natural radar-scattering shapes, near-silent propeller-driven flight, and low-trajectory flight paths.

The zeppelins would be launched under cover of darkness on night bombing missions from bases in northern Germany. Here only a relatively small stretch of French territory separated Germany from the English Channel. The zeppelins would be launched in packs of half a dozen or more per mission sortie. The commanders would take advantage of prevailing winds to speed the lighter-than-air flying machines across the Channel where they would silently and stealthily penetrate into British territory and drop their bombs.

When the explosions started, the zeppelins would inevitably become sitting ducks for British triple-A fire, and because they were filled with hydrogen, which unlike helium is a highly flammable gas, they usually burst into flames and were quickly destroyed. When a searchlight beam pinned one of the invading airships, the zeppelin—which had less speed and maneuverability than the Goodyear Blimp—was as good as history. Few, as a result, ever made it back to Germany again.

Because of this it quickly dawned on the Germans that zeppelin raids were one-way missions, and these early stealth bomber missions soon became a footnote to military history.

# CHAPTER 3

# STEALTH WARFARE IN WORLD WAR II

As we've seen, stealth warfare has been practiced since antiquity in various ways, shapes, and forms, and even primitive technology can be adapted for deception and camouflage operations.

We've also seen that as military technology—especially in the realm of surveillance and reconnaissance—becomes more sophisticated, stealth becomes an almost inevitable quality of subsequent development of new hardware, tactics, and combat doctrines. The examples from World War I include the necessity of camouflaging artillery because of the widespread use of aerial surveillance.

Today the military abbreviation C$^4$ISR, which stands for command, control, communications, computing, intelligence, surveillance, and reconnaissance, covers that part of the electronic order of battle (EOB) in which stealth warfare has a wide-ranging place. We will come to a broader discussion of C$^4$ISR later on in this book. For the moment it's a handy term to keep in mind as we consider the next phase in the evolution of stealth warfare, one that has taken it beyond its origins and brought it squarely into the realm of the modern.

# THE RADAR WAR

This next phase was based on a technology that came of age in the early years of the Second World War that forced military scientists and war planners to rewrite the rulebook, and eventually gave rise to the need to counter it by stealth: radar.

Radar, an acronym for radio detection and ranging, was one of the most critical developments on the Allied side. Because Nazi Germany did not have radar capability as advanced as its enemies or possess that capability earlier, it was brought one notch closer to defeat. In World War II, there was a practice of referring to several "wars" that were fought in support of the main battles of fighting men and war machinery in the battlefield. Of these, the two most important were the "weather war" and the "radar war." While both of these sub-wars were fought in the realm of clandestine operations, they involved real and often bloody combat; this was especially the case in the weather war. It was imperative to deprive enemy forces of accurate weather data, critical to launching, coordinating, and supporting air, land, and sea actions of every kind.

Deception operations were key to both sides in protecting their assets from interdiction and destruction by the opposite side. During the weather war, for example, the Germans went to great lengths to disguise their far-flung network of weather stations from attack. Many of their seaborne installations were camouflaged as merchant vessels, and remote weather outposts on land were disguised to blend into the landscape. At the same time false reports were generated by the British in attempts to confound German forces about weather conditions in the theater.

By the same token the so-called radar war involved more than just electronic countermeasures and counter-countermeasures. Military operations were undertaken to attack enemy radar stations, and at least in one instance to actually steal an advanced radar set right from under the noses of the Nazis.

## The Birth of Radar

The technology of radar was first developed at the dawn of the twentieth century by the German scientist and inventor Christian Hulsmeyer, who called his invention *Der Telemobilskop* or Remote Object Viewing Machine. Hulsmeyer received patents in Germany, the United Kingdom, and the United States for *Der Telemobilskop* in 1904. The device, which had a three hundred meter range, was originally intended to prevent ship collisions. Like many another invention ahead of its time—including the digital computer invented by Charles Babbage in 1850—*Der Telemobilskop* was considered of no practical value and was forgotten.

It wasn't until 1930 that engineers from the U.S. Naval Research Lab stumbled onto the rediscovery of radar's basic working principles. More importantly, they also discovered how radar might be used in warfare. The naval engineering team had been conducting signal strength measurements on a radio transmitter antenna when it found a noticeable change in signal strength when an aircraft on a landing strip near the antenna crossed the radio beam. This meant that by collecting radio waves that bounced off an object, that object's presence could be remotely detected.

By 1935, after the so-called Daventry Experiment which proved that an aircraft could be detected by a radio device, a crash program in England was ordered to develop radar that could be used militarily. At this stage sound locators were the only available means of detecting inbound bombers. Apart from being inaccurate, they were also only effective at relatively close range—too late to provide enough lead time for useful defensive measures to be taken. That same year a French naval vessel was outfitted with collision avoidance radar, and in 1936 the French also tested their *barrage electronique*, a form of ground radar.

## The Need for Radar

The need to develop radar was all too pressing by this point. By the early 1930s it was apparent that the world was again on the brink of war. In Asia, the second Sino-Japanese War had broken out in 1931. In Italy, the Fascist regime under Benito Mussolini had come to power, leading to Italy's conquest of Ethiopia in 1936, an event that showed that the League of Nations was impotent to stop aggression.

In Germany, the Nazis were in power and since the early 1930s had also flouted both the League of Nations and the Versailles Treaty by reindustrializing the Ruhr valley, a 100-square-mile area of factories, steel mills, and railway depots, and by going about rearmament in a way that could only lead to war. Although that war did not materialize in 1938 when the Munich Pact ceded Czechoslovakia to Hitler without a shot being fired, Britain would declare war the following year after the Nazi invasion of Poland.

Under Herman Göring, air minister for the Third Reich, and later under Albert Speer, Nazi Germany was developing aircraft of revolutionary design, capable of long-range missions, and was turning out these aircraft at a frantic pace. The British too were developing long-range fighter and bomber aircraft with the range to take the war to the German heartland. (They had in fact developed the Meteor jet fighter simultaneous with its counterpart, the German Me 262, but never fielded the aircraft.) The British were aware that in this coming war with Germany their homeland could no longer escape the danger posed by enemy air raids on major population centers and other strategic targets on the home island.

Radar was not only a means of detecting incoming bombers far enough away to take measures and to accurately target them once they came in range of defensive triple-A guns, but it was also necessary for flight control operations with friendly aircraft. Radar would also be necessary to operations at sea, and operations at sea would prove critical to the outcome of this impending war.

In World War I, Germany had launched wolf pack raids using its U-boat fleet against transatlantic Allied shipping. New U-boats under development by Germany with greater range, speed, and submergence capabilities would mean an even more dangerous repeat of this performance. Radar would also be needed in surface naval operations of all kinds, a fact especially appreciated by the U.S. Navy as it faced the prospect of a war in the Pacific against the Japanese.

In Britain this led to the establishment of the first modern radar network, the Chain Home system. Chain Home (CH) radars were what are today known as low pulse repetition frequency or PRF radars, a form of pulse-Doppler radar. These radars worked by transmitting short pulses of high-frequency radio energy at a suspected target, quadrant of the sky, or other area in which targets might be expected to be found.

The Doppler shifts of the pulse train that echoed back from solid objects struck by this radio energy were measured by electronic circuitry in the receivers and the result displayed as a trace or blip on a cathode-ray-tube scope. The position and strength of the blip indicated information about the target or targets, including relative range, speed, inbound trajectory, and size or density of the attacking force.

## Ultra and Radar Improvements

By 1939 Britain also knew that Hitler was planning to invade across the English Channel. The British knew this because of another milestone in the battle of deception that was to define World War II as a battle fought as much by stealth as by force of arms—they had Ultra, which was signals intelligence gained from deciphered German radio traffic encrypted on an Enigma coding machine. Because the Germans never caught on to the fact that their encoded messages were readable to the enemy, possession of Ultra meant that the Allies could learn about the military plans of the Third Reich before many of the principles even knew of them.

> Ultra was a code name originally taken from an old British Admiralty codebook.

Years before, the British had come into possession of the top-secret Enigma cipher machine that had been developed by the Nazis prior to World War II. When linked to typewriters, Enigma was an advanced device that could quickly encode or decode outgoing and incoming messages using a series of electrically powered wheels and cylinders. At a secret location at Bletchley Park, the British intelligence service had set up a facility whose sole purpose was to unlock the secrets of Ultra intercepts. To do this they had built a special computer known as "the Bomb" or "the Oracle."

Through Ultra intercepts the British knew of Operation Sea Lion, Hitler's invasion plan. They were also well aware that should it succeed they were doomed. The previous year the British Expeditionary Force (BEF) in France had been driven to the sea after Guderian's surprise tank blitzkrieg through the Ardennes that turned the supposedly impenetrable Maginot Line like a vast hinge. Moving with lightning speed, Guderian's

Panzer army had quickly enveloped the British and French and squeezed the BEF into a thin column in the center of pincers.

The Brits retreated to the Normandy coast with the English Channel at their backs. It was a defeated army that had returned to England, leaving all its equipment behind. The BEF had gotten away only because, at the last minute, Hitler had countermanded Göring's orders to bomb them with the might of the Luftwaffe. The führer had entertained hopes of an Anglo-German alliance and had spared his enemy in the belief that in defeat England would sue for peace on terms favorable to Germany.

About this he was as mistaken as he was about many another thing. Instead of waving the white flag as Hitler had expected, Prime Minister Winston Churchill, as pugnacious as the bulldog he resembled, rose in Parliament and in ringing terms promised to fight the enemy to a standstill. With his plans thwarted Hitler planned a diabolical revenge on England that included reducing London to ashes by subjecting it to concentrated incendiary bombing and, later, when the means appeared possible, nuclear attack.

Through Ultra and also through the *Swartze Kapelle*, or "Black Orchestra," the anti-Hitler underground in the German High Command, the British knew the details of Hitler's plans. They also knew that in order to achieve his objectives Hitler had first to gain mastery of the skies over England, which meant destroying the fighter planes of the Royal Air Force (RAF) fighter command which, despite the losses in France, had since made a remarkable recovery.

Once the Luftwaffe owned the skies it could then bomb London, the seat of British government, into submission. Reducing it to a pile of smoldering rubble would break the nation's morale and speed the way to German victory. But in order to achieve these ends the Nazis would also need to deal with Britain's CH radar network, which, though top-secret, they knew existed through surveillance and espionage. The Luftwaffe would also be assisted by a technical breakthrough on the German side in the field of electronics, the Knickebein blind-bombing system that used long-range radio beacons to guide munitions-laden Heinkel heavy bombers to their targets.

Not only had the British extended their radar coverage by the time the Luftwaffe raids and aerial dogfights that collectively came to be known as the Battle of Britain began in 1940, but they had achieved a breakthrough that was to result in radar far more powerful than anything Germany possessed at the time.

This was the invention of the cavity magnetron. Radar transmitters originally used wire-tuning coils to make radio waves resonate at the proper frequencies, but there was a downward limit to the size of the wavelength that could be produced by this method. The smaller the wavelength, the more accurate and powerful the radar.

By substituting a hole drilled in a bar of metal for the hollow inside a wire coil, a then-miraculous wavelength of one tenth of a meter could be reached, more than ten times as short as the shortest radar wavelength then in existence. A second development was the Blumlein modulator, a device that, among other things, helped produce a sharp, clear image on a radar scope at closer ranges than ever before.

These critical improvements in radar came along at just the right moment in history. Together they enabled the British to gain vital advantages in advance warning and a critical advantage in ground control interception and airborne interception. Prior to this the "smeller" system used by the British only enabled night fighters to approach to within twelve hundred feet of an enemy bomber and was considered unreliable. With the Blumlein modulator, aircraft could now be guided to within five hundred feet of their targets, close enough to make visual identification even on the darkest night by sighting on the faint glow of the bomber's exhaust pipes. Once this sighting was made, the pilot could track and aim his weapons at the plane by its silhouette.

Using a combination of Ultra intercepts, which revealed the Luftwaffe's strategy, and their advanced radar, which enabled accurate plotting of the air war, the British were able to prevail at this critical juncture of history. It was a final Ultra intercept that revealed to them that Hitler had called off Sea Lion until the following year.

To Churchill this meant that the threat of invasion had been permanently averted, because the Allies already had plans on how to deal with the Nazis by this time. It was not until the spring of 1943, when a British

Lancaster bomber was brought down by German antiaircraft fire near Rotterdam, Holland, that the Germans discovered the existence of the advanced British H2S radar based on the cavity magnetron. Although they immediately put a reverse-engineering effort underway, only a few examples of the advanced "*Rotterdamgerat*" or "R-gerat" radar sets that were developed as a result were in operation by the war's end.

## U-boats and Radio

On the high seas, the combination of Ultra and exploitation of the radio-wave spectrum in the form of a secret device called "Huff-Duff" proved of critical importance to stemming the predations of German submarines in the U-boat war. Because the German navy had few reconnaissance planes of its own, and because it was not provided with aircraft in sufficient numbers by the Luftwaffe, it had to devise other means of locating Allied shipping targets in the Atlantic.

U-boat wolf packs therefore developed the practice of prowling for their prey in small groups along known shipping lanes. When a sub spotted a convoy it would send out a radio call to headquarters giving bearing coordinates of the sighting. Other U-boats would then be directed from land control stations to converge on the convoy, forming a skirmish line from which the subs could torpedo the ships.

The Germans believed their radio locator signals were safe from interception. Not only were they were encrypted but they were sent as burst transmissions of one second or less. The Germans assumed that Allied direction finders on land might be able to get a general fix on a wolf pack's position, because in order to accurately raid a convoy, a constant series of radio signals had to be transmitted between the wolf pack and headquarters, and between individual submarines, but they deemed the risk acceptable because the wolf pack would be long gone before any help arrived. Besides, the Allies would quickly get that same general picture once the attack was launched anyway.

What the Germans didn't know was that since the beginning of the U-boat war in which shipping had suffered near-catastrophic losses, the Allies had developed a portable and highly accurate radio direction finder that was secretly placed aboard the combat vessels that escorted the merchant ships in transatlantic supply convoys. These high frequency direction finders, abbreviated as Huff-Duff, began to be placed aboard ships in the summer of 1942. The Allies also used airborne and shipborne radars to detect submarines, and the Germans, who assumed that it was these radars that were responsible for the increasing efficiency of the Allied counterattacks, never caught on to the existence of Huff-Duff, which was far more efficient here than radar.

## Sonar

Also coming into widespread use was a technological weapon developed late in World War I known as ASDIC. This was early sonar. Once the U-boats were located by ASDIC they could be damaged or sunk by depth charges or, if found on or brought to the surface, could be attacked by deck guns or even rammed. At night special "Leigh" lights were used to light up or "mark" the target either for cannon or machine-gun fire or aerial bombardment from night-fighting planes.

As might be expected, these early forms of antisubmarine warfare countermeasures gave rise to various counter-countermeasures intended to protect U-boats from detection and attack. Among the most interesting of these for the purposes of our study of stealth warfare was the discovery by German technicians of a substance they colloquially referred to as *Schornsteinfeger*, which literally meant "chimney-sweep."

*Schornsteinfeger* was an experimental compound made up of graphite particles bonded with rubber which, when applied to the hulls of submarines was found to substantially dissipate radar energy striking the hull and so weaken returning radar echoes.

Unfortunately for the Germans, *Schornsteinfeger* only worked while the U-boats were in dry dock because once the U-boat put out to sea a layer of salty water would form around it which in itself was a strong radar reflector. Despite the fact that *Schornsteinfeger* didn't work, the Germans had unwittingly stumbled onto what today is known as a RAM skin, a layer of radar-absorbent material that is a primary component of stealthy aeronautic or maritime hulls.

### Radar Countermeasures

Another discovery made during this period was dipole chaff, which the Allies code-named "Window." Dipole chaff, which are tiny strips of aluminum foil or aluminized glass fiber that are one half wavelength long by approximately two millimeters in diameter, were found to be highly efficient microwave reflectors.

Chaff, which falls slowly and takes on the velocity of the prevailing winds, was dropped from planes in a "seeding" operation to produce clouds or corridors that produced extremely large radar echo signals in the frequency bandwidth in which it was designed to operate. This, in other words, gives it a large radar cross section or RCS, which is the direct opposite of what a stealthy plane, ship, or any other protected object might have. Another secret of modern stealth had been discovered, only in reverse.

Finally, the development of jet aircraft by the Germans gave rise to a number of radical new designs, among which were the flying wing designs of the Horten brothers. These flying wing designs were originally intended to maximize the speed of an aircraft and the distance such new, advanced planes could fly.

These factors were considered of special importance because as the war progressed Hitler cherished the dream of attacking New York City with a nuclear weapon. When the HO1, the first working prototype of this new all-wing aircraft, was test-flown, German engineers made a startling discovery: The new aircraft were also invisible to radar.

The secrets of stealth were becoming known, piece by piece, and bit by bit. They would wind up permanently standing the concept of warfare on its head.

## CAMPAIGNS OF DECEPTION

Before getting to the subject of the radical aircraft that the German Luftwaffe was experimenting with—and in some cases actually flying—during the Second World War, and how the United States came into possession of the secrets of this technology, we must first consider several other aspects of stealth warfare. As mentioned in the introduction to this book, stealth warfare is not only about aircraft fuselages or ships' hulls coated with RAM skins: It is a philosophy of warfare that pervades every aspect of the order of battle. Moreover, as the definition of the "battlefield" has changed, so stealth warfare has come to play a principal role in cyberwarfare, counterterrorist warfare, and internal security operations.

Deception is as old as warfare. It could also be accurately defined as the underlying objective of all stealth. The Trojan horse and the stealth bomber both have the same purpose—to hide the existence of the weapon or strategy from adversaries so that an attack may be made where and when they are unprepared to defend against it. Although this seems to be the direct opposite of conventional concepts of fairness, honor, virtue, and all the rest, these qualities have been honored more in the breech than in the act throughout military history.

In London, which seems to have the most museums on earth, a visitor can descend beneath the streets of Westminster into the war rooms that were used by the British Ministry of Defense in World War II. Preserved in this underground bunker is a sanctum sanctorum dedicated to the military art of deception. Still to be found on one of its walls is a plaque bearing an excerpt from *The Soldier's Handbook*; the words, written in 1869 by Sir Garnet Wolsely, a former commander in chief of the British army, were there to address any concerns about fair play that those who routinely met in this chamber of deception might have as they went about their work:

> We are bred up to feel it a disgrace ever to succeed by falsehood—we will keep hammering along with the conviction that honesty is the best policy, and that truth always wins in the long run. These pretty little sentiments do well for a child's copy book, but a man who acts on them had better sheathe his sword forever.

The group that met in this inner sanctum was known by the acronym LCS, which stood for London Controlling Section, which was an elite group within the Allied Joint Planning Staff responsible for devising and coordinating strategic cover and deception schemes in all theaters of World War II. It was created as part of a massive effort to confound an enemy that outstripped the British by a wide margin in troops and war matériel, which had already dealt them a crushing blow, and which was getting ready to administer the coup de grâce with Operation Sea Lion, the planned invasion of Britain, which MI-6, their intelligence service, already knew was in preparation.

On taking office, Churchill, who favored indirect warfare and special means to combat Nazi Germany, ordered a raft of far-reaching plans to be immediately put into effect. By contrast with the preceding Chamberlain government, whose policy of appeasement had given Hitler Czechoslovakia without a shot being fired, it was clear that Churchill had committed his side to a policy of total war, one in which virtually any means that promised victory were to be used. From now on the Third Reich would find its plans for world domination contested at every turn. Since the stakes were all or nothing and the enemy held most of the cards there was no other choice.

This is not to imply that in the Nazis didn't also have deception weapons in their bag of tricks. They certainly did. In fact it could be argued that World War II began with a deception campaign on the part of Nazi Germany that set the stage for all the rest that followed.

It was to be Germany's blitzkrieg conquest of Poland in 1939 that led to a declaration of war by Britain and thus the start of the global war that soon began. Hitler, who had used the pretext of nonexistent persecutions of Germans in the Czechoslovakian Sudetenland to justify his annexation of Czechoslovakia, intended to use a similar pretext to justify his invasion of Poland. In the so-called Danzig Corridor (a German zone of the Polish city of Gdansk, known to Germans as Danzig), the Reich claimed that their fellow nationals were also being persecuted.

Therefore to precede the Nazi blitz on his next target of opportunity, Hitler ordered that a deception campaign be launched to give him an excuse to invade, however flimsy it might be. An operation of special means was to be carried out. It was called "Operation Himmler" in honor of the number-two man in the Third Reich hierarchy. Heinrich Himmler was head of the *Schutzstaffel*, better known by its abbreviation, SS. The SS was, among other things, Hitler's praetorian guard and chief enforcement arm. As head of the SS, Himmler held tremendous power; but he wanted more and always had an eye out for how to get it.

Himmler entrusted the job to a younger man who had become his trusted protégé and would before long become his archrival, Reinhard Heydrich. Later in the war, after Heydrich had been felled by grenade shrapnel in a partisan ambush staged by British intelligence, it would be generally assumed that a clandestine radio transmission giving MI-6 information vital to the hit had come directly from Himmler. Such were rivals dealt with in the Third Reich.

At this stage, though, Himmler considered Heydrich the perfect subordinate. Heydrich was both ambitious and the perfect exemplar of an SS officer's ideal Nordic physical type, according to precise guidelines that Himmler had established to recruit SS members—guidelines which, I note in passing, would have also made guitarist Johnny Winter a prime candidate on this same basis, since existing photographs of Heydrich show an uncanny resemblance to the albino performer who wrote "Rock and Roll Hoochie-Koo."

Heydrich, head of the Reich Security Service (*Sicherheitsdienst* or SD), the intelligence branch of the SS, had been chosen by Himmler to plan the daring mission. Himmler had come up in the Nazi ranks since the death of his archrival Ernst Röhm after the infamous "Night of the Long Knives" in which Hitler set about to liquidate the *Sturmabteilung* or SA. The brown-shirted private army led by Röhm, whom he increasingly viewed as a challenge to his leadership, had helped propel him to power.

The SA had been about 3,000,000 strong at the time of the purge. By comparison Himmler's fledgling SS had only about 50,000 members at that point. With the SA gone, Himmler headed the sole military organization that Hitler could count on to perform special operations, including intelligence and internal security. The Polish operation would be Himmler's greatest coup yet and increase his stature with Hitler by a quantum jump.

Himmler entrusted the mission planning to Heydrich, who in turn entrusted the execution of the mission to his own protégé, one Maj. Alfred Naujocks of the SS, a man identical to his master in brutality, though lacking Heydrich's superficial polish and cold intelligence; in time Naujocks would rival the infamous Otto Skorzeny in reputation for being one of the Third Reich's deadliest commandos. Knowing Hitler needed a frontier incident of some kind to justify an attack on Poland, Heydrich devised a two-pronged operational plan. First, SD agents, masquerading as Polish rebels, were to attack the German radio station at the Polish frontier town of Gleiwitz, broadcast what Maj. Strasser in the movie *Casablanca* termed "the foulest lies," and then disappear.

At the same time, Polish-speaking Germans from Upper Silesia dressed in Polish army uniforms would seize the German customs office near Hochlinden and stage a mock battle with SS troops stationed there. This was intended to draw real Polish troops into the skirmish. A Polish army defector was to act as an agent provocateur, haranguing the Poles to enter the fray. As a crowning touch, corpses from the nearby Dachau concentration camp dressed in Polish army uniforms would be dumped at the customs house and radio station.

Hitler gave the plan his blessing. At 4:00 P.M. on August 31, 1939, the führer issued two historic orders. The first was to commence the invasion of Poland at 4:45 A.M. the following morning. The second was to Himmler: Heydrich's operation was to proceed that same evening. At 4:00 P.M. on August 31, Naujocks, stationed at a hotel room in Gleiwitz, got a call from Heydrich. The mission was on.

Shortly before eight that evening, a German engineer named Foitzik, working at the Gleiwitz radio station, saw armed men mounting the stairs to the broadcasting studio. Foitzik demanded to know where they thought they were going. In answer he got a gun barrel shoved between his eyes. With Foitzik and the rest of the staff handcuffed and held prisoner in the building's basement, Naujocks and his crew began staging the mock "takeover" of the station by Polish troops.

They got the part about shooting up the place right, but hit a snag when it was realized that none of the raiders knew how to operate the radio equipment. Thus none of the "foul lies" they were to spread against innocent and helpless Nazis could be broadcast. After frantically flipping switches, turning dials and kicking and swearing at the equipment, one of the SS technical geniuses finally managed to press the right button—an emergency switch that allowed overriding of broadcasts in progress.

At this Naujocks's Polish-speaking "announcers" went into action. Anti-German statements inflammatory enough to give a barrel of sauerkraut a case of heartburn were broadcast, with the chatter of gunfire in the background to convince listeners that the German radio station was under attack by bloodthirsty Poles. About five minutes later, with the uniformed Dachau corpses—referred to as "canned goods" by the SS—scattered around for effect, Naujocks gave the signal to clear out.

While this was taking place, another SS detachment staged the second mock attack on the German customs station at Hochlinden, leaving more corpses in Polish uniforms in their wake. No matter that rigor mortis had long ago set in and the bodies were by this time as stiff as boards. The führer's will had been done. Hitler now had his *casus belli* for blitzing Poland. Even before the two SS detachments had returned to their bases, the Panzer tanks, Stuka dive-bombers and divisions of Wehrmacht and Waffen SS troops were on the move toward the Polish border.

As the attack was underway, Hitler radioed his troops that Germany was invading because "the Germans in Poland are being persecuted with bloody terror and driven from their homes." Germany would no longer tolerate this outrage. "To put an end to these mad acts I can see no other way but from now onwards to meet force with force," the führer went on. Capt. Renault would no doubt have added, "I'm shocked! Shocked, I tell you!"

As it turned out Hitler got a lot more than he bargained for. Not only was Nazi aggression met with the armed might of nations who would no longer idly stand by while Germany carved up the world and swallowed it piecemeal, but Hitler's Reich would in future also be met with deception operations that made "Operation Himmler" seem like crude child's play by comparison. Such operations included a British operation using "canned goods" known by the code name Mincemeat based on the same principle as the Himmler op, but far more sophisticated.

This brings us back to the inner sanctum beneath the pavements of Westminster, and the deception operations that were pioneered there and which later were also carried out by the United States in Europe and in the Pacific Theater against Imperial Japan, and the secret that those in the LCS guarded as key to victory.

It was a secret deemed so vital to the British cause that extraordinary lengths were taken to safeguard it including, in more than one instance, deliberately sacrificing the lives of noncombatants and friendly forces so that the Germans wouldn't learn that the Allies possessed it. It was to prove the heart of all Allied deception operations in World War II, including those that preceded the critical invasion of the Normandy beach heads on D day, and the determining factor in Allied victory in major battles against German forces. The secret's name was Ultra.

The British, and later the Americans and Russians (the last on a limited basis) who were also made privy to Ultra, could thereby anticipate German military offensives before these were carried out and devise counteroffensives tailored to defeat the German plans. Having access to Ultra also meant that deception and cover operations could be staged with maximum effectiveness by Allied forces.

But before Ultra could be used, the impossible first needed to be accomplished. The Enigma coding machine used by the German high command was a specially modified model based on an earlier Enigma originally developed for business purposes. The Enigma machine, as described in the memoirs of F. W. Winterbotham, who was entrusted with Ultra security throughout World War II by LCS, was described as ...

> ... A complicated system of electrically connected revolving drums around which were placed letters of the alphabet. A typewriter fed the letters of the message into the machine, where they were so proliferated by the drums that it was estimated a team of top mathematicians might take a month or more to work out all the permutations necessary to find the right answer for a single cypher setting; the setting of the drums in relation to each other was the key which both the sender and receiver would no doubt keep very closely guarded.

Physically, the Enigma used by the German general staff was a box-like device approximately 24 inches square and 18 inches high. Like many aspects of the Ultra operations, the appearance and operational characteristics of Enigma are still shrouded in secrecy some 60 years after the end of World War II. Published descriptions of Enigma since that time hint at a typewriter-like device, much like the "Lektor" coding machine in the James Bond movie *From Russia With Love*.

This is, and has been, deliberate disinformation. Enigma was essentially an electromechanical computer, an early information appliance that could encrypt and decrypt messages passing through it quickly and efficiently. In order to encode or decode using Enigma, two electric typewriters were connected to ports on the central unit. One of these typewriters was used to input either plain text for encoding or encrypted text for decoding. The output—in code or in clear—was printed out on the second typewriter.

To encrypt a message, the operator would first select the correct cipher for the time of day from his key book, accordingly set the controls on the Enigma unit, and then type the message in plain text on the left-hand typewriter. Minutes later, after processing inside Enigma, the right-hand typewriter would spit out the encoded message. This could then be sent by courier or retransmitted by a wireless operator in Morse code. On receipt, an Enigma operator at the other end would repeat the process in reverse to decode the message.

Prior to the development of Enigma the only absolutely secure method of sending messages in code was to use the one-time pad system. Since this system was extremely time-consuming and cumbersome, it was unsuited to the requirements of a modern military service and needed to be replaced. One-time pad cipher books also needed regular replacement because these codebooks—which contained the cipher keys—inevitably were lost or stolen and because with repeated use even one-time codes could be partially deciphered by the enemy.

Enigma did away with all the disadvantages of using one-time pads— messages could now be encrypted on-the-fly and quickly decoded. No codebooks needed to be kept because the machine contained the cipher keys, and even should an Enigma machine fall into enemy hands no ciphers would be compromised because the dial settings on the outside of the machine, which were constantly changed by headquarters, determined which cipher keys were used.

Because of these qualities and because it was deemed totally secure, Hitler and the three armed branches of the Wehrmacht trusted Enigma implicitly and used it throughout the war with complete assurance. Yet all the while the Allies were reading virtually every word of the messages they transmitted. Not even after D day, when it should have been apparent that the Allies were staging operations countering Nazi moves that they could have only known about in advance, did OKW or Hitler suspect that their commands, messages, and orders of battle were being read at virtually the same moment they had been sent.

Placing unquestioned faith in Enigma was arguably the greatest blunder that the Third Reich—or anybody else—made in the history of warfare. By all accounts, not even the otherwise shrewd Erwin Rommel caught on to what was happening. Although Rommel and a few other generals did on occasion entertain doubts concerning the security of their war plans, intelligence leaks were always attributed to the work of spies and informers—never Ultra.

More than mere possession of an actual Enigma coding machine enabled the Allies to read German transmissions at will. Since Enigma ciphers could be (and were) changed several times daily, only an inside knowledge gained through espionage could afford reliable access to Enigma-encoded messages. This, of course, meant that while the Allies might otherwise have succeeded in reading German messages some of the time, they would normally be expected to be unable to do this in any meaningful way, which is the main reason the Germans considered Enigma impregnable. And the Germans would have been right—except for the fact that the Allies had "the Bomb."

The Bomb, otherwise known as the Turing Engine or Turing Universal Machine, and called by Winterbotham "the Oracle," was the key to continuous decipherment of Enigma transmissions throughout the war. Without the Bomb there would have been no Ultra. The Turing Engine was a machine specifically built to duplicate the performance of the thousands of Enigma machines that would come into being during the war. To do this it would need to extrapolate the constantly changing keying procedures of every major German command ordered every day and night, year-in and year-out, and it would have to make its mathematical calculations at speeds beyond anything humanly possible.

Until the British succeeded in actually building one, the Turing Universal Machine existed only in the theoretical imagination of its inventor, whom many considered a crackpot. Yet the Turing Engine was actually built and did work, deciphering Enigma-coded messages throughout the war and providing the Allies with the vital intelligence that turned the tide of battle.

When it's considered how close Hitler came to bringing off his insane visions of world domination even with the Allies having the benefit of Ultra, it's chilling to consider that without Ultra Hitler might very well have succeeded. Even had the Nazis had another year to extend the war, they might have achieved technological breakthroughs in nuclear weaponry, long-range stealth aircraft, guided missiles, and many other areas that might have swung the war around in their favor. The existence of Ultra could very well have spelled the difference between victory and defeat.

Although there were some glaring failures—such as in Allies' miscues in response to "Case Yellow," Hitler's early offensive into Belgium and the Netherlands, Ultra was used to great advantage throughout the rest of the war. Yet at no time was it more critical than during the preparations for D day and the aftermath of the Allied invasion of Europe.

## Crossing the English Channel

In support of this massive undertaking, possibly the most extensive and complicated campaign of cover and deception operations in the history of warfare was staged by the U.S.-U.K.-Soviet alliance under the code names Bodyguard and Fortitude, with dozens of suboperations under these headings, with names such as Glimmer, Taxable, Big Drum, Ironside, and Diadem.

The Allies realized they had to eventually return to Europe in order to win the war. A large-scale invasion was considered inevitable by the alliance and the Nazis alike. Yet while Hitler and his generals justly feared this impending attack, they also viewed it as an opportunity to destroy their enemies in one fell swoop. In this case the führer's optimism, usually met with justifiable scorn by his subordinates as not being grounded in reality, was to a large extent shared.

It was taken for granted that the Allied assault on Europe, when it came, would be through France; if so the landings would have to be made either at the Pas de Calais or the beaches of Normandy on the southwestern French coast. Because the Pas de Calais was the narrowest point between England and France, Hitler's generals believed this was the likeliest place to expect the attack. Hitler, on the other hand, believed that the more hostile landing zone would be the beaches of Normandy. A compromise was reached between the führer and his advisors and both parts of France were garrisoned, while on the Normandy coast Hitler ordered the construction of a line of massive fortifications called the *Atlantikwall*.

The Germans had every reason to feel optimistic that their preparations would result in stopping the invasion in its tracks and throwing the invaders back into the sea, splitting the alliance and leaving the Nazis in complete mastery of Europe. Though they didn't know it the Allies were equally concerned about the prospects of success. The United States and Britain had come to a crossroads in the war and the alliance was in jeopardy of splitting apart.

Where Washington pressed for a direct, all-out assault on Europe across the English Channel and through the French west coast, the Brits first refused to budge from Churchill's "soft underbelly" approach; insisting that the invasion be through Italy and the Mediterranean coast. The United States in 1943 was thus in a position similar to that preceding the 2003 assault on Iraq. While the United States pressed for a single, concentrated strike on the enemy via the most direct route, its Allies favored a gradualist strategy that the United States viewed as self-defeating. The British, sobered by their experiences in 1940 on the continent following the destruction of the Maginot Line, were fearful of the consequences if troops were bogged down or forced to fight grinding land battles reminiscent of World War I.

If the invasion failed, all bets were off. The Allies, who would need to commit every military and political resource in their arsenal, would have shot their bolt. A bloodbath on the shores of France in 1944 would have also meant that President Roosevelt, who would be up for reelection that year, would almost certainly be defeated by an isolationist opponent and the United States would pursue the "Pacific First" policy advocated by many prominent members of government and business.

Roosevelt's presidential administration rested on shaky ground at home. In 1943, there had even been an open attempt by right-wing forces to stage a *coup d'état* and replace the president with a retired World War I general. While the United States turned its energies to combating the Japanese and left the war in Europe to the British before deciding on whether to attempt a second invasion, Hitler would be able to concentrate his full might on defeating the Russians.

The result would almost certainly have been a negotiated settlement to World War II, which would have left Hitler as conqueror of Europe. But this would ultimately (probably by 1950, when according to Albert Speer's memoirs Hitler had planned to have rebuilt Berlin as the capitol of the New World Order and fully consolidated his power) have led to World War III, a war begun with surprise nuclear attacks on New York and London by German stealth bombers and advanced V-2 missiles carrying nuclear warheads.

Speer records how Hitler gleefully fantasized about turning London and New York into blazing nuclear infernos and was especially thrilled about reducing the skyscrapers of Manhattan to radioactive dust. Speer stated that he had not the slightest doubt that had Hitler possessed the means to carry out these aims he would have done so without hesitation.

Even without the knowledge of how far along the Nazis had gotten in secret technology projects, the consequences of Allied defeat in an invasion of Fortress Europe were all too apparent. Bickering between the U.S. and British general staffs went on until the Quadrant conference in Quebec, during which the alliance hammered out an agreement and set the date for the invasion as May 1944. Its code name would be Overlord, and the landings themselves would be called Neptune. In its aftermath, Winston Churchill pondered how the advantage could be placed with Allied forces. According to his memoirs, published in the six-volume *History of the Second World War*, the answer was summed up in a single word: surprise.

And so it was that plans Bodyguard and Fortitude were devised. While the aim of both of these was to deceive the Nazi Reich as to the time, place, disposition, and objectives of D day, the two plans embraced different aspects of the overall plan. As Churchill went on in his memoirs, the enemy had to be persuaded that the Allies "were landing somewhere else and at a different moment." Bodyguard was the code word for the overall Allied strategic deception plan in support of D day, and its primary aim was to con the enemy into making erroneous strategic dispositions of every kind.

## Fortitude

Fortitude, the tactical part of D day deception operations, encompassed the nuts-and-bolts end of the deception campaign, and was especially geared to misleading the Nazis after preparations reached the point where they could no longer be totally concealed from Berlin. It was intended to confuse Hitler about the true invasion site and bleed off fighting divisions that would otherwise oppose the landings.

Originally called Plan Jael, after the Biblical heroine who used guile to lure a foe of the Israelites into a tent where she later hammered a stake between his eyes, the plan was renamed after the Allied strategy conference in Tehran, where Churchill made his famous statement that in war, "Truth must be protected by a bodyguard of lies."

The Allies had already effectively used strategic deception to fool the Germans about the landings in North Africa that had taken place the previous year, and a brief mention of this campaign, code-named Operation Mincemeat, deserves to be made before continuing with Bodyguard.

The centerpiece of the Mincemeat deception was the famous "Man Who Never Was," a corpse released from a submarine in the waters off the port of Huelva, Spain, a town infested with Nazi spies. The corpse, whose true identity was never revealed, carried documents identifying him as the nonexistent British Royal Marines major William Martin.

Chained to "Martin's" wrist was a briefcase containing military plans for the invasion of Greece. Like Martin himself, the plans were complete fabrications designed to convince Berlin that the Allied invasion was coming off in Greece instead of Sicily. Operation Mincemeat worked perfectly and caught the Germans with their pants down on July 10, 1943, when the landings actually took place.

## Bodyguard

Bodyguard would go far beyond this or anything else ever attempted before or since. It was a multilayered disinformation and deception plan that involved an interlocking web of diversions, dirty tricks, electronic snooping, radar spoofing of German reconnaissance planes, flipping of double agents, engineered intelligence leaks, an impersonation of at least one Allied commanding general, and the creation of several bogus armies.

The overall goal was to present the German intelligence arm with a box of puzzle pieces that, when assembled, would present the Nazis with a picture of the Pas de Calais instead of Normandy. Bodyguard's task was to put the pieces into the box and hand the box to the Germans; it was up to them to assemble the jigsaw as the Allies intended them to do and hoped that they would.

Even a partial blow-by-blow account of Bodyguard—described by one principal as a plan of "Proustian complexity"—is well beyond the scope of this book, but here are some of the more notable examples of deception and information warfare operations that were part of it.

One was the so-called wireless game, the specialty of the XX Committee, an organization run by British MI-5 in conjunction with LCS and in concert with X2, the counterintelligence and agent manipulation branch of the American OSS. Since the Germans were also skilled at the wireless game—they called it *Englandspiele* with a nod to the British, or *Funkspiele* (literally "wireless game")—both sides experienced their share of victories and defeats.

The main object of the wireless game was to capture enemy radio operators along with their sets and then flip them to work for their captors as double agents. They could then be used to broadcast deceptive reports concocted by their new masters. Alternatively, once a spy's cover was blown, he or she might unknowingly be fed false information designed to mislead the enemy to whom the spy was transmitting. Using the wireless game, a great deal of misleading information concerning D day was broadcast to the Germans. The key to effectively playing the game was to make sure that enough reliable information was mixed in with the deception, so that the other side would continue to trust the transmissions enough to swallow the bait whole.

A refinement of the wireless game was known as the cipher trick. This gambit was played by sending operators into enemy territory with ciphers that the sending side knew the receiving side would be able to decrypt. Here too the key to making it work was in lending verisimilitude to the capture of the ciphers, which inevitably meant the capture of the agents bearing the ciphers, and which in turn meant the inevitable deaths of those captured at the hands of the Nazis.

Because agents parachuting into German-held territory were generally accompanied by air drops of arms, ammunition, explosives, money, and other agents, playing the cipher game also meant setting up all of these assorted assets for capture and—in the case of the other agents—execution by the Germans. Yet this is precisely what the British did on several occasions as revealed in court documents prepared by representatives of French and Dutch partisans after the war's end.

Another accusation—in my view also probably true—made after the war was that the British set up an inordinate number of women agents in playing the cipher game, on the grounds that the Germans believed that no Englishman would be so ungallant as to set up a woman to take a fall in an espionage operation.

By one count some 70 agents were deliberately set up in the cipher game for capture and death in order to feed the enemy false tactical and strategic information. But that's the game of espionage. There are black metal stars on the white marble wall in the lobby of CIA headquarters at Langley, Virginia. Each of those stars indicates a secret operative who died in a covert operation. More than a few of those stars were earned under circumstances similar to the cipher trick. The game hasn't changed. It never will.

Another way Bodyguard used radio deception was to deliberately increase the level of radio traffic at certain times and between certain points of reception and transmission. Even when encrypted electronic transmissions could not be deciphered by enemy eavesdroppers, it was axiomatic in intelligence that an increase or decrease in traffic could in itself be indicative of increased military activity; if a particular operation was in the offing, it could then be inferred that the increased traffic meant that this anticipated operation might be nearing the go stage.

This was one of the deception stratagems used in Bodyguard's FUSAG operation, especially since it was known that the Germans set high store in monitoring Allied radio traffic in Britain toward determining the strength, disposition, location and destination of troops. FUSAG stood for First

United States Army Group, an almost completely fictitious Allied military force stationed in that part of southeastern England known as East Anglia.

Supposedly FUSAG was made up of the totally nonexistent 14th U.S. Army and the real 4th British army. In reality neither bogus nor actual army was anywhere near East Anglia. FUSAG was one mammoth mirage, a grand *maskirovka* utilizing phony barracks, radio loudspeakers to simulate the movements of troops, and other subterfuge. Its intended purpose was the invasion of Europe via the Pas de Calais.

The capstone of the operation was the disinformation operation to convince the Germans that Gen. George S. Patton was FUSAG's commanding officer, a gambit sure to lend credibility to the fiction that the Pas de Calais was the actual D day landing site because of the high regard that the German high command held for Patton. The Germans considered Patton the quintessential warrior, a soldier they would have been proud to call their own.

Their assumption was that if Patton were heading FUSAG, then FUSAG had to be a genuine force, and ipso facto, its planning invasion site, the Pas de Calais, was also real. The only reality about the entire plan was that Patton, whose forced retirement was demanded by numerous parties after his infamous face-slapping incident at a field hospital in North Africa, was simultaneously being kept out of mischief and given a chance to redeem himself by Ike, until the real invasion got underway.

As it was Eisenhower came to regret the sentimentality that led to his sparing the old war-horse from an early demise, since Patton flouted Ike's orders to stay in East Anglia every chance he got, and on at least one occasion came perilously close to spilling the truth about D day's actual landing site at Normandy to a crowd of reporters.

As D day approached, Bodyguard's final deception plans were put into effect in an effort to tie down the Wehrmacht and Waffen SS in the south of France rather than at Normandy. Starting on June 1, Allied aircraft began attacking tactical targets between Calais and Le Havre with increasing intensity, striking coastal guns and beach defenses. Electronic jamming of radar installations between Cherbourg and Le Havre was carried out. Some 105 RAF aircraft and 34 small vessels of the Royal Navy were used for three pre-invasion feints: Operation Glimmer, directed at Boulogne;

Operation Taxable, at Cap d'Antifer; and Operation Big Drum, at Pointe Barfleur.

Shortly after dark on June 8, 18 small naval vessels steamed toward Cap d'Antifer, north of Le Havre, towing barrage balloons intended to produce echoes on German radar consistent with a massive force of inbound bomber aircraft and an armada of invading warships. As many as a hundred radar posts were located between Brest and Borkum on the North Sea. Scopes were lighting up like neon signs all along the coast of Calais.

Above the phantom fleet, B-17 bombers circled and dropped bundles of Window, the codename for dipole chaff—radar-reflective aluminum or metallized Mylar strips—to further spoof German radars into returning false echoes consistent with a large convoy sailing across the channel. Smaller vessels carried loudspeakers which broadcast the sounds of this ghost armada approaching the Pas de Calais.

The combined operations were successful. As late as June 20, Erwin Rommel, who was in charge of Hitler's *Atlantikwall* defenses, still expected an attack on the Pas de Calais; von Runstedt, the general in charge of Wehrmacht defenses, believed the Normandy invasion to be merely a tactical feint in support of the main landings in the south.

All these operations were continuously supported by spurious FUSAG radio intercepts indicating that Patton's First Army was positioned for a cross-channel invasion via the south of France. While the Germans were duped into drawing the wrong conclusions, the real 12th Army group mobilized for D day's actual attack site.

The pre-D day deception strategies were so effective that even after the Allied breakout from the Normandy beachheads the Germans still staunchly held onto their Pas de Calais defenses, in anticipation of a second invasion from that direction. In fact, they had even reinforced them with two fresh divisions diverted from the Russian front.

All in all, approximately 20 German divisions were pinned down in the Pas de Calais, awaiting a ghost armada that never appeared, when those divisions might well have succeeded in stopping D day in its tracks had they instead been at Normandy.

## Battle of the Bulge

Credit for the final major deception campaign of the war goes to the Germans, who used deception operations to sow discord behind American lines during the winter offensive in the Ardennes that came to be called the Battle of the Bulge. It also marked the first time in the war that preparations for a major offensive were cloaked by a stringent security blackout on the part of the German high command. Berlin still believed unreservedly in the security of Enigma and still knew nothing about Ultra. Strict secrecy was imposed because Hitler gave orders that no chances were to be taken. This was to be the last roll of the dice with everything staked on the final throw. The führer believed that fate would come to his aid at this, the Third Reich's eleventh hour, just as it had once plucked Frederick the Great, another German leader, from the verge of defeat.

Elements from approximately 28 infantry and tank divisions were gathered for the decisive blow through the Ardennes forest—the same route through which Guderian's Panzer army had come crashing to turn the Maginot Line and rout the British in 1940. This time Hitler had learned his lesson from the defeats in Russia and had equipped his troops with the best available gear, including heavily insulated white winter fatigues. This time the Wehrmacht would not freeze in the snow. The weather would also serve the German cause; Hitler had waited until dense clouds and snowstorms ruled out Allied air operations before launching the offensive.

He took one final step that set this operation apart from all others that preceded it. Sending for his chief enforcer, SS Colonel Otto Skorzeny, Hitler outlined his plan. Skorzeny, who had earlier staged the daring escape of overthrown Italian dictator Benito Mussolini from a ski lodge on top of Grand Sasso mountain in which the Italians were holding their former leader prisoner, was now ordered to prepare for a deception operation to support the offensive.

Skorzeny was to assemble a force of handpicked German commandos, most of whom were able to speak English. They were to be dressed in American uniforms—the sector was in American hands—carry G.I.-issue gear, including rifles and pistols, and wear captured American uniforms and helmets. Skorzeny—who knew full well about the contempt in which Americans held Hitler's infamous commando rule, which stated that any enemy commandos captured in German territory were to be treated as spies and executed—was justifiably anxious about his new assignment behind U.S. lines, but orders were orders.

While German troops clad in snow-white parkas—some elements on skis—poured virtually unopposed through the Ardennes sector, gaining so much territory with such speed that a "bulge" developed behind the American perimeter, Skorzeny's commandos spread havoc behind the lines. After it became clear that armed, English-speaking Germans in G.I. uniforms were circulating around in the midst of American forces, the panic level rose to the point where even Eisenhower was affected.

Skorzeny had started a rumor that a force of his operators was on a mission to assassinate the American commanding general. As a result, Eisenhower was removed to a special mobile headquarters and kept under round-the-clock guard behind a wall of troops. With his movements restricted, Ike had even more trouble in coping with what was happening in the Ardennes and issuing effective orders. It wasn't until the weather finally cleared and American planes could fly again that the momentum of battle shifted against the attackers. After that, the German winter offensive quickly petered out, and in its aftermath the last precious reserves of equipment and manpower available to the Third Reich were lost forever.

The Battle of the Bulge marked the last great turning point of World War II. If nothing else it demonstrated what might have happened during previous offensives had the Allies not possessed Ultra, or worse yet, had the shoe been on the other foot and the Nazis had a pipeline into the deepest secrets of the Allied joint command.

# CHAPTER 4

# WW II GERMAN STEALTH RESEARCH, INCLUDING STEALTHY AIRCRAFT DESIGNS

Radar, as noted earlier, was a key development in military technology during World War II, and one that both sides were actively pursuing in a "radar war."

Although the Third Reich had a few rocket scientists working for it, it didn't take one to figure out that warfare had entered a new era, in which the ability to see and hear enemy forces without being seen or heard, and to counter or defeat the ability of unfriendlies to do this to your side, was as integral to the order of battle as tanks, planes, bombs, bullets, or troops.

This perception led to the development of what later became known as stealth by the Nazis during World War II. Yet while, as we'll see, the Third Reich gets the credit for inventing stealth, it's also true that stealth came into being in an indirect way, more as a by-product of research and development in other areas than a technology pursued for its own sake.

The main German approach to countering Allied advances in radar that gave the Nazis' enemies a critical edge wasn't to make their own side's aircraft harder to see on radar. It was instead to develop aircraft that would fly higher, faster, and farther than anything the United States or Britain had in the air, making Allied radar detection irrelevant.

Obsessed with overpowering the world, Hitler's mind-set was to simply create a juggernaut that would overwhelm the opposition. This was the doctrine of blitzkrieg translated into armaments design and production. The German military term for this philosophy was *vernichtungschlag*, which meant a battle strategy geared to no less than total annihilation of the enemy. It was in pursuit of this goal that the führer ordered a raft of advanced aircraft production efforts.

Helping to push for this, and convincing Hitler that these new secret Luftwaffe weapons could win the war, was Hermann Göring, former World War I fighter pilot and chief of the Nazi Luftwaffe, which is a compound word made up of *luft*, or air, and *waffe*, or force—air force.

Göring, who had been a morphine addict for years, wasn't the best person to listen to, but Hitler and he were kindred spirits when it came to grandiose schemes for world domination. The push to develop an awesome array of superplanes and superweapons was to be crowned by Göring's "thousand by thousand by thousand" directive, which was Luftwaffe shorthand for the need to build an aircraft capable of flying a thousand kilometers carrying a thousand kilograms of weapons at a thousand kilometers per hour.

This ambitious master plan went hand in hand with the effort to develop a nuclear weapon that the plane would carry. The main goal of a long-range intercontinental bomber of this type would be to strike the United States.

In the later stages of development of this aircraft it was discovered that its flying wing airframe was inherently stealthy. The plane's shape deflected radar energies in such a way as to make the large aircraft show up as a very small return on radar scopes. In military parlance it had a low radar cross section or RCS.

## CHAPTER 4: WW II GERMAN STEALTH RESEARCH, INCLUDING STEALTHY AIRCRAFT DESIGNS

Another innovation was the application of what today might be called a RAM skin or coating of the fuselage with radar absorbent materials (RAM). Combining RAM in the form of a RAM skin and special fittings made of RAM at key radar hot spots with a radar deflective fuselage design enhances the stealthiness of an aircraft or other stealth platform.

Col. Philip Corso, who has written and lectured about the part he played in alleged alien technology transfer, has speculated that RAM, like stealthy flying wings or discoid fuselage designs associated with stealth, was part of the treasure trove of extraterrestrial technologies taken from aliens by Germany, the United States, Britain, and Russia during and after World War II. This is doubtful, since the Third Reich's scientists had previously developed RAM as an application for an entirely different sector of its war effort prior to its use in advanced aircraft prototypes.

This substance, code-named *Schornsteinfeger*, literally meaning "chimney sweep," was a compound made of graphite and rubber. It possessed proven ability to absorb radar energy and weaken radar echoes bouncing off treated surfaces. Chimney Sweep, which used the same essential components as iron ball paint—the outer RAM skin applied to the F-117A and B-2, so-named because the paint is impregnated with microscopic particles of iron—was originally developed by the German navy as a means of protecting its U-boat fleet in the Atlantic.

Though having taken a heavy toll on Allied transatlantic shipping in the early stages of the war, by 1943 countermeasures—many based on secret Ultra intel—had decimated Germany's U-boat force. Allied radar played a key role in U-boat detection, since U-boats needed to regularly surface in order to recharge their batteries and replenish their supplies of breathable air. Once on the surface they were prey to Allied radar carried on ships and especially surveillance aircraft. Once detected they were quickly and efficiently dealt with by aerial bombardment or sea-launched torpedoes.

Chimney Sweep was seen as a way to counter the threat posed by radar. It worked effectively but proved useless due to a single, fatal flaw—when immersed in salt water it became useless, since the salt crystals and water formed a layer that nullified Chimney Sweep's radar-defeating qualities. This didn't apply to aircraft, though, for obvious reasons. Variations on

Chimney Sweep were applied to the Luftwaffe's superplanes under development during the war.

## THE HORTEN WING

The Nazis launched several main initiatives in advanced aircraft during this period, such as the Heinkel 178, the first military jet, which flew in 1929; the Messerschmitt 262, the first and only jet fighter to see active service in World War II; and one-man rocket planes such as the Komet, which also flew in the war. The aircraft most closely resembling modern stealth aircraft in concept and design, however, were those built as prototypes under the direction of the Horten brothers, a design generically known as the Horten Wing.

The so-called "flying wing" design, with its most recent use in the B-2 Spirit stealth bomber and the U.S. Navy's canceled A-12 AX project, though long associated with the Hortens, didn't begin with them.

In fact an all-wing airframe was an early concept dating back to the dawn of modern aviation. Because an aircraft's fuselage and tail section produce anywhere between thirty and fifty percent of the drag acting on the airframe, eliminating these from the aircraft translates into increased speed and more efficient fuel consumption. The flying wing was a natural design concept derived from the earliest observations of the behavior of aeronautic lifting bodies, and aviation pioneers, including Northrop, Lippish, Dunne, Lilienthal, and Chanute built and flew early planes based on the design.

In the wake of the First World War, Germany's aircraft production was severely curtailed by the Versailles treaty but the Luftwaffe got around the lack of pilot training facilities by organizing national glider clubs. The Hortens developed their early designs from membership in the clubs between the two world wars. By the early 1940s, they had already designed and built prototypes of designs based on the flying wing concept.

In 1942, under the Luftwaffe's advanced aircraft programs—and partly in response to German intel that Northrop in the United States had also designed a flying wing aircraft—they developed the Ho IV, and soon thereafter the more advanced Ho V. Both were all-wing aircraft, with the Ho V equipped with a hybrid propeller-jet engine propulsion system.

In early 1944, under Göring's order to produce a fast, long range bomber mentioned earlier, the Horten Ho IX prototypes were built.

These prototypes featured more cantilevered wings and an all-turbojet propulsion system using two large Jumo 004B engines which, with diameters of 80 centimeters, were considerably larger than spec, which was set at 60 centimeters. The result was two bulging engine nacelles at the upper rear of the fuselage, directly between the wing roots.

The Luftwaffe's orders called for an initial production run of 20 of the first Ho IX design. During flight tests of the Ho prototypes an astounding discovery was made—the all-wing aircraft failed to show up accurately on radar. Radar echoes bouncing off the Ho's airframe produced indistinct radar signatures more consistent with those returned by flocks of birds than by man-made aircraft.

At first this discrepancy was deemed a result of equipment failure, but it was soon discovered that the flying-wing shape of the airframe itself was deflecting radar beams and dissipating the strength of returning echoes. The result was an image on radar scopes that was far weaker, and therefore far smaller, than would have ordinarily been expected.

Fired with this revolutionary discovery, the Horten brothers, who were familiar with the German navy's Chimney Sweep experiments, used various forms of the *Schornsteinfeger* compound on the fuselage of succeeding Ho models. Test results confirmed that with the application of this primitive RAM skin, the aircraft were even harder to detect on radar than they'd previously been.

It is not known whether the major flaw in these early stealth aircraft—the huge Jumo engines referred to before—was considered. The compressor blades of ramjet engines are especially good radar reflectors, and the hot exhaust produced by the big Jumos would have been easily detectable by infrared imaging (which was in experimental stages then).

Nevertheless, the placement of the engines on the upper fuselage so that the heat and light they generate is hidden from ground observers is very definitely a stealth application and one that was used in both F-117A and B-2 stealth designs. This argues that even though the engines of the Ho were not deeply cocooned in shrouded nacelles as with modern stealth designs, stealth was a concept that figured in this area of the Ho IX's design, too.

Be this as it may, time was running out for Hitler's Reich and within months after first test flight of the Ho IX under turbojet power, the war was over. On April 14, 1945, U.S. forces, racing both the Russians and the British to reach production plants at Goatharwoerken, were in possession of the most advanced of the Ho IX models, the Go 229s.

One of these prototype models was placed in the Smithsonian Air Museum in Washington, D.C. where it still can be seen. It's been reported that in the 1980s technicians from the Lockheed Skunk Works carefully studied it for use in the secret Have Blue concept demonstrator program which ultimately led to production of the F-117A Nighthawk.

Considering the progress that the Nazis had made in advanced weapons technology it's chilling to ponder the impact on the outcome of the war had the Third Reich not been defeated at that precise historical juncture. The race to develop a stealthy intercontinental jet bomber capable of carrying an enormous war load by 1940s standards was coupled with the Nazis' desperate efforts to develop a functional nuclear weapon.

That the combination of the two developments was intended to make possible a strike on the United States, specifically New York City, is not conjecture but fact. Albert Speer, who as armaments minister was in charge of many of the Reich's most ambitious weapons programs and had access to information concerning both Ho aircraft development and nuclear programs, wrote in his biography, *Inside the Third Reich*, that Hitler made it plain that he wouldn't have the slightest qualms against nuking New York.

Although it's not clear that a nuclear weapon would have been available to Germany within a reasonable enough time to make a difference, it is clear that, given even an additional six months, the Ho IX might have become fully operational. In that case Nazi Germany would have been in possession of a fleet of long-range stealth aircraft that were virtually invisible to Allied radar. Even carrying conventional munitions they could have unleashed firestorms on British and American cities that, though non-nuclear in origin, would have had much the same effect.

Fortunately the story of Nazi stealth is about a superplane that never got off the ground.

## CHAPTER 5

# POSTWAR U.S. STEALTH RESEARCH AND DEVELOPMENT

The history of postwar stealth research is also the history of black aircraft programs and exotic aerospace technologies. These programs are links between the early visionaries of aviation, who began designing unconventional flying machines at the turn of the century, to the first true stealth aircraft whose existence was revealed in the 1980s, and on toward the future of stealth warfare. Because secrecy still shrouds these black-world projects—many of which have never been declassified—the extent to which disinformation still shrouds knowledge of these programs is to a large extent unknown.

## COLD WAR SURGE

One thing is for certain, and that is that immediately after World War II and from the earliest years of the Cold War onward, development of exotic aircraft surged. While many if not most of these programs had the attainment of high altitude ceilings and multimach speeds as primary goals, stealth was also a consideration to greater or lesser degrees.

The new bipolar world where two superpowers confronted one another across a divide of continents and oceans, and where each viewed the other as an imminent threat, created the perceived need for an entirely new global defense posture. To U.S. policymakers, the growing arsenal of ICBM-deliverable Soviet nuclear weapons posed a clear and present danger.

On the one hand the United States felt it needed the capability to see what the Soviets were up to so that it could take defensive action. On the other hand Washington wanted to have the capability to strike deep into the Russian heartland with its own nuclear forces should World War III break out. Strategies and policies to meet these objectives obsessed presidential administrations from Eisenhower's to Reagan's.

## COLD WAR AIRCRAFT

Manned aircraft were considered the best ways of achieving both end results. Moreover in the early phases of Cold War, confrontation, piloted planes were the only viable "overhead" assets available. Spy satellites that could do the strategic reconnaissance mission were still decades away.

To accomplish these missions, such aircraft needed to be stealthy as well as fast-moving. Recce birds and strategic bombers alike would also need to outwit Soviet radar coverage over the Russian homeland and outmaneuver Soviet guided missiles and MiG fighter aircraft during surveillance over-flights or bombing runs.

And while the term *stealth* as we understand and use it today is a neologism of later coinage, the term "low-observable" was certainly in use and its implications understood by postwar and Cold War aircraft designers.

Lockheed aircraft designer Ben Rich, who worked for Clarence "Kelly" Johnson at Lockheed's Skunk Works wrote that "a low observable aircraft has to be good in six disciplines—radar, infrared, noise, smoke, contrails, and visibility—otherwise you flunk the course."

That these considerations figured in postwar advanced aircraft designs is self-evident even just from the standpoint of fuselage designs—stealth is right in front of you if you have eyes to see it. Although the aerospace industry and the Pentagon tried to keep stealth research secret, stealth was always part of the program.

As mentioned earlier, the bulk of the programs of this era were black, that is, clandestine projects. Even those few projects whose existence was grudgingly revealed, such as the U-2 and A-12/SR-71 Blackbird family spy planes, were never entirely declassified.

As Churchill observed, in war the truth must sometimes be protected by a bodyguard of lies. Divulging information about critical capabilities of military aircraft can and will give adversaries valuable clues to counter-measures it can use against them. For this reason it has to be assumed that a great deal of deliberate disinformation surrounds even the most familiar of white-world projects.

## OPERATION PAPERCLIP (BLUE SKY)

Another reason for the secrecy that cloaked special postwar aircraft pro-jects is that much of it was based on captured prototypes and research done by Nazi technicians, many of whom were now working in the United States under government auspices and official protection. Public recognition of these facts so soon after the war would have aroused a national outcry. The intelligence and defense establishments who had put those ex-Nazis to work needed to avoid such a scenario.

A cloak of secrecy also surrounds the technology transfer issues that gave rise to postwar advanced aircraft programs. At the close of World War II, the United States came out the winner in a race by the three vic-torious Allied powers to grab the cream of Nazi weapons technology and the Reich's brain trust. The Russians got the throwaways, while the Brits got little or nothing, except for what the United States let them have.

Because stealth technology is in the service of clandestine intelligence missions, a word must be said about the programs that gave Nazi special-ists sanctuary in the United States after the war. Operation Paperclip, known also by its disinformation name, Blue Sky, was the code name by which the commandeering of Nazi brain trust and technology was known. As we've seen, the Third Reich was the birthplace not only of rocketry but of advanced aircraft and stealth technologies as well. As Army G-2 debriefed captured Nazi scientists, technicians, and others in-the-know, intelligence agents were startled to discover the extent of the advances that the enemy had made.

The Allies held the edge in radar, fielding airborne radars in the giga-hertz range while the Germans didn't even believe that performance above eight hundred megahertz was possible. The Germans were behind the curve in nuclear weapons, largely because their best physicists had gone over to the United States early in the Nazi regime to escape persecution by Hitler who called physics "a Jewish science," and thus, to him, a bas-tard discipline of no practical value. Otherwise the Germans were ahead of the curve in every other technology area, scoring breakthroughs in jet propulsion and rocketry that put them beyond much or all that the Allies had accomplished in these same fields.

The postwar intelligence discoveries meant that, had the war continued, Hitler's boast of Nazi superweapons might not have been that far-fetched. It also meant that there would be inevitable technology leakage in the postwar world, and the side that had the most toys could declare itself the winner. Facing the new postwar order and a Cold War between the USSR and the United States, it was deemed imperative that America be the win-ning side.

The alternative was to leave the Soviets holding all the aces, and that was clearly no alternative at all. Via Paperclip, former Nazi scientists were repatriated as U.S. citizens and put to work making use of their skills to produce a new crop of weapons for the United States. That many of them, such as Werner Von Braun, had been ardent Nazis fanatically loyal to Hitler was unquestionable.

But the end was felt to justify the means. At the same time the United States continued to work along the lines of its homegrown stealth re-search. As already mentioned, American air pioneers were part of the ros-ter of early stealth visionaries. Northrop, Lockheed, and other aerospace defense contractors made efforts to develop a new breed of advanced, low-observable aircraft of many types. In facilities like the Skunk Works, based at Burbank, California, stealth was secretly being explored and the fruits of the research applied to next-generation aircraft.

## OPERATION MAJORITY (MAJESTIC)

Another postwar secret project connected with stealth research also bears mentioning. This is Operation Majority, also known by a disinformation code name Majestic. That Majority allegedly concerned contact between the U.S. government and extraterrestrials should not exclude it from a well-informed discussion of stealth.

That most or all of Majority might have been disinformation is irrelevant since disinformation contaminates all discussion of the postwar black projects, including (it must be repeated) those later openly acknowledged. Bolstering Majority have been the claims of retired Col. Philip Corso who has stated that several key military technologies, including the silicon microchip itself, were retrieved from crashed UFOs. Although a good deal of Corso's claims are compelling, other aspects require leaps of faith.

Be that as it may, there is evidence to support allegations of research into discoid aerospace vehicles by both the Nazis and in the United States after the war, and some of these will be covered in the following chapter.

> The discoid form is inherently low-observable. Devoid of radar reflective angles and projections, such as wing roots, weapon pylons, air intakes, and the like, discoid aircraft present small radar cross-sections. If powered by exotic propulsion technologies that, unlike turbo-ramjets or other air-breathing systems, don't show strong signatures at the infrared end of the spectrum, such aerospace vehicles would also be low-observable to thermal imagining. They would also be far quieter, if not altogether silent. Obviously discoid aircraft would satisfy Ben Rich's six disciplines of stealth to a T.

## SUBMARINES

Naval operations were also key enablers for the gathering of strategic intelligence on the Soviets and other intelligence targets during the Cold War, and therefore there was a need to get in close in order to see and hear what adversaries were saying and doing. It was during these years that submarines became the stealth platforms of the ocean as aircraft were in the skies.

Like aircraft, submarines also performed reconnaissance and attack missions. Not only were subs used to emplace and retrieve listening devices hidden on the seabed, deliver special forces troops to covert landing zones, and listen in on Soviet and East Bloc transmissions, but they also became increasingly critical as the third leg of the United States's nuclear defense triad of land-based missiles, long-range bomber aircraft, and maritime weapons platforms. A new generation of nuclear submarines could remain submerged for months at a time without needing to resurface. These were designed with curvilinear shapes and coated with anechoic skins highly resistant to sonar detection.

Propulsion systems that reduced propeller cavitation—the undersea equivalent of the heat generated by ramjet engines—that were the strongest producers of sonar signatures were also part of the design, as were communications systems that were resistant to hostile interception. At the same time, better, more sensitive sonars were also developed to counter the increased stealthiness of the opposition's submarine forces. As a result, oceans of the globe became the scenes of deadly games of tag between the stealthiest weapons systems possessed by the superpowers.

## THE CHANGING DEFINITION OF STEALTH

In these years the definition of stealth would change, too. The deception operations of the war years characterized by Ultra intelligence were played out against a new global backdrop, but Cold War espionage, as a peacetime operation, was taking on a distinctive character of its own. Stealth warfare, in its embryonic form, was becoming the province of machines that sped through the air and the edge of atmospheric space or prowled the hidden regions of the deepest seas. Deception operations continued, of course, but warfare began to be stealthy because of the need to remain hidden and strike from afar, and at the same time to catch the enemy napping before he had a chance to catch you unaware.

At the same time the very nature of mechanized warfare was beginning to change. The word *kill* itself might no longer refer to human lives, and more and more frequently became associated with the inanimate machinery of warfare. The robotic weaponry of future conflicts had its origins at the dawn of stealth.

# CHAPTER 6

# U.S. PRECURSORS OF STEALTH

The B-35 and B-49 "flying wing" aircraft programs are among the few declassified projects of the postwar years. The programs led to the production of a tail-less all-wing lifting body. These aircraft were initially powered by turboprop engines and then later by ramjets. A special point of interest is that of all the U.S. postwar special aircraft design projects, the B-35 series bore a striking resemblance to the Ho IX Go 229 both in silhouette and in profile.

The B-35 principally differed from the Horten wing in its size. It was designed to carry a crew of nine plus a relief crew of six. It was intended to be a long-range bomber, capable of striking out to a 10,000-mile range and delivering a 40,000-plus pound bomb load. The B-49 replaced the propeller-driven propulsion system with eight jet engines, increasing the size, weapon load, range, and striking power of the aircraft.

Like the Ho IX, the stealth capabilities of the flying wing aircraft were known to flight engineers, and yet also like the U.S. aircraft's German predecessor, range, speed, and bomb load were primary considerations while the plane's radar-evading qualities were "gravy." At least this is the official version. The flying wing program has its white and black history and it may be that stealth was more of an operational concern than is openly acknowledged.

Other mysteries surrounding the B-49 concern whether the development program was canceled following the well-known crash at Foley Air Force Base in Nevada on June 5, 1948, that killed the aircraft's five-man crew, including its pilot, Captain Glen W. Edwards, for which Foley was renamed Edwards Air Force Base . Reports that the B-49 program was in fact not canceled and was used in stealthy reconnaissance missions over the Korean peninsula during the Korean War and on recce flights over mainland China after that have persisted and have some credence.

If true, the reports of B-49 covert reconnaissance and surveillance flights would tend to confirm that the low-observable qualities of the flying wing airframe were far more important to mission planners than was officially let on. One such report is a case in point: RB-49F reconnaissance variants of the B-49 flying wing flew over Red China on intelligence gathering missions. The aircraft were supposedly piloted by Republic of China Air Force (ROCAF) personnel, the air force of Nationalist China based on Taiwan. Six RB-49F aircraft were secretly sea-lifted to Taiwan. They were based at Taoyuan, an air base from which U-2 spy plane missions also staged.

Both programs are said to have been black CIA-run operations. Along with the planes came a team of 12 ROCAF pilots secretly trained at Edwards AFB, 10 of whom returned to Taiwan in 1961 to form the "Black Bat" recce unit—a name similar to "Black Cat" which was the U-2 squadron's code name.

Indeed the similarity of names could well have been intended as part of a deception operation to convince Russian and Chinese agents that only the U-2 was flying surveillance missions, a cover story that would hold up because surveillance targets knew about U-2 overflights—their SAM (surface-to-air missile) radars could see them—but were only sporadically effective against them because of their extremely high flight ceiling.

The RB-49Fs, on the other hand, returned an extremely low radar cross section or RCS and flew a low-altitude surveillance vector while the U-2s drew the attention—and often the fire—of the hostile SAMs, allegedly resulting in several shoot-downs of the U-2 but none of the RB-49Fs. All 10 of the flying wings were to have been returned to the U.S. by 1970 and the program, it is said, classified deep black.

There are other reports concerning flying wing overflights of North Korea during and after the Korean War, and if the program was in effect for nine or ten years, it could have well been flown over Soviet Russia as well.

Still other reports indicate that stealthy unmanned aerial vehicles which were capable of electronically spoofing enemy radars with a bogus U-2 signature, and thus hiding the existence of these advanced remotely piloted surveillance drones, were also used in recce missions over China, North Korea, and later Vietnam.

There are precedents for giving credence to these reports. The Eisenhower administration used aerial spy assets to gather information of nuclear weapons test and missile launch facilities over the Soviet Union. Although virtually everything remains classified, enough has leaked to indicate that there was a vast surveillance effort carried out to spy on communist China, Korea, and the Soviets beginning early in the Cold War and continuing over the next three decades.

## THE U-2

The U-2 spy plane program, as already mentioned, was another covert aircraft program that flew surveillance missions around the world. While it's a precursor of stealth, and deserves mention, the U-2 is less interesting to this work than some other advanced recce planes because it was probably the least stealthy platform of them all. Although the U-2 did boast a black coating of iron-ball paint on its fuselage and the use of radar absorbent materials at radar reflective junctions on the airframe, stealth was not the U-2's long suit.

The U-2's greatest protection lay in its extremely high flight ceiling, one that placed it generally beyond the lethality envelope of existent SAM systems. In fact, the capability to fly higher than missiles could follow was a key reason for Lockheed's Kelly Johnson having recommended the construction of a very high-altitude surveillance plane in 1954, which was subsequently approved by Eisenhower as a CIA asset, since the Air Force had already turned down this same proposal.

The U-2 could fly exceptionally high and stay in the air for long periods of time. This made it the perfect aerial surveillance aircraft for gathering intel on the items of interest to the United States regarding the two main communist states of the era, Russia and Red China.

Both of these communist regimes had been established in countries with vast, inhospitable land masses that could not be penetrated by any other means at the time. Covert bases were established in nearby countries friendly to the United States, such as Turkey, Iran, Pakistan, Japan, and the already mentioned nationalist Republic of China on Taiwan.

Hundreds of missions were flown to gather intel on the development of nuclear weapons programs and missile launch facilities in the target countries, both by U.S. and foreign pilots. While photographic intelligence (PHOTINT) derived from U-2 missions showed CIA and NSA analysts sights never before beheld in a pre-satellite age, the U-2's high-observable profile made it the subject of controversy during a period of building Cold War tensions, where mission success was a tradeoff between good intel and worsening U.S.-USSR relations.

East-West tensions reached their peak after the 1960 shoot-down of a U-2 flown by Francis Gary Powers over Sverdlovsk, Russia, and spelled doom for the U-2 surveillance program. The U-2's successor, the TR-1, continues to fly, albeit under a far different set of geopolitical contexts than its Cold War predecessor. From the standpoint of stealth, other aircraft development programs of the era stand out far more than does the U-2 program.

## THE FDL, X-15, AND DYNA-SOAR PROGRAMS

During the early 1960s, the USAF Flight Dynamics Laboratory (FDL) devised new and unconventional shapes for hypersonic vehicles. The planes—FDL-5, FDL-6, FDL-7, and FDL-8—were designed with the intention of sustained hypersonic flight (both gliding and powered) and reentry. Even at hypersonic speeds, they were capable of lift-to-drag ratios as high as 3:1. The tail and fin arrangements were all different, but they all shared one characteristic: They were all 75-degree triangles.

In the late 1960s, Lockheed and the USAF FDL built a full-scale mockup of a hypersonic research vehicle using the FDL-5 shape. This configuration used a stabilization technique called "compression sharing" and featured flip-out wings to reduce its landing speed and retractable fairings in front of the split windshield. Fuel for initial acceleration was to be carried in two conformal tanks that fitted around the aircraft's nose like a collar.

The USAF FDL projects paved the way for future projects involving orbital, transatmospheric, and hypersonic flight. These projects include the Transatmospheric Vehicle (TAV) and the Maneuvering Reentry Research Vehicle (MRRV).

The X-15 and Dyna-Soar projects were other early projects that were forerunners of modern stealth aircraft. Both planes were conceived as high-altitude and high-speed vehicles capable of operating on the fringes of space. The X-15 was intended to reach operating speeds of Mach 6, and in its more than 300 test flights did in fact reach a top speed of Mach 7.4 and reached an altitude of 354,000 feet. Though an air-breather, the X-15's ramjet engine was fitted with a rocket-like nozzle that optimized performance at high speeds and altitudes.

Dyna-Soar, officially called the X-20, was conceived as a follow-on program to the X-15. It was developed by Boeing to function as a small, single-pilot, recoverable space plane that could land on a conventional runway. The small, delta wing lifting body would launch like the space shuttle—which, with its blunt-edged wings and nose, it distantly resembled—boosted into suborbital flight by a modified ICBM such as a Titan missile.

Unlike the X-15, which was also seen as space-capable, there was little pretense about Dyna-Soar's use as a near-space research vehicle for NASA. The Air Force saw the X-20 as a tool of space-based reconnaissance and a possible platform for future space-based weapons.

The manned space-plane was to have been used to sneak up on Soviet satellites and examine them at close range for evidence of reconnaissance devices or orbital nuclear weaponry (there was no bilateral nonproliferation treaty for space-based weapons at the time). The Dyna-Soar could then return to Earth, land at any conventional military runway, and be quickly turned around for another mission.

The Dyna-Soar project was canceled in late 1963 largely because of advances in satellite-based reconnaissance systems and East-West treaties against space-based nukes. Although the X-20 was canceled, the X series of reusable space planes continued well into the 1970s with the X-24 series, which were to be launched from piggyback rails atop various mother ship aircraft. The X-24 project was canceled, too, but the technological lessons learned from it are believed to have been transitioned to other clandestine programs such as Aurora, which I discuss more later on.

## FLYING DISKS

As already mentioned, saucer-shaped aircraft designs are inherently stealthy, affording virtually no angular surfaces to reflect radar echoes. For this reason and others—including the fact that the Germans had very likely developed at least working prototypes of saucer designs which were captured along with the designers by the U.S.—saucer-shaped aircraft or "flying disks" were also developed after the war under clandestine programs.

One such secret development program that came to light accidentally was the Avro, named after the U.S. company at which one of Nazi Germany's leading specialists in saucer aircraft, Walter Meithe, worked in the postwar years, the defense aerospace contractor A.V. Roe and Company. The existence of the Avro came to light when one was photographed by freelance cameraman Jack Judges. The photo found its way into the newspapers and the Air Force acknowledged its existence, releasing an official photo of the craft but providing few details. In fact the Avro was developed under the secret Project Silver Bug which sought to develop radical-design vertical takeoff and landing (VTOL) aircraft for a variety of uses, including carrier operations.

It's speculated that at least some of the flying disk sightings of the immediate postwar years, and even the famous crash at Roswell, New Mexico, might have been results of U.S.-developed flying disks rather than those of extraterrestrial origin. A lengthy discussion of flying disk programs is beyond the scope of this book, but saucer-shaped vehicles do seem to have been under study by the United States as advanced aircraft prototypes.

## THE BLACKBIRD PROGRAM

By far the stealthiest of all modern stealth precursors are those aircraft designed, built and flown under the A-12/YF-12/SR-71 Blackbird family programs, and it's with the SR-71 that the first truly modern stealth aircraft makes its appearance.

In the mid-1950s, after it had become apparent that the Soviets were deploying new SAMs and MiG fighters that might one day shoot down even the high-flying U-2, the CIA and Department of Defense began to rev up efforts to perfect the U-2's successor.

In 1956, the CIA's Richard Bissel, who ran virtually all U.S. clandestine spy plane missions as a personal fiefdom, had already begun working with the Skunk Works's Kelly Johnson on the aircraft that was eventually to become the SR-71 Blackbird. The new aircraft was to be built for speed and stealth. It was to fly far higher than the U-2 yet far faster—pulling Mach numbers of 3 or better—and yet be far less visible to search and track radars of Soviet SAM sites, MiGs and other threats.

In June, 1960, President Eisenhower signed an executive order for the first prototype aircraft, yet "on low priority, as a high-performance reconnaissance plane for the Air Force in time of war." Eisenhower didn't think there would be much chance of the new recce bird being used in peacetime, but he turned out to be very wrong in this assumption. The Blackbird and its predecessors became one of the longest-running aircraft programs in the history of military aviation, and the planes are still flying today. The major reason for Eisenhower's lack of enthusiasm for the newer spy plane lay in the fact that he believed that manned aircraft tools of surveillance and reconnaissance were growing obsolete.

In 1958, Bissel and his boss, Director of Central Intelligence (DCI) Allen Dulles, had persuaded Congressional leaders to approve secret funding for the first U.S. spy satellite, code-named CORONA. In February 1959, Ike told the CIA that U-2 flights "should be held to a minimum pending the availability of this new equipment," anticipating satellite intel that was finally available in August, 1960.

CORONA's overhead imaging was far superior to the intelligence take that the U-2 had previously brought back. Once he'd seen the capabilities of the new space-based system Eisenhower clearly didn't think there was much future in another piloted surveillance aircraft, no matter how fast or stealthy it might be.

To an extent he was correct in this sober assessment, because the SR-71 presented Lockheed engineers with formidable difficulties in design and construction, problems that were not entirely solved until the mid-1960s when the first A-12 prototype came off the assembly line. By this time it had also become apparent that satellites were not a surveillance panacea but only one form of intel collection asset that a country had to have in its bag of tricks if it was to effectively spy on its adversaries.

(USAF)

*The SR-71 Blackbird spy plane in flight.*

# CHAPTER 6: U.S. PRECURSORS OF STEALTH

Like other assets, satellites had their weaknesses, the foremost being that their orbital paths were as predictable as the rising and setting of the sun and moon, and for many of the same reasons. The Russians didn't have a way to shoot U.S. satellites down—yet—but if they knew when to expect them to pass overhead, that was almost as good as killing them. To evade and confuse U.S. spy satellites they developed camouflage and deception to a high military art, one called by the uniquely Russian name, *maskirovka*.

Dubbed "perhaps the most enigmatic aircraft in service," by one observer, the Blackbird began its service life as a pinch-hitter, flying intelligence missions too short-notice or low-altitude for satellites and too dangerous for other manned spy aircraft. Like the U-2 and other spy aircraft, the SR (as the SR-71 is frequently called by insiders) flew surveillance tracks along Soviet borders and made incursions into Soviet airspace.

The length of a Boeing 727, flying at speeds of Mach 3 or better at ceilings approaching 90,000 feet, painted matte black with muted USAF markings, and almost invisible to Ivan's radars during these maiden overflights, the Blackbird quickly became the bane of the red air force. Reports indicate that by the early 1980s SRs had eluded well over 1,000 attempts by Soviet and other air forces to knock the troublesome recce bird from the skies.

Delivered almost completely assembled by two trucks and a special trailer to the Air Force's classified Groom Lake flight test facility (also known as Dreamland, The Ranch and, of course, Area 51) in southeastern Nevada in mid-January of 1962, the first "Article" (a CIA catch-all term that includes all Agency-funded and operated aircraft), an A-12 bearing the serial number 60-6924 was reassembled over a period of weeks in one of several large Groom Lake hangars and prepared for its first flight. Following preliminary ground and taxi tests that led to a first hop on April 24, the first official flight was successfully staged on April 26.

The first public acknowledgment of the existence of the Blackbird came on February 29, 1964. Republican presidential front-runner Barry Goldwater was then accusing Lyndon Johnson of being more interested in social legislation for the Great Society than in the military defense of America. In an effort to deflect Goldwater's criticism LBJ decided to take the wraps off what had been one of the most closely held secrets in America. The fact that the spy plane program had been inaugurated during Eisenhower's watch and brought to completion by the Kennedy administration didn't prevent LBJ from claiming credit for it.

Johnson stated, "The performance of the A-11 far exceeds that of any other aircraft in the world today." Yet LBJ had made a mistake: The aircraft was in fact called the YF-12A. Reportedly, LBJ misread "AMI" (advanced manned interceptor) as "A-11."

The misreading was allowed to stand. It was known that Lockheed's designations for the test prototypes of the Blackbird ran from A-1 to A-12. This lent credence to the A-11 designation, but mainly nobody came forward to correct the chief executive because few wanted to incur the wrath of LBJ's famous temper if it could be humanly avoided.

After the original gaffe was smoothed over, LBJ made further statements about the secret aircraft that included yet another faux pas. When he followed up his A-11 announcement of February 29 with a July 25 revelation of the development of the SR-71, he juxtaposed reconnaissance strike (RS-70)—as the canceled XB-70 bomber had been designated—into strike reconnaissance.

Once again, though he'd gotten it wrong all over again, Johnson's name for the new plane stuck. From there on out the Blackbird family would bear the SR designation.

The first public unveiling of a Blackbird spy plane took place at Edwards Air Force Base in the fall of 1964. The YF-12A, announced the press, was an interceptor aircraft that would guard U.S. shores from hordes of Russian bombers lurking just over the horizon. The spy aircraft was initially reported as being the follow-on to the North American F-108 Rapier, which was to have been the escort fighter for U.S. heavy bombers on their way to drop nuclear weapons in the Soviet heartland (the fighter was later canceled).

In operational service, the Blackbird, as its name implies, is painted black from nose to tail. The composition of the paint is officially classified, but the fact that it has radar-absorbing properties that contribute to the stealth characteristics of the SR-71 is well known. The black paint is probably a variation on the iron-ball paint developed by the Lockheed Skunk Works as early as the mid-1950s and applied to earlier aircraft projects.

It's so-called because of the minute iron particles used in its pigmentation. These dissipate electromagnetically generated energy and effectively lower the radar signature of the aircraft. The paint is also optimized for high heat emissivity and actually radiates significantly more friction-generated heat than it absorbs at the SR's Mach 3 cruising speeds.

The blended airchine surrounding the fuselage center-body is another early stealth characteristic. Although the chined fuselage of the Blackbird is, with the delta wing configuration, part of the lifting body strategy toward providing lift at the speeds and altitudes the SR was to fly, the rounded chine that forms a discoid shape when viewed from certain angles presents few angular surfaces to easily reflect radar echoes. The exact RCS of the Blackbird is still classified, but it is considerably smaller than that produced by a flock of small birds. This is large by comparison to the RCS of an F-117A, which is said to be smaller than a bumblebee's, but quite small in comparison to other pre-stealth aircraft.

The addition of a reconnaissance systems officer (RSO) as a "backseater" in the SR's second cockpit was another innovation that contributed to the stealthy characteristics of the plane. The RSO's duties were not only to operate the array of cameras and electronic sensors that scanned the terrain below while the pilot flew his "black line" across the skies, but also to conduct electronic warfare, and as a "wizzo" or weapons system operator much like the backseater of jet fighter aircraft.

The SRs were stealthy, but as just noted they were not in the same league as F-117As. Enemy SAMs, MiGs, or other hostile aircraft could frequently get a good radar skin paint on an SR. When they did, the backseater was equipped with an array of electronic countermeasures to enable jamming and spoofing of enemy search and track radars.

Deception-jamming was one of the RSO's primary electronic stealth weapons, enabling him to generate false targets on enemy radar scopes, or use deception repeater signals to make the SR seem to jump around in the sky, enabling the RSO to break missile acquisition locks. The RSO could also receive RAW, or radar advanced warnings, of the approach of still-distant hostile contacts with enough advance warning to change course, if necessary.

# THE D-21 DRONE

The D-21, a Mach 4-cruise, ramjet-powered drone, was carried by two specially modified A-12s atop a pylon mounted on the empennage be-tween the A-12's two vertical tail surfaces. Like the Blackbird itself, the drone, which had a wingspan of 19 feet, a length of approximately 40 feet, and a gross weight of approximately 20,000 pounds, possessed very low radar and infrared signatures.

Code-named Senior Bowl, the D-21 program resulted in the construction of some 38 drones by Lockheed's Skunk Works. The drone program was short-lived, though, as there were continual problems with launching the drone in flight during experimental testing.

On what was to be the final test of the D-21, the drone pitched sharply upward from its A-12 mother ship on launch, sending the plane into a tail-spin. The drone was destroyed and the backseater killed in the aftermath of the accident. As a result, and also because of changing strategic align-ments, the D-21 program was canceled soon after the crash. Nevertheless, although the D-21 never again flew from a Blackbird mother ship it did fly again, as we'll see later on.

Because the Blackbird program was sponsored by the CIA, details of the D-21's service career remain shrouded in mystery. Only limited information concerning its exact performance specifications and physical characteristics has surfaced, even with the passage of several decades.

It's known that the D-21 was to be treated as an expendable surveillance asset. Following a mission the drone was to fly to its canister recovery zone. There it would eject the film canisters on which surveillance data was stored. The canisters would fall to earth by parachute. As they drifted down a specially equipped C-130 Hercules would scoop them up in mid-air. The drone would then either self-destruct or be remotely detonated by an internal explosive charge. It could also be deliberately crashed to achieve the same end result.

# THE SR-71

The SR-71, first ordered in an initial batch of six aircraft in December 1962, soon became the best known of the Blackbird family. The SR was a major redesign of the original A-12 configuration which, by 1967, was beginning to reach the end of its service life and also was becoming redundant to more advanced intelligence systems then being developed by the CIA and the Pentagon.

The last A-12 flight took place in June of 1968. Following its retirement all missions requiring A-12 capabilities were flown by the newer SR-71A. The surviving A-12 fleet of approximately eight aircraft were moved to Beale Air Force Base in California for long-term storage. They remain there in mothballs to the present day.

Bigger, heavier, and internally more spacious than its predecessors, the SR-71A offered increased range and a slightly greater payload while also accommodating a second crew member. The latter, eventually referred to as an RSO (reconnaissance systems officer) was a technical specialist whose primary concerns were the aircraft's extensive array of electronic and optical sensors, and its passive and active electronic warfare systems.

The SR-71 was deployed to Kadena Air Base, Okinawa, and to RAF Mildenhall in the UK. Blackbirds were based permanently at both locations throughout the Cold War and until the Blackbird program's official cancellation in 1989. Following the Gulf War the Blackbird was again brought back into service. With the spy plane fleet retrofitted with new avionics and surveillance equipment the SR is still in service, making it the longest-lived stealth aircraft in aviation history.

# PART 2

# AIR AND SPACE OPERATIONS

In this part of the story of stealth we'll examine the low-observable aircraft that have flown yesterday's most critical missions and will be equally important tomorrow as stealth aircraft are called upon to fly under conditions they've never before encountered.

# CHAPTER 7

# THE F-117A NIGHTHAWK

In the early morning hours of Thursday, January 17, 1991, stealth first proved its mettle in the dark skies over downtown Baghdad. This date marked the first night of the air assault phase of the Gulf War, Desert Wind. Pilots of the 415th Tactical Fighter Wing had been tasked with striking the initial blows of the air assault, having trained for the mission since August 21, 1990, but nobody had predicted that Iraqi defenses would open up before incoming U.S. tactical air was even detected.

As F-117A Nighthawks out of King Khalid Airbase in Saudi Arabia some 1,000 miles to the south approached the glimmering lights of the city below, stealth pilots saw to their chagrin that they were flying into the teeth of the enemy's defenses. Triple-A tracer fire from gun emplacements on the rooftops, so dense at times it appeared like vast sheets of flame, rippled angrily into the skies punctuated by the blazing exhaust contrails of SAMs boiling up and exploding into cascades of fire.

*(Department of Defense)*

*An F-117A Nighthawk in flight.*

Having learned, shortly after midnight, that the air assault had been launched, and assuming that U.S. stealth aircraft would form the spearhead of a strike to be followed by a massive assault by conventional TACAIR assets, the Iraqis opened up blindly with everything they had. The Mother of All Battles was upon them, they knew, and the reception they had prepared for the Nighthawks was intended to hurl a dense curtain of AAA and SAM fires into the air from the approximately 1,300 triple-A pieces positioned around Baghdad, "a massive pillar of fire that the Yankee lackeys of Zionist imperialism would not dare enter," and from which nothing could emerge unscathed.

As they flew toward this lethal incandescent cauldron, several pilots were prepared for what they assumed would prove their inevitable combat deaths. And though the fire suddenly slackened and stopped altogether as the first assault wave penetrated the airspace over Baghdad (a cease-fire had been issued at 2:56 A.M. to prevent overheating and permanent damage to the Iraqis' overworked guns) the barrage started up again once the F-117As had destroyed their targets downtown.

The black planes were in the thick of it as they began their return flights. On debriefing, many pilots confessed to having had initial doubts about stealth's ability to cloak them from detection. But as they cleared hostile airspace all realized that stealth worked: The enemy had in fact not seen them. "They were shooting up in the sky because they felt we were coming, but they didn't have a clue to where we were coming from," said one stealth pilot after returning to King Khalid AFB. Like Shadrach, every member of the sortie had passed through the furnace without apparent harm.

That night the 415th TFW's stealth pilots proved a maxim of modern war, if not all wars: You can't hit what you can't see; you can't kill what you can't hit. Consequently weapons and weapon platforms that can steal up on targets undetected offer a decisive advantage to attack forces in modern warfighting.

That night the F-117A brought stealth into modern combat. First-look, first-kill systems that permit the operators of distant weapon platforms, such as tactical fighters, to select targets at standoff range, launch their armament loads, and score kills before the targets can even recognize their presence, serve the same objective. In both cases low-observable (LO) technology, otherwise known as stealth, is the force multiplier of choice.

After the F-117A proved itself successful as an invisible fighter in Desert Storm, the Lockheed Skunk Works proposed an upgraded carrier version for the U.S. Navy. The A/F-117X would have been modified with reduced sweep wings that would have allowed the Seahawk stealth fighter to comfortably fit on carrier decks and two horizontal tail surfaces for added lift to help give the aircraft stability during shipboard takeoff and landing. The Navy was cool to the Lockheed proposal, preferring to pursue development of the AX stealth fighter program. In the end, neither A/F-117X nor AX ever got off the ground. The future stealth aircraft for the U.S. Navy will be the carrier-deployable version of the F-35 Joint Strike Fighter.

# THE NIGHTHAWK IN ACTION

Of all the advanced tactical and strategic warplanes that have been developed thus far, the F-117A Nighthawk is the only one to have flown in three regional conflicts.

The faceted or angular stealth of the Nighthawk began with the secret DARPA-run Have Blue program in the 1970s. The Nighthawk flew its maiden mission in Panama in 1989, proved its mettle in the 1991 Gulf War and again flew stealth combat missions into Iraq in March and April 2003.

Actual nose-camera images from laser-guided bombs in flight to their targets released to the news media demonstrated the ability of the stealth fighter to deliver its ordnance with pinpoint accuracy. Gun camera video of surgical bombing strikes, including the placement of a laser-guided bomb down the airshaft of Baghdad's "AT&T" tower during Desert Storm, convinced even critics that stealth research paid off. In both Gulf campaigns, USAF Nighthawks flew undetected by enemy threat-seeking radars into Iraqi airspace. The F-117As even passed through the heavy Triple-A and SAM defenses over central Baghdad without a single plane being hit.

All the same (and for similar reasons to those cited later in connection with the B-2), the F-117A can sometimes be a hard plane to maneuver in flight. The strange geometries of the aircraft's aerodynamic control surfaces, the mainstay of its faceted stealthiness, make it inherently unstable when flown.

In fact, without its sophisticated, computer-controlled inertial navigation system (INS), the stealth fighter would get about as far as a broken kite in a high wind. Even with this computerized augmentation, the plane has had some notorious handling problems, especially while refueling. Pilots who have flown the F-117A refer to the stealth by the less-than-honorific title of the "Wobbly Goblin."

In 1996, an F-117A attached to the 49th Fighter Wing crashed on the Zuni Indian Reservation in New Mexico, an area populated by members of the Pueblo and Zuni tribes. While the crash is the first publicly acknowledged incident of its kind, it is not the first time an F-117A has experienced serious in-flight control problems, at least while on test or training runs.

Because of in-flight instability, all components of the F-117A fleet had their INS systems upgraded with an improved version by 1998, promising greater aerodynamic stability for the aircraft. This is the Ring Laser Gyro/Global Positioning System Navigation Improvement Program system or RNIP-Plus retrofit, which is designed to integrate the F-117A's INS with

GPS data from the array of 24 global positioning satellites currently in orbit around the earth. Test pilots who've used it say that it significantly reduces the aircraft's tendency to drift off course. RNIP-Plus also increases targeting precision, aligning target crosshairs to more precise calibrations during missile launch and bomb delivery.

Because of maneuverability and other issues concerning the F-117's design features, the Nighthawk will only strike under the cloak of darkness. In daylight combat operations, the F-117A would become extremely vulnerable to even mediocre enemy fighter planes chancing to sight it visually, although continuing to remain invisible or extremely hard to see by other means, such as on airborne search radars. Once sighted, though, it would become an easy target of opportunity. At a maximum airspeed of Mach 1 the stealth fighter is not fast enough, nor is it maneuverable enough, to escape a true combat fighter, and its air-to-air ordnance is virtually nil. The stealth is optimized for covert offensive strike missions and for little else.

This is one reason why the stealth will continue mostly to fly night combat missions and will be only used against high-value targets whose destruction merits the hazard of exposing any one of the fleet of multi-million dollar aircraft to any form of danger, however slight or intangible that risk might be. Daylight stealth will have to wait for a new generation of advanced strike and reconnaissance aircraft, already flown as prototypes, such as Bird of Prey (we'll discuss these later on).

## HOW THE F-117A'S STEALTH WORKS

From cockpit canopy to tail assembly, the F-117A exhibits low-observable features designed to enable the Nighthawk to evade radar and survive enemy air defenses.

The edges of the cockpit canopy, like all surfaces on the F-117A, have no right angles, which are strong reflectors of radar. Working from the assumption that the F-117A would most likely meet the first hostile radar signals head-on, the plane's frontal profile was designed to foil enemy defense radars in the first stages of the Nighthawk's mission.

The glass in the five flat canopy windows is made of a laminate that allows the pilot to look out but prevents radar waves from entering the cockpit and bouncing off unstealthy items inside. Without this coating, the reflection from the pilot's helmet, for example, would be greater than that from the entire aircraft.

The wing's leading edge is ruler straight and swept back at a 67° angle. Its design reflects radar waves to the side and rear of the aircraft instead of forward—and back toward enemy radar receivers—as is normally the case. Signals from other bearings, such as radar side lobes, are deflected by the F-117A's flight surface panels which are tilted at least 30° from vertical. The tilted surfaces deflect most wavelengths upward instead of back toward the enemy.

Sawtooth edges are also used extensively on the forward portions of the airframe in order to deflect radar waves away from hostile receivers. Any seam or ridge that runs perpendicular to the path of a radar wave will reflect the wave directly toward the sender. The forward edges of the Nighthawk's windows, canopy, and the five-sided bay above the nose would normally be excellent radar-reflective surfaces. Because the saw-tooth surfaces present jagged surfaces to oncoming radars, the waves are deflected to left and right, again away from hostile receivers.

An aircraft's air intakes pose another set of very good radar-reflective surfaces. They contain compressor blades for the turbofans of the aircraft's ramjet engines, and these are among the most highly radar reflective surfaces on any aircraft. The F-117A's air duct inlets are covered with a fine grille made up of small rectangular grids. The grille is composed of intersecting knife-edged blades and coated with radar absorbent material. The compressor blades are completely shielded behind the grille, which presents a flat, upward-tilting surface that, like other parts of the fuselage, reflects radar away from the aircraft's forward line of flight.

The Nighthawk's wings are swept back at a high angle from the fuse-lage. This is unusual in a subsonic aircraft such as the F-117A. The reason for this wing alignment is to again give the plane low-observable qualities by deflecting radar waves away from the front of the plane.

Other alignments on the faceted airframe serve the same purpose. They were all designed to deflect and dissipate radar echoes bouncing off the airframe away from the line of travel. Because inside corners, such as those formed by the junctions of wing roots with the aircraft's center body, are extremely good radar reflectors and can't be avoided, these all face to the rear of the aircraft. The twin butterfly tail fins at the rear of the F-117A are also designed to deflect radar energies away from hostile receivers. The fins are faceted instead of cambered as with traditional designs.

## LOW-OBSERVABLE (LO) TECHNOLOGY

Low-observable (LO) technology, otherwise known as stealth, is a combination of methods designed to defeat radar identification of combat aircraft by reducing that aircraft's radar cross section (RCS). An RCS is produced whenever the beams of search radars come into contact with aerodynamic surfaces on an aircraft's body, reflect off (backscatter), and are in turn picked up by receivers located on the ground or in the air.

When there is high backscatter of radar pulses, the aircraft shows up on radarscopes in high definition and is said to have a large RCS. When radar energy is absorbed and backscatter is dissipated, the RCS is correspondingly small and the plane is said to be low observable.

Reducing an aircraft's RCS affords it with a number of advantages over easier-to-see or "visible" aircraft. For one thing, it forces enemy radars to increase their transmission power and to emanate more strongly as they sweep the skies. Stealth has the effect of making these radars more visible to friendly forces and therefore easier to detect and destroy.

Low RCS also enables the design of special surfaces on the fuselage of planes designed to induce errors in enemy detection systems—they can, for example, spoof an incoming missile's homing systems into an inaccurate target picture by dazzling its radar or glinting its infrared trackers with thermal noise.

Further bonuses of low RCS include the reduction of the power of electronic countermeasures needed to jam enemy electronic warfare and to reduce the size of decoys and the quantity of radar-reflective chaff carried by any given warplane, thereby affording more room for offensive weapons payload. In short, a low RCS makes for an overall enhancement of platform survivability in a stress-filled combat environment, and gives the plane or other combat system a better strike and defensive capability.

The Nighthawk's twin General Electric engines are also designed for stealth. They're buried deep in the fuselage, to reduce their heat signatures, and their intakes are protected by a radar-deflecting grille as already mentioned. The engines have shallow "platypus" exhausts, which consist of long rectangular openings broken up by a series of vertical guide vanes.

The exhaust produces a wide, shallow plume of hot gases, which is deflected upward to mix rapidly with cool air outside the plane. Ceramic tiles that dissipate heat are also incorporated into the trailing edges of the engine exhausts to further reduce the F-117A's thermal and infrared signatures.

Finally, a coating or radar absorbent material covers the entire fuselage. RAM coating is comprised of a coating of carbonyl iron serrite, creating a magnetic field of alternating polarity which dissipates radar waves hitting the aircraft. This RAM skin is now sprayed onto the surface of the plane, whereas it was originally applied in cumbersome flexible sheets. RAM putty and tape are used to join seams and local patching and repairs to the RAM skin.

The composition of the F-117's RAM skin is a closely held secret but is thought to be similar in makeup to the iron-ball paint first used on the SR-71. Whatever it's made of, the purpose of the RAM skin is to absorb radar energies and further reduce the strength of returns.

# THE B-2 SPIRIT OF ST. LOUIS

From its first clandestine test fight in 1982, to its official unveiling in 1988, to its first successful test firing of a precision guided standoff munition in 1997, and even to its most recent combat flights in the Second Gulf War, the B-2 Spirit advanced technology bomber has remained the most secret of high-level aircraft projects.

At current production costs of some $2,000,000,000 per aircraft, the B-2 is easily one of the most expensive pieces of military hardware in the history of aviation warfare. In an age of post–Cold War budget cutbacks, the fact that the B-2 ever flew represents a victory for the plane. Despite years of controversy regarding its ability to live up to its advertised capabilities and a radical change in its original combat mission, Congress continued to fund the plane, and the Air Force has flown it on several combat missions.

*(Department of Defense)*

*A U.S. Air Force B-2 Spirit stealth bomber refuels from a KC-135 Stratotanker on April 6, 1999, during an air strike mission in support of NATO Operation Allied Force against targets in the Federal Republic of Yugoslavia.*

Politically speaking, the B-2 continues to fly high while other advanced aircraft programs have been shot down in flames, a fact that made the B-2 a survivor before it ever saw combat. At present, there are officially 21 fully operational B-2 bombers attached to the USAF's 509th Bomb Wing at Whiteman Air Force Base in Missouri—the same number of operational planes planned back in 1993 when Congress capped future acquisitions at 20 additional aircraft.

The B-2 has been called the "jewel in the crown" of U.S. tactical air (TACAIR) assets. In fact, the warplane is considered too valuable to fly into any combat environment where it might entail the risk of being downed by blind fire despite its stealth characteristics. It did not fly a mission over Baghdad in the 2003 Gulf War until other aircraft and missiles had suppressed Iraqi antiair defenses.

# CHAPTER 8: THE B-2 SPIRIT OF ST. LOUIS

In 1990, the then–commander in chief of the Strategic Air Command (since renamed Strategic Command or STRATCOM), Gen. John T. Chain told the House Armed Services Committee "I cannot see putting very many [B-2s] at risk during a conventional conflict if they were going to be exposed to high threat, dense type of activity in a small geographic area." This turned out to be an understatement—when Desert Wind, the air offensive over Iraq and Kuwait, commenced in January 1991, not a single B-2 was committed to the attack (or at least no indication of this can be determined from a close study of open sources).

The less-advanced F-117A Nighthawk and refitted Cold War era B-52H bombers were sent out as the primary heavy strike aircraft in bombing missions over Baghdad and on strategic targets in the Iraqi desert. Only after first successful firing of standoff weapons in the mid-1990s did it appear likely that the B-2 might be flown in combat. The Spirit's maiden combat mission had to await the 1998 Desert Fox campaign against carefully selected strategic targets in Iraq.

The B-2 combines the stealth and survivability of the F-117A Nighthawk with the range and payload of a B-52H strategic bomber. It is estimated that a force of six B-2s could put as much firepower on target as was delivered in the 1986 Libya bombing raid but launch from the continental United States instead of Europe with only a single in-flight refueling. Such a strategic scenario comes close to the original mission for which the B-2 was developed during the late 1970s. This mission called for stealthy aircraft that could defeat Soviet radar coverage, penetrate deep into Soviet airspace, and deliver nuclear payloads on high countervalue targets such as missile silos, nuclear weapons plants, hardened command and control bunkers, and major industrial centers.

The B-2 was developed as a strike aircraft with intercontinental range that could fly in undetected at a high-altitude envelope. On reaching its initial points for ordnance release, the B-2 would either launch long-range cruise missiles, such as AMRAAM, or fly a radar-evading low-altitude vector to strike harder targets with laser-guided bombs.

The B-1B Lancer was developed to fly a similar mission, but as a general-purpose heavy bomber. If the Cold War had turned hot, B-1s would have barreled in after the B-2 spearhead destroyed Soviet defenses and cleared a safe corridor for the Lancers. Though not a stealth aircraft in the same right as the B-2, the B-1B's design does incorporate a number of stealth features, such as shielded engine intakes, and it has a radar cross section about one fourth that of a B-52. The Lancer is equipped with advanced terrain-following flight capabilities enabling it to make blind, low-level attacks, and has almost three times more weapons payload capacity than the B-2. It would have swept in under the Soviet radar curtain to carry out bomb and missile strikes against very large or hard-to-destroy targets, such as well-camouflaged or buried installations.

In the wake of the Soviet Union's collapse, critics claimed that the B-2's mission no longer existed and that plans for more than the additional two already delivered to the USAF should be scrapped. These criticisms were bolstered by new revelations of design defects, including deficiencies in its radar cross-section or RCS—meaning the aircraft was less stealthy than advertised—structural cracks in its aft deck, avionics malfunctions including problems with critical terrain-following and terrain-mapping radars, and lack of software for various functions, including some weapons delivery.

Finally, there were no advanced standoff weapons, such as AMRAAM, available at the time, which would be necessary for the B-2 to function in its new, post-Cold War mission as a force-multiplier in regional theater conflicts, taking out high-leverage targets and opening a corridor for "visible" warplanes like the B-52H or B-1B through which to fly follow-on bombing sorties. This would support a shift in strategy from the Cold War–era deterrence by threat of punishment to the contemporary strategy of deterrence by denial that has figured in regional conflicts in which the United States has been engaged since the end of the Cold War.

# B-2 PROGRAM DEVELOPMENTS

Since delivery of the first fully operational Block 30—which designates combat-ready planes—B-2 (AV-20) to the 509th Bomb Wing, most of the bomber's major functional problems had been addressed. The twentieth Block 30 B-2, delivered in May 1997, featured a number of new enhancements, including full-capacity terrain-following/terrain-avoidance radar, improved navigation, all-weather operation, and weaponry enhancements including carriage of the joint direct attack munition (JDAM), which the B-2 dropped on targets in Iraq, including Saddam Hussein's bunker complex, during the shock and awe campaign of Gulf War II.

At this writing the United States has a heavy bomber force composed of 66 upgraded B-52H, 95 B-1B Lancer series, and 21 B-2 bombers. This adds up to a total of 182 of all three types in the inventory, enough aircraft to deal with the contingencies of two simultaneous major regional conflicts (MRCs) and peacetime training requirements.

Nevertheless, during the last two Quarterly Defense Reviews (QDRs) by the Pentagon, the role of the B-2 in fighting future wars has come under fire by critics in Congress and elsewhere. This time the "B-2 killer" argument was ironically focused on weapon systems whose former absence was cited as a reason for canceling the B-2 by earlier critics.

These weapon systems include AMRAAM and JSOW, cruise missiles whose fire-and-forget capabilities allow them to be fired from extreme standoff ranges outside enemy territory with high kill probabilities. Global Hawk, Darkstar, and other unmanned aerial vehicles could also be used in similar roles when outfitted as weapons platforms. This being the case, critics have continued to ask whether such a development doesn't negate the B-2's core mission—to stealthily penetrate enemy airspace and fire or drop munitions at close range.

More than any other military aircraft, with the possible exception of the wasp-like SR-71 spy plane, the B-2 Spirit seems the physical embodiment of stealth and predatory striking power. From its arrow-pointed nose to the sawtoothed trailing edges of its wings and aft fuselage, the black warplane aptly lives up to its name. The Spirit is every inch the ghost plane for fighting twenty-first century ninja war.

A unique blending of curved and angular stealth characteristics lend the B-2 its distinctive shape. The warplane's fuselage, wings, and other aerodynamic surfaces are fashioned from radar-absorbent materials composites and covered with about a ton of energy-dissipating iron-ball paint.

The air intakes and compressors of its twin GE-100 turbofan engines are mounted well back from the wings' leading edges, their W-shaped front configuration designed to break up radar returns—auxiliary air intakes used on takeoff are located behind blow-in doors that shut once the plane is airborne to preserve its seamless contours.

The troughs behind the intakes from which engine exhaust gases are emitted are wide and coated with a carbon-rich compound to reduce energy (the gases themselves are mixed with air to cool them, and they can be mixed with CFCs—chlorofluorocarbons—to eliminate visible contrails). The engines are also specially baffled to reduce their acoustic signatures—the B-2 is as silent an aircraft as it is stealthy.

The plane's weapons bays are conformal, the hatch doors blending seamlessly with the undercarriage of the B-2 when closed. All upper surfaces are likewise blended together into a computer-designed whole, their individual parts dovetailing with the precision of a carpenter's mortise and tenon. The parts are joined using special, classified, high-technology processes that reduce seams to microscopic tolerances.

Combined with internal electronic warfare systems that jam, spoof, and otherwise counter enemy detection measures including, but not limited to, radar, the B-2 is said to be as hard to detect on enemy scopes as a bumblebee despite having a wingspan measuring almost two thirds the circumference of a football field.

Shrinking the B-2's radar cross-section by the "shaping-and-masking" techniques previously described is one of the primary elements of the plane's stealthiness. It formed the object of years of research and development, both when the Spirit was funded as a covert or black program and after its official 1988 unveiling. But using shaping-and-masking approaches to stealth design place, certain performance penalties on the airframe of any aircraft depending on modified aerodynamic and control surfaces to lower its observability.

Stealthy cutout and ogive shapes (for example, shapes resembling a pointed arch) such as those used in the B-2 and F-117A, make the planes much harder to see on radars. But at the same time these same measures make them much harder to control by conventional electrohydraulic methods.

To compensate for the tradeoff between low RCS and in-flight instability, the B-2 is equipped with an advanced avionics suite. This includes a computer-controlled fly-by-wire system that's hardened against the electromagnetic pulse (EMP) effects of nuclear explosions and which automatically compensates for the inherent instability of the Spirit's airframe.

Another critical function performed by the B-2's advanced avionics suite is to enable the aircraft with terrain-following/terrain-avoiding performance capabilities.

These features also contribute to the high stealth characteristics of the Spirit by allowing the B-2 to fly a ground-hugging, nap-of-the-earth trajectory and enable it to get in beneath the downward limits of enemy radar coverage, by flying under the curtain when it needs to.

## A VIEW FROM THE FLIGHT DECK

All the B-2's systems, including navigation, flight control, targeting and ordnance delivery, countermeasures detection and management, and secure communications, are accessed from the cockpit of the B-2. Virtually all the information the bomber's two-man crew is likely to need during a mission is displayed in color on four multiple-mode CRT screens.

The number of screens has increased from three since the first operational B-2 was delivered, the fourth screen replacing panels containing analog gauges. Further study by the author of B-2 cockpit photographs taken between 1993 and 2003 shows a general trend to replace analog gauges and push-button controls with digital screen technology. It's also possible that even more radical command interface technologies using virtual reality and interactive video might at some time be included in future block upgrades of the plane.

The B-2's cockpit is spacious—the plane is 69 feet long, approximately the same length as a typical New York City brownstone apartment—and so the crew has room to stretch out during missions estimated to be in the vicinity of ten hours at a time. In fact there is room enough on the flight deck for a third crew station, which may be added in future B-2 upgrades. Wraparound windows—two front windshield panels and two side panels, both incorporating energy absorbent technology—give the crew members a panoramic view of the sky and, depending on flight conditions, of the ground below.

The windows do not appear to be removable, though, prompting questions about safely storing the aircraft in the baking heat of non-air conditioned desert hangars or hardened aircraft shelters (HASes).

To the left of the crew cabin sits the pilot, whose tactical screens include navigation and flight control data and to whose right is a set of commercial airline-style throttles. To the right of the cabin sits the B-2's copilot/"wizzo" or weapons systems officer, whose front-mounted display panels reflect offensive weapons availability and targeting as well as electronic warfare and other soft-kill capabilities.

Both crew stations are equipped with advanced-design HOTAS (hands on throttle and stick) controllers studded with red and black "pickle" buttons enabling both crew members to carry out a wide range of control and offensive functions.

As alluded to earlier, the flight deck of tomorrow's B-2 might include the addition of what is officially termed an ILS or integrated large screen display. Others call this the "god screen" concept. By whatever name, the ILS would be a large, integrated flat panel display screen in which all tactical and operational data are available to B-2 crew members. It would do more than just depict ongoing events; it would be responsive to eye, voice, and hand/gestural commands, and it might include digital links to head-mounted displays (HMD), virtual reality interfaces that would enable all crew members to closely interact with and control all aspects of the warplane's performance and weapons systems.

The technology for such advanced control systems is available today—voice recognition, eye-trackers and data gloves, and the large, flat panel displays, including the computer processors necessary to tie the system together, are all commodity items, therefore procurable as COTS or common-off-the-shelf technology components.

The B-2 is capable of delivering both nuclear and conventional munitions of many varieties. With a payload capacity of about 40,000 pounds, it carries roughly the same amount of ordnance as the well-respected B-52H, a plane justly known for its formidable saturation bombing capabilities. And like the B-52H, the B-2 is capable of dropping dumb, laser-guided, or GPS-guided iron bombs at short distances from the target.

The Spirit also carries cruise missiles that can be fired from standoff ranges and strike distant targets.

One of the staples of the B-2's weapons inventory is AMRAAM or advanced medium range air-to-air missile, an air-breathing cruise missile that, like Tomahawk, flies a meandering, ground-hugging flight trajectory toward deep penetration targets to destroy them with surgical accuracy.

Variants of the joint standoff weapon (JSOW) are also part of the Spirit's payload. The baseline model of this cruise missile design carries combined effects submunitions—bomblets that separate from the main dispenser to strike preprogrammed ground targets.

Follow-on versions of JSOW will be equipped with a high-explosive BLU-108 single warhead and will be terminally controllable from the Wizzo's station by a camera mounted in the missile's nose. For those missions that call for free-fall weapons, the JDAM or joint direct attack munition is available, the aerially delivered bomb's guidance system linked to GPS or the Spirit's own inertial navigation system (INS) for accurate targeting.

Also part of the B-2's ordnance payload is the N-1 tactical nuclear bomb, a low-yield, sub-megaton weapon optimized to penetrate hardened facilities located deep underground. JDAM, a conventional munition, was the weapon of choice in striking the Hussein regime's bunker system beneath downtown Baghdad in March 2003. If a time ever comes when nuclear weapons are again used in combat by the United States, it's a good bet that it will be the B-2 that will put the first of them on target.

# CHAPTER 9

# ADVANCED TACTICAL FIGHTER PROGRAMS

The most currently advanced production fighter aircraft in the world is the F-22 Raptor air superiority fighter. The F-22 will replace the F-15 Strike Eagle which will be 31 years old by the year 2010 and will face challengers to the title of world's foremost air superiority fighter from advanced-design Russian and European aircraft. These are likely to include the MiG-37 and EFA 2000 Eurofighter.

Russian MiGs and Sukhois would be the F-15's chief global contenders, especially because of the former Soviet Union's shift from a policy of politically motivated arms sales to an aggressive marketing strategy in the years following the collapse of the USSR.

The Russians today sell their best technology to virtually any buyer with the hard currency their hard-pressed economy needs to survive, regardless of political alignment, and the Russians show no signs of changing direction in future. Next-generation weapons systems and air defense systems will have also improved to the point where today's first-line fighter aircraft would not only have lost superiority but even forfeited parity.

With the Raptor operational, the United States will continue to maintain the margin of technological advancement that will enable its air assets to prevail over any known or foreseeable challenge that may arise.

# THE F-22 RAPTOR

The F-22 multimission fighter plane embodies a blending of stealth, speed, and high maneuverability. It can draw first blood in an aerial dogfight as well as slip through radar defenses to deliver smart munitions to high-priority targets. It's fast and agile enough to quickly outdistance and outfly pursuit aircraft. When cornered, it can stand on its tail and fly rings around other planes, and some missiles too, that are chasing it through the skies. In short, the Raptor's blend of design features and avionics give it a first-look, first-shoot, first-kill capability bar none.

Current Pentagon requirements are for a wing of 38 F-22s to meet combat needs into the first decade of this century. The small force of F-22 Raptors flying by 2010 will be the force-leveraging spearhead of a mixed air combat arm made up of advanced technology fighters, stealth aircraft, and last-generation planes like the F-16.

The Raptor force will perform the roles of an assortment of different aircraft. To quote from the USAF's vision statement, Global Engagement, the force is intended to "pack more lethal punch into a smaller package" than ever before. And because the F-22 is likely to be the last major fighter plane developed along the lines of Cold War force requirements, it may be the last true superfighter ever produced in production quantities. Barring drastic returns to past superpower confrontation (which are unlikely), future generations of warplanes will not likely embody as radical improvements over the F-22 as the F-22 embodies over the F-15/F-16 generation of fighters.

## Capability and Design

The current generation of fighters achieves speeds just below Mach 1, the speed of sound, using standard military or "dry" power. To achieve multi-mach speeds, high-performance turbofan engines have afterburners built into them. These spray fuel into the engine and burn it at a much faster rate, in the process supplying more powerful thrust.

Flying on afterburner consumes fuel at far higher rates than does normal thrust, which significantly reduces the time that a fighter can spend in the air. It also produces a great deal more heat energy, which increases the plane's radar and thermal signatures and makes it a more acquirable target to the homing radars and infrared seekers of air-to-air missiles.

The F-22's supercruise capability means it can cruise at supersonic speeds without afterburner in "dry" mode—supersonic speeds are therefore a standard part of the Raptor's normal operating envelope. Its twin Pratt & Whitney F119 engines have a far higher thrust-to-weight ratio than those found on previous-generation fighters. This means there is less inertia caused by the plane's mass for the engine to overcome in propelling the aircraft through the sky, making it far more agile than its predecessors.

The F-22's engines are also thrust-vectoring. The engine nacelles can be made to swing upward and downward in order to direct engine exhaust to enhance the power and agility of the plane during in-flight maneuvers. The Raptor's acceleration capability is approximately twice that of the Tomcat and F-15C and nearly a third better than the muscular SU-27. Its engines give it a 25 percent increase in combat range over the F-15.

It should be obvious from these statistics that the F-22's propulsion system makes it very well suited to high-g combat maneuvers involving sharp turns, dives, and wingovers. This has mandated certain advances in the design of the Raptor's fuselage to accommodate advancements to its power plant and propulsion systems.

The F-22's fuselage has a high titanium content—nearly 70 percent in the aft part of the plane—needed to withstand the tortuous gravitational stresses that the plane will endure during combat and to enable it to withstand the massive thrust potential of its engines. Approximately 25 percent by weight of the aft fuselage is composed of large, electron-beam welded titanium subassemblies called "booms."

The boom construction technique was devised to give the plane greater structural integrity and to improve stealth characteristics; the booms reduce the amount of rivets and welds in the airframe by about 75 percent over previous aircraft models. The fuselage was designed entirely on CATIA, a computer aided design (CAD) system.

The F-22's wings, like the fuselage, were also designed using CAD technology. Each wing weighs approximately 2,000 pounds, made up of titanium, composite materials, aluminum, steel, and other materials in the form of fasteners, clips and miscellaneous parts. Each wing measures 16 feet by 18 feet in length.

The wings are designed to cruise at supersonic speeds for extended periods of time and to withstand high gravity maneuvers and are interchangeable from plane to plane. Unlike the wings of today's aircraft and some of tomorrow's fighter designs, they bear no weapons pylons or "strakes." Weapon bay doors are conformal, dovetailing into the undersurface of the fuselage. The weapons carriage is internal, and a special dispenser lowers missiles into firing position once the bay doors are opened.

The F-22 is a stealthy fighter, far stealthier than any existing air superiority or air dominance fighter now flying. Its fuselage is made up of a mix of curvilinear stealth features similar to those of the B-2 bomber and the asymmetric stealth surfaces used in the F-117A Nighthawk fighter-bomber. Radar-absorbent materials are used to blunt echoes from fuselage hot spots and line engine intake ducts, while stealthy sawtooth shapes are used extensively in the rear of the plane.

Like all true stealth aircraft the Raptor's silhouette differs radically with the observer's viewing angle. Diamond shapes dominate the airframe when viewed frontally, with front fuselage, air intakes, and canted twin tails sharing the same 48° angle. The arrangement of parts deflects and soaks up enemy radar energies. Similar surface architectures are found elsewhere on the fuselage, with most of these being aligned at the same 48° angle to deflect radar beams away from enemy transmitters. As a result the Raptor has an extremely low RCS, approaching that of the Nighthawk. To further enhance its stealth qualities, the Raptor is equipped with an array of electronic countermeasures that can actively jam and spoof enemy radars, such as those carried by its nearest equal antagonist, the Su-27 Flanker. The F-22 is equipped with a stealthy radar as well, a low probability of intercept (LPI) radar that has long range and yet is extremely hard to detect and jam.

As mentioned earlier, the Raptor carries its war load in internal bays. These are located along the sides and bottom of the fuselage. Absent are the highly radar-reflective wing strakes and pylons found on the F-15 and F-16. For a missile shot these conformal doors snap open and the missile is ejected clear of the plane into the airflow before its motor ignites. Hostile thermal imaging can pick up the missile exhaust plume only after the Raptor has flown clear of the launch area and is in another part of the sky.

Stealthy though it may be, the Raptor isn't quite as stealthy as either the F-117A or B-2. But it doesn't need to be. When combined with its stealth characteristics, its high speed and formidable maneuverability make it hard to see and hard to hit even if detected, either by other advanced fighter aircraft or by the radar seekers of Russian-built SA-8 and higher surface-to-air missile installations.

## The Raptor's Advanced Avionics

Adding to innovations in the plane's overall flight performance is an advanced avionics suite that includes innovative radars, ladars (laser-radar), and other new sensors. The enhanced sensor capability affords the Raptor pilot greater situational awareness. He will track, identify, and fire at the threat before his opposite number can detect the F-22's presence. Sensors can provide information on type, location, speed, and direction of enemy aircraft; type and location of surface threats; effective range of enemy radar and weapons; targeting priorities and solutions; and all relevant information concerning the F-22's wingman and other friendly aircraft.

The sensors deliver their information to digital high-resolution cockpit displays and the pilot uses advanced controls to fly the plane and fire its ordnance. Many systems currently requiring the pilot's attention will increasingly become automated, such as monitoring engine performance, hydraulics, fuel consumption, and the effects of g-forces on key structural elements and components of the airframe.

Mission data, including threat identification and navigational data, will be available to the pilot on a bank of multimode flat panel display screens capable of exhibiting high-density color graphics overlaid with alphanumeric combat data. All data will be in real time and will be derived from several sources.

The principal source will be the Raptor's main active sensor array featuring a 32-bit processor based on PAVE PILLAR architecture, VHSIC modular circuitry, and ADA-based software. Other sources for the data fused together for the pilot will include airborne surveillance assets such as Joint Stars (JSTARS) and AWACS aircraft, ground-based C4ISR stations, and military satellites in orbit around the earth.

The plane's onboard processor will fuse this data into a comprehensive picture of the combat environment. Threat envelopes from SAM sites, for example, would appear as graphical "balloons" surrounding high-definition pictorials of the ground below, while a projected flight path graphic would also overlay the imagery.

The conventional HUD or head-up display found in the F-15/F-16 fighter aircraft will be replaced with a lightweight head-mounted display (HMD) system similar to but more sophisticated than those currently worn by military helicopter pilots.

The HMD system will be a "HUD in a helmet" that will project mission data, including high-density graphics and pictorial overlays, directly in front of the pilot's eyes. Flight controls will be integrated into the HOTAS—hands-on throttle and stick—system that will enable the pilot to control flight systems and weapons systems directly from the throttle. Armament of the Raptor is to include advanced airborne weapons, for example, the AMRAAM, AIM-9X and JASSM missile systems.

## THE JOINT STRIKE FIGHTER (JSF)

For long-range strikes, air superiority fighters such as the F-16 and F/A-18 have been the weapons of choice. Yet the Air Force and Navy view both aircraft as approaching the end of their service lives and in need of replacement. The F-35 Joint Strike Fighter is to be developed for both conventional runway takeoff and carrier launch for both U.S. and British military air arms, and possibly other NATO nations as well.

The JSF will be a multiservice aircraft with international variants poised to supersede or replace planes currently in service by the USAF, USMC, and British Royal Navy. These countries may be joined by other strategic partners in the multinational development program that is intended to produce 3,000 operational aircraft by 2015–2020.

Exactly when rollout will occur is a conjectural matter at this stage of JSF development. Nevertheless, an aircraft such as JSF will be necessary to fill fighter-bomber roles currently served by aging F-16s, A-10s, and to some extent even B-52 heavy bombers (strategic aircraft deployed tactically during the Gulf wars) when the next regional conflict erupts. In two cases, the survivability and lethality of the  previously named aircraft should by then be seriously threatened by parity with other aircraft and vulnerability to next-generation SAMs; in the case of the A-10, that plane should no longer be in service.

## The YF-23 and A-12 AX

In general appearance and aerodynamic characteristics—and probably in performance, too, ultimately—the JSF bears an uncanny resemblance to the YF-23 ATF prototype, one of the two original contenders for the advanced tactical fighter (ATF) program of the 1980s. Demonstrator testing of both designs culminated in the selection of the YF-22 for development by the USAF. The YF-23 has a larger, more muscular airframe than the F-22, a more powerful ramjet engine and a more blended stealth configuration than the somewhat more angularly stealthy F-22.

During the ATF trials it became apparent that the YF-23 was an aircraft optimized for long-range missions, somewhat less agile and less maneuverable, and generally less of a "hot dog" plane than the F-22. These aspects made the YF-23 design less attractive to the Air Force as a plane that would replace the F-15, an air-superiority fighter optimized for the dogfight role, not an air-dominance fighter like the F-16, whose missions included deep-strike bombing runs.

Though the YF-23 was canceled, it was apparent that the worthy design of the aircraft was destined to be resurrected when an F-16 successor was sought, and this now seems to be the case. The factors that doomed the YF-23 to cancellation in the 1980s currently make the plane's design characteristics, transitioned to the JSF, attractive as a replacement for the F-16, A-10, A-67, and F/A-18A.

Another canceled ATF plane project with a technology base that was transitioned into JSF is the former Navy AX program. The A-12 AX was to have been a low-observable multirole fighter-bomber with an airframe based on a radical flying wing design. The AX would have been optimized for deep-strike and antisurface warfare roles and capable of carrying all existing USN missiles except for the Phoenix AAM.

## Requirements and Production

The JSF will fly missions that require endurance, range, penetration of air defenses, and delivery of bomb loads per sortie in the medium bomber ballpark. It's to be a plane that can hit targets far inland when launched from carrier flight decks or from more distant land bases separated from the theater by hundreds or, with air-to-air refueling (AAR), thousands of miles.

The high production numbers projected for the JSF are another factor making the plane a viable component of tomorrow's combined arms battlefield, as is the JSF's planned performance envelope. The current roster of next-generation strike aircraft are "crown jewel" assets. Their high production and maintenance costs have been justified by their ability to successfully attack well-defended, high-value targets that could not be effectively engaged by any other means. But conducting a successful air campaign requires more than just a precision scalpel. It also takes the cheap and dirty sledgehammer of round-the-clock saturation bombing to attack unfriendly infrastructure on a massive scale and disrupt enemy morale and will to fight. This means having a large enough number of aircraft continually flying a large enough number of mission sorties to get the job done. Less expensive to build and maintain than the F-22, more flexible in the types of missions that it can fly, the JSF will be a day-night, all-weather warplane that delivers maximum bang for the military buck.

One reason that the JSF will be less expensive is its modular design approach, intended to produce variants based on a basic technology set. Once the core technology has matured, all variants of the JSF could then be assembled on a single production line.

Use of composite materials and off-the-shelf (COTS) subsystem components are other cost-reduction measures incorporated into the JSF design philosophy. Modular, upgradable, and yet technologically advanced, the JSF will be inexpensive enough to field in relatively large numbers, if current plans materialize along predicted lines.

The JSF will be built in three basic variants, two naval versions and an air force version. The USN wants a survivable, first-day-of-war strike fighter aircraft to complement its current first-line fighter, the F/A1-8E/F. The USAF wants a multirole fighter plane to replace the F-16 and the A-10, the latter of which has been retired.

The USMC and the British Royal Navy want STOVL—short takeoff/vertical landing—versions that can lift vertically from the flight decks of aircraft carriers and other ships capable of carrying aircraft. Currently, the only production aircraft that can perform this feat is the Sea Harrier, which is in service with the Royal Navy and also scheduled to be replaced with one of the JSF variants. If successful, a STOVL-capable JSF would lessen the need for large flat-top aircraft carriers with long flight decks and the elaborate system of steam catapults and arresting pendant assemblies that are currently necessary for the effective takeoff and landing of naval warplanes at sea. This isn't to suggest that a STOVL JSF would spell the end of the modern nuclear aircraft carrier. It would not, at least not in the foreseeable future. What it would do, however, is make feasible the development of stealthier, cheaper, and perhaps even faster, but definitely smaller, types of aircraft-carrying ships that could be used to spearhead a global strike capability in line with the Navy's Copernicus vision statements.

According to the Joint Initial Requirements Documents released by the U.S. Defense Department (JIRD-I and JIRD-II) the JSF will be a plane that can take a beating yet continue performing over and over again. Its "enhanced sortie generation rate" (SGR), says the JIRD, "can deliver impressive combat power as a force application tool available to the Joint Force Commander (JFC)."

This document goes on to state that the JSF will have a "lean logistics footprint." This means that JSF will be optimized to fly more sorties than present-day fighters of its class, with less turnaround time per mission. It also means it will be able to carry a larger and more sophisticated weapons load than preceding generation fighters.

The JSF will be sent out in the initial phases of tomorrow's MRC. It will be among the first planes in and among the last planes out of the combat theater. Its primary mission will be to kill short-dwell and mobile targets such as tanks, APCs, towed artillery, and mobile SCUD launchers, and also to slam fixed tactical targets such as hardened communications nodes and aircraft hangars, supply depots, radar installations, and the like.

Desert Storm and subsequent war-gaming analysis have demonstrated that suppression of this set of targets is critical to a quick and decisive victory in a future MRC. Studies conducted by the Defense Intelligence Agency (DIA) calculate that a range of approximately 400 nautical miles (NM) into enemy territory will enable the JSF to strike about 90 percent of its designated targets. Naval versions of the JSF set the range at between about 450 and 550 NM while the USAF version will carry enough fuel to take it out to 600 NM without requiring refueling in flight.

The new joint standoff weapon (JSOW), an air-launched cruise missile that is effective in the mission the JSF is intended to fly, is the primary weapon system that the JSF will carry in its internal bay. Other weapons systems the JSF may deploy will be the JDAM and various general purpose bombs, mines and rockets, such as the projected two 2,000-pound laser-guided bombs that each JSF will be able to carry.

## INTERNAL AND EXTERNAL WEAPONS CARRIAGE FOR THE F-35 JSF

One of the lessons of the Gulf War was that once enemy C⁴I (command, control, communications, computing, and intelligence) was suppressed beyond a certain point, the opposition was effectively blind, and stealth was no longer as necessary as it had been during the opening phases of the air war. As a result of this lesson, F-35 Joint Strike Fighter variants will be designed for both internal and external weapons carriage. Internal weapons such as JDAM (Joint Direct Attack Munition) and JSOW (Joint Standoff Weapon) would be carried during stealth missions. After the initial "shock and awe" phase, JASSM (Joint Air-to-Surface Standoff Missile) and the AIM-9X Sidewinder and Storm Shadow cruise missile could be carried on externally mounted racks to maximize the amount of ordnance the JSF could put on target.

## THE JSF'S AVIONICS SYSTEM

The JSF's avionics system will possibly incorporate an integrated off-board information management system for the pilot in the form of an integrated helmet-based head-mounted display (HMD) that would be responsive to voice, brain wave, or touch commands, or a mixture of some or all of these control interface command sets.

Preliminary tests have indicated that such an advanced pilot control system for the JSF may be less expensive to field than conventional HUD and stick systems and also afford better control characteristics to the pilot. The IHAVS system, an integral helmet audiovisual system, has already been tested in JSF proof-of-concept demonstrations and has proven superior to conventional HUDs—head-up displays—found in current-generation fighter planes such as the F-15, F-16 and F/A-18.

## POSSIBILITIES

The F-35 Joint Strike Fighter will probably be the last major first-line fighter plane production model fielded by the United States for the next half century. Like its sister aircraft the F-22 Raptor, the F-35 will need to be stealthy in order to fly its mission, and it will incorporate many of the same stealth characteristics as previously discussed concerning the F-22. There are reports that the F-35 might incorporate visual stealth character-istics, such as shadow-defeating fuselage design and active light panels, to make it far stealthier in daylight operations.

These stealth innovations are likely, because a stealthy, long-range strike aircraft capable of daylight penetration of enemy territory would complement the capabilities of the F-117A and B-2 bombers, and because it's likely that other aircraft, such as the Bird of Prey, have already been used as development test beds for visual stealth. However, although likely, the bottom line is that it's too soon yet to tell precisely what the F-35 will have in its bag of stealth tricks.

# CHAPTER 10

# ROTARY-WING AND UNMANNED AERIAL VEHICLES

Prowling the lowest tactical envelope of the air war, 30, 40, or 50 feet off the ground, helicopter gun ships will contribute their formidable firepower to the accelerated tempo of tomorrow's battle space. Helicopter gun ships will support infantry, kill tanks, hunt mobile and stationary SCUD launchers, identify targets of many varieties, and perform a range of other gritty "down-in-the-weeds" jobs.

Because of the usefulness of helicopters and the comparative simplicity of the technologies necessary to build them, and also because rotary-wing aircraft are inherently stealthy, next-generation stealth warfare will see many strong contenders in this area of procurement and development.

Tomorrow's combat choppers will be much stealthier than yesterday's helicopters, with both a reduced radar cross-section and a reduced auditory signature. They will be better armed as well and more responsive to pilot commands due to advanced onboard avionics systems.

# RAH-66 COMANCHE

Of the many combat helicopter development programs that have been started in the last 10 years, by far the most revolutionary has been the U.S. Army's LHX (Light Helicopter, Experimental) program, the goal of which was to develop an advanced combat rotorcraft that could perform missions that other combat choppers, like Apache or Cobra, could not do and go places they could not go. The end result of the program is the current RAH-66 Comanche helo.

The Comanche was originally planned to have a light transport version in addition to scout and attack variants, but successive budgetary cuts have done away with the former and have whittled down the final production numbers to an approximate 120 production models in the last Quadrennial Defense Review (QDR).

The Comanche's main role is to be armored reconnaissance. The helo's mission is to seek out and destroy enemy forces and to designate targets for other weapons systems, primarily the Apache combat helicopter. It will also spot for artillery and fighter aircraft higher up in the envelope.

To help it perform its mission, the Comanche has a low-observable design that includes a carriage of weapons internally and radar-deflecting aerodynamic surfaces similar to those found on stealth warplanes. The doors of the Comanche's internal weapons bay can also double as defensive weapons platforms with three hard points each for missiles such as Hellfire or Stinger, or it can alternatively be mounted with rocket pods.

For attack weapons or auxiliary fuel tanks for long-range missions, stub wings can be added onto the sides of the chopper. The wings can support a maximum Hellfire missile payload of eight missiles, four under each wing in Apache-type two-plus-two racks.

With room for an additional six missiles in its internal bay, this gives the Comanche a total weapon load for the Hellfire of fourteen rounds. The Comanche can also be adapted to accept other weapon mixes as well and new weapons types as they become available.

The main gun for the Comanche is the GE Vulcan II twin-barrel 20 mm machine gun. The lightweight electric-powered chain gun is housed in a special trainable turret developed by GIAT Industries, a French weapons consortium. The Vulcan's gun barrels can be shrouded by a radar-absorbent fairing for added stealth characteristics when entering heavily defended airspace, although this means an extra weight penalty and consequently a possible reduction in weapon payload per mission.

The Comanche features advanced avionics integration and logistics support integration, meaning that its weapons and flight control systems are all electronically assisted and crisply responsive to human control. A wide field-of-view HMD will incorporate real-time video, forward-looking infrared (FLIR), and digital map display overlays piped through a high-speed data bus of very high-speed integrated circuit- (VHSIC) based computers. The electro-optical Aided Target Acquisition/ Designation (ATA/D) and Longbow Night Vision Piloting Systems (NVPS) will also be part of the Comanche's avionics package.

The main onboard communications system of the Comanche will be the ICNIAS lightweight integrated communications, navigation, and identification avionics system. Subsystems under ICNIAS will include SINCGARS and HAVE QUICK 2A radios, a GPS satellite navigation system and the HF SBBV, a location and identification system utilizing the Mk12 anti-jam IFF (identification friend or foe) transponder.

The multiyear Comanche development program ranks as one of the longest in Army aviation history, but its results in the fielding of what is probably the most advanced helicopter design ever flown will undoubtedly pay large dividends in ensuring battlefield supremacy for friendly forces in the next major regional conflict where enemy armor is a threat. Though this was not so much the case in Gulf War II, the Comanche would have certainly been useful in the combat environment of the First Gulf War where the Iraqis did field heavy armor.

In the next major military engagement faced by the United States, friendly infantry and tank formations will especially look on Comanche as a low-altitude guardian angel, while their enemy counterparts will surely see it as a nightmare draped in black.

## OTHER STEALTHY ROTARY WING PROGRAMS

Because manned helicopters such as Comanche make excellent stealth aircraft it could be argued that unmanned helos could also be effectively used as stealth unmanned aerial vehicles (UAVs). Such is the case. There have been a number of programs to develop rotary wing UAVs and these have resulted in some interesting designs, some of which have gone into production and been deployed in active combat roles.

The CL-227 Sea Sentinel is nicknamed the Peanut because it resembles a giant goober standing on end. This peanut shape gives the UAV a compact footprint, which makes it well suited for launch from the helipads of warships.

The Sea Sentinel uses a system of contra-rotating rotary wings to provide lift and stability. The Peanut earns its nickname in another way, too: it's extremely small and lightweight by UAV standards, standing just under six feet in height and yet capable of carrying a 100-pound payload. The Sea Sentinel is launched vertically and remotely piloted. On return the UAV is recoverable by an automatic deck-lock system that engages special latching mechanisms on the four metal feet that project downward from the Peanut's base.

Miniature helicopters have also been designed for the UAV role. These unmanned helos are virtually identical to piloted designs except for their size and their optimization for long-range reconnaissance and surveillance. In Britain the Phoenix battlefield surveillance UAV system is a miniature drone helicopter whose hull is packed with a variety of cameras and sensors, such as synthetic aperture radar imaging pods.

Other helicopter-based UAV prototypes include the R-50 UAV concept demonstrator and the RoboCopter, both built under a NASA program in tandem with Japanese companies, and both applicable to military and peacetime roles.

One of the most interesting rotary-wing UAVs is Sikorsky's Cypher multimission reconnaissance surveillance UAV. The Cypher is nicknamed the "Flying Saucer" because of the discoid shape of its fuselage. Inside the disk is a rotor-blade propulsion system that provides vertical lift and control.

The exterior of the disk contains a variety of cameras and sensors capable of real-time transmission of tactical data to remote command and control stations. At the top of a mast projecting above the main body is a thermal imaging sensor. The Cypher has an extremely small footprint and its hollow, semispherical shape makes it a naturally low-observable platform with a small radar cross section.

The granddaddy of the Cypher was a manned flying disk known affectionately as the Flying Flapjack to aviation buffs. Officially called the V-173, the aircraft featured a contra-rotating propeller system, and although the propellers were frontally mounted, the Flapjack maneuvered in flight much more like a helicopter than a plane. The fuselage was made of a wood-and-fabric composite material, which helped give the plane radar-defeating stealth properties. The discoid shape of the fuselage also proved to be a highly stealthy design. Although only a single prototype of the V-173 was ever made, at least some of the design innovations of the Flapjack were incorporated into next-generation stealth warplanes, including the B-2 stealth bomber.

## UNMANNED AERIAL VEHICLES AND UNMANNED AERIAL COMBAT VEHICLES

Unmanned (sometimes uninhabited) aerial vehicles (UAVs) were among the first stealth platforms ever fielded and are important experimental test beds for stealth technology. They will continue to be important test beds as both stealth and remote warfare technology develop. UAV programs are also among the most clandestine research projects. The very existence of some have been the subject of stubborn official denials even in the face of strong documentary evidence.

Remote-piloted aircraft not only can function autonomously like cruise missiles during combat missions but can also be controlled by human operators at distant command posts far from the mission area. This makes UAVs useful in reconnaissance and surveillance operations that would be too hazardous for manned aircraft, such as those flown over heavily defended areas or at very low altitudes, or those that require very long loiter times that might subject pilots to extreme fatigue. Small, stealthy, silent, and smart, UAVs are capable of being crammed with gear that can collect and disseminate real-time battlefield intelligence to remote command and control centers.

Other roles proposed for UAVs are that of "surrogate satellites," which could be deployed at high altitudes and relay battlefield communications along with functioning in the surveillance role, and as robotic fighter aircraft, as small, agile decoys for advanced combat aircraft, as mechanical moles or ferrets that could sneak into underground installations and report back on what they have found, or even as hummingbird-sized micro-UAVs that could be carried by the infantry and sent to reconnoiter ahead of small units in combat.

When UAVs are equipped with weapons, they are known as unmanned combat air vehicles (UCAVs). While future UCAVs with advanced performance capabilities are currently under development, UCAVs, as we shall see, have been in use for quite some time under a variety of names and special project code names.

As we'll also see, stealth technology has figured in UAVs and UCAVs from early postwar days. UAVs played an important role in the First Gulf War and proved their worth in battle; for this reason this war marked a watershed in UAV development.

What is probably the first unmanned aerial vehicle flight was also the first powered, sustained, and controlled flight by a heavier-than-air aircraft. This Aerodrome No. 5 was a pilotless, steam-powered plane built by Dr. Samuel Pierpont Langley which flew across the Potomac River on May 6, 1896, on an approximate one-minute flight.

A few years later, in September 1903, Carl Jatho flew a small pilotless plane powered by a gasoline engine over a distance of 196 feet at a height of 11 feet; this was farther, faster, and earlier than the Wright Brothers flew. As mentioned earlier, World War I saw the marriage of cameras to planes for aerial surveillance.

By late in the war a weaponized drone aircraft designed by Charles F. Kettering, known as the "Kettering Bug," was under development. A biplane with a 12-foot wingspan powered by a 40 horsepower Ford engine, the Kettering Bug could carry a bomb load equivalent to its own 300-pound weight and drop it on distant targets by means of fold-up wings that sent the Bug into a vertical dive at a remote radio signal.

Launched from a wheeled trolley, cheap to manufacture at around $400 per drone, and hard to hit by the enemy in the trenches, the Bug was ordered in large quantities in the waning months of the Great War. The Armistice was signed before the first Bugs reached the front, though, and only a few production models were produced before the project was canceled shortly thereafter.

## PROJECT OPTION

Between the wars, and during World War II, several other pilotless aircraft development initiatives were made, both in aerial recon and surveillance roles and as remote-piloted weapon platforms. The most important of these for the purposes of this book are the drone aircraft developed in the early years of the war under Project Option.

These remote-piloted bomber aircraft, the TDN-1 and its successor the TDR-1, first flew in combat in July 1944. The TDN-1 was a sleek, shark-nosed twin-engine aircraft able to carry a torpedo or 2,000-pound bomb at a 175 MPH cruising speed. The bombs were slung from the underfuselage, between the wings.

Although this model never flew in actual combat and was used as a trainer only, the TDR-1 was deployed in combat under the Navy's Special Task Air Group One (STAG-1) in the Pacific theater in the fall of 1944, during which 46 missions were launched. It boasted a 50 percent success rate.

## ENEMY UAVS

Some might credit the Nazi V-1 "Doodlebug," and the Japanese Ohka (meaning "cherry blossom" but code-named Baka, meaning "fool," by the Allies) as other early UAVs. Yet while they were certainly drone aircraft, they reached their targets by means of preprogrammed guidance systems, not remote control in real time by a distant human operator. (Here I'm referring to the original pilotless versions of both weapons; manned versions of both Ohka and V-1 were built later in the war.)

Of more interest to this study, and probably considerably less known, are German radio-controlled glider bomb projects, which include the FZG-76, the Henshel Hs-293, and the Fritz-X (or PG-400X). The latter was used successfully in an attack on the Italian fleet in September 1943, sinking the cruiser Roma, and was later successful against British warships off the coast of Anzio in January 1944. Nearly 1,000 FZG-76s were launched against targets in Britain during Operation Rumpel Kammer, in which Heinkel He-111H heavy bombers launched from Venlo, near the Dutch border, exerted remote control. While few of the FZGs reached their targets, the more advanced Hs-293s were used to blow up bridges over the Oder River in efforts to slow the Allied advance in March 1943. These, like the FZGs, were launched from Heinkels and remotely piloted by means of a joystick controller by operators in the Heinkel's nose. Project Mistel (Mistletoe) aircraft—unmanned Junkers Ju-88 light bombers packed with almost 10,000 pounds of high explosive—were also used to attack the Oder bridges.

In the Mistel system an Me-109 or FW-190 fighter was mounted above the cockpit of the Ju-88 in a composite resembling gigantic mating wasps; the combined aircraft had the code name Beethoven. The manned fighter flew the unmanned bomber to the strike zone, and once the pilot aligned on the target, he released the Mistel which was guided the rest of the way down via automatic pilot.

Mistel attacks were staged on D day and later against the Oder bridges under Operation Eisenhammer (iron hammer). All known examples of the aircraft were destroyed in USAAF bombing missions in April 1945.

## POSTWAR AND COLD WAR UAV PROJECTS

UAV/UCAV projects were continued during the postwar years and, during the Cold War, they made technological breakthroughs. Three such projects produced early stealth aircraft. These were the D-21, Lightning Bug, and Compass Arrow projects—all three still cloaked in secrecy both because of the sensitive nature of the clandestine missions they flew and because of the secrets of stealth design that they embodied.

### D-21

We've already talked about the D-21 in connection with the SR-71 Blackbird spy plane family. The D-21, also designed by the Lockheed Skunk Works, was a Mach 3.3 UAV with a 3,000-mile range that piggy-backed onto a launch pylon atop and to the extreme aft part of an A-12 and the later SR-71s that succeeded it.

In tandem, the piloted aircraft took on the designation M-12, the M standing for "mother" as the D in D-21 stood for "daughter." Like the Blackbird, the D-21 was designed for speed, altitude, and stealth. Its delta-wing shape and chined fuselage, incorporating blended curved surfaces, gave it good low-observable characteristics from its flanks, underside, and top, while the tapering nose that ended in the sharp spikes of the ramjet engine inlets made for good frontal stealth.

In addition, radar-absorbent materials were applied to radar "hot spots" on the fuselage, wings, and engine ducts to thwart hostile radars. Kelly Johnson and his Skunk Works design team decided to put a number of innovations in stealth technology into the D-21 as they had with the SR-71, and tests in radar-echoic chambers were made to determine the fuselage design.

Of special importance was the RAM coating just mentioned. It was an early version of the RAM applied to later Skunk Works stealth planes, such as the F-117 and the B-2. Johnson referred to it by the code name "plastics," and this disinformation ploy is one reason why the stealth program connected with the SR has been little known.

The D-21 was designed to provide the SR-71's RSO with a remote-piloted outrider surveillance drone. This would have allowed the SR to fly its "black line" along the border regions of the world's trouble spots while its UAV gathered surveillance intel high over political and military hot spots.

With its multimach speed and operational flight ceiling of more than 80,000 feet, to say nothing of its stealth qualities, the D-21 would have been invulnerable to attack. Yet no operational M-12/D-12 flights ever took place because of an accident over Area 51 at the Groom Lake airfield on March 5, 1965, when a D-21 went haywire on launch, sending the mother plane crashing to earth. Although both pilots ejected safely, Ray Torick, the RSO onboard the doomed test flight, drowned after splash-down in the sea 150 miles off the California coast by the time a rescue helicopter reached them. After that the program was canceled.

This didn't spell the end of the D-21, however. After further testing with B-52s as launch and remote control mother ships, the UAV went into production as the D-21 Tagboard. Hot missions were first flown in the late 1960s and early 1970s, the first taking place in November 1969 over China. Although the UAV disappeared soon after launch, more missions continued until the project's final cancellation in March 1971.

Some observers believe that D-21 research was transitioned into the Aurora Project, which is also claimed to be or to have been an unmanned, remote-piloted vehicle capable of hypermach speeds.

## Lightning Bug

Less redolent of mystery, but equally innovative in stealth, are the AQM-34N Firebee UAVs flown under Project Lightning Bug during the Vietnam War. These UAVs flew more than 130 missions over North Vietnam between 1967 and 1971, sparing U.S. pilots the dangerous job of running missions into the heart of the enemy's heavily defended northern stronghold.

Lightning Bug's origins lie in the secret stealth feasibility studies successively called Red Wagon and Lucy Lee. These studies, still officially classified, were conducted by Ryan Aeronautical (later Teledyne Ryan Aeronautical) for the USAF in an attempt to devise ways of reducing the radar signature of a modified Q-2C Firebee target drone.

The techniques, which included placing a radar-retarding screen across the intake of the ramjet engine's air scoop, blanketing the fuselage with conformal strips of RAM, and then painting the UAV with antiradar paint, led to a reduction in the Firebee's radar signature.

Less stealthy AQM-34s, which were stretched and modified target drones, were flown on hot missions under the aforementioned Lightning Bug, setting out from Kadena AFB in Okinawa, Japan, slung from the launch pylons of Hercules DC-130 mother ships, and then released on photo-recce runs deep into the interior of China or over Hanoi and elsewhere in North Vietnam.

Black operations under the Big Safari program are said to have used UAVs in the AQM-34N series that had been modified with the then radical stealth characteristics developed under the Ryan studies. In addition to being extremely stealthy, these UAVs were equipped with all the options of clandestine surveillance including high-resolution cameras and early detection and jamming gear that enabled them to skirt SAM sites with impunity. Some of the missions were to have been flown in tandem with RB-47s, RB-49 flying wings and U-2 spy planes (see Chapter 6) to gather electronic intelligence about Chinese and Russian-made radars supplied to the North Vietnamese.

After 1970, Big Safari UAVs were outfitted to gather signals intelligence from opposition aircraft in China and other regional hot spots. In the early 1970s, further modifications to the Firebee resulted in the BQM-34B "Sad Hippo," which was a UCAV that could carry a formidable array of weapons, including Maverick and Stubby Hobo missiles, and Mark 81/82 ATGMs.

In this configuration the remote piloted vehicle was planned as the first of a new generation of unmanned long-range bombers that could strike deep into Soviet airspace. The project was canceled in favor of manned strategic bombers, such as the B-1A.

## Compass Arrow

The Compass Arrow Project was perhaps the most advanced stealth project prior to the development of modern stealth aircraft in the 1980s. Compass Arrow was considerably more advanced than preceding UAV projects, incorporating new digital microwave transmission technology and a super-accurate camera-system with an optical resolution of 1 foot directly below the flight path and an inertial navigation system for guidance.

Stealth was engineered into the system by engineers at Ryan, which used the company's prior experience with Firebee UAVs to minimize the new UAV's radar cross section by ...

> contouring the structural shapes, shadowing the engine intake and exhaust ducts and by using radiation-transparent and radiation-absorption materials.
>
> Infrared suppression has been achieved by positioning the engine on the top area of the aircraft, extending the fuselage aft of the engine, shadowing the tailpipe by the twin-canted vertical fins and using engine inlet air to cool the engine ejector nozzle.

This is according to declassified documents.

Clandestine test flights using captured Russian and Chinese SAM radars showed that the UAV was virtually impossible to lock on to.

Although the program was funded and the UAVs were ready for action, the project was put on hold and then canceled in the aftermath of President Nixon's rapprochement with China. It's alleged that all 28 known existing models of the UAV were destroyed by the USAF in order to protect the secrets of stealth they embodied.

## MODERN UAVS: TIER III MINUS AND TIER II PLUS

At 2:25 A.M. on March 29, 1996, a small unmanned robot plane with a discoid body and two long, narrow wings jutting out at its rear took off from a remote desert airstrip located at Edwards Air Force Base in Northern California. The airstrip was located at the Air Force Flight Test Center, a facility that has for several decades been no stranger to an array of arcane flying devices.

The UAV's name was Darkstar, officially known as Tier III Minus and developed under the High Altitude Endurance Unmanned Aerial Vehicle program (HAE UAV) managed by DARPA for the Defense Airborne Reconnaissance Office (DARO).

Darkstar is characterized as a "high-altitude, endurance unmanned air vehicle optimized for reconnaissance in highly defended areas" by DARPA. The Darkstar UAV flew for 20 minutes, during which it reached an altitude of 5,000 feet and executed a series of preprogrammed flight maneuvers. It then returned to the launch site and landed. Darkstar did everything autonomously, acting completely on its own.

Darkstar can operate out to a range of 500 nautical miles from its launch site. It can loiter over its target area for over eight hours at an altitude of 45,000 feet while its electro-optical (EO) or synthetic aperture radar (SAR) imaging payloads (the UAV does not carry both simultaneously) transmit high-resolution graphics of whatever it's been sent out to spy on far below in near-real time (NRT) over either satellite communications (SATCOM) relay or line-of-sight (LOS) communications links.

Darkstar's big brother is Tier II Plus, a 13-ton, single-jet engine aircraft with a 116-foot wingspan otherwise known as Global Hawk. The size of a single-engine plane, Global Hawk is a sleek drone aircraft with a fuselage that seamlessly blends into a huge ramjet intake at the rear and flares into a rounded sensor bulge at the front, with long, slightly swept, glider wings sprouting from its sides. The combination of design elements gives it the look of a winged monster blindworm full of cold, sinister intelligence—which is not very far from what it is.

Global Hawk is intended to fly long endurance missions that require it to stay airborne—or, as it's said in military parlance, loiter—for as long as 25 hours before returning to base. During that time it will be able to aerially survey approximately 40,000 square nautical miles, a target area equivalent to the state of Illinois, with a resolution of objects as small as 3 feet in diameter (spot-mode scanning enables it to surveil a much smaller area with a resolution of objects down to 1 foot in size).

Like Darkstar, it's also equipped to carry EO and SAR imaging payloads. Unlike Darkstar, however, it will be able to carry both systems and a third infrared (IR) system simultaneously while operating at altitudes of greater than 66,000 feet—the UAV can be crammed with up to a ton of cameras, radars, and other sensors. Global Hawk will also transmit NRT data via LOS data link and SATCOM relay, although these channels will enable transmissions of higher resolution than will Darkstar.

A variant of Global Hawk might also be built as an armed drone equipped with weapons to enable it to shoot SCUD missiles out of the air. In pursuit of this objective, a joint U.S.–Israeli program called MOAB (which stands for Missile Optimized Antiballistic Missile System, and is not related to the Massive Ordnance Airburst Bomb, an air-to-ground munition with the same name) uses a kinetic energy (KE) weapon capable of firing projectiles at ultrahigh speeds at ballistic theater missiles while in their boost phases.

This is similar to what the Patriot missile defense system does, although using a different approach. Unlike Patriot missiles, the KE projectiles are not explosive warheads per se. Their extreme velocity causes them to transfer tremendous amounts of energy to the target, which if struck, will be broken up in flight. Approximately $31,000,000 will have been spent on this project through fiscal year 2004. MOAB-armed Global Hawk UAVs could also theoretically be used to kill other UAVs, enemy aircraft, and even satellites in low earth orbit.

While Darkstar and Global Hawk are large, unmanned planes, far smaller UAVs are also being developed. At the other end of the UAV size-spectrum are MALD and MAV.

---

### COMPASS COPE AND THE UNMANNED U-2

In 1976 the Lockheed Skunk Works proposed an unmanned variant of the U-2 spy plane. The secret initiative was intended to compete with remotely piloted vehicles being developed by Boeing and Teledyne Ryan under the code name Compass Cope. The uninhabited aerial vehicle version of the U-2, designated the U-2U, was turned down by the U.S. Air Force. The idea was revived in the early 1990s and proposed to DARO, DARPA's Defense Airborne Reconnaissance Office, but rejected again as being too expensive and representing an investment in a technology that was at least 40 years old at the time and originally designed for manned operations.

---

## MALD AND MAV

MALD stands for miniature air-launched decoy. MALDs would be carried onboard fighter and other aircraft and released when enemy radars threatened to acquire friendly aircraft as targets. The MALDs would then use their onboard computer systems to jam and spoof the radars, creating false echoes and other effects, while the actual plane executed high-speed evasive maneuvers.

Smaller than even MALDs would be MAVs or micro-air vehicles. The extremely small size of MAVs will optimize them to perform military missions that larger drones could not accomplish because of stealth, maneuverability, or other issues associated with their size.

MAVs the size of hummingbirds might be sent out to detect bio-chemical agents in contaminated areas, act as tiny communications satellites or radar decoys, be used as nasty little flying antipersonnel or antiarmor mines, and also fly down air shafts for peeks into buildings in urban warfare environments.

# CHAPTER 11

# STEALTHY AIR-TO-AIR MUNITIONS

**General Powell:** ... This was the target for tonight, and all of the TLAM missiles which were fired at the complex were at this headquarters section of the complex.

**Q:** How many were fired, General?

**General Powell:** A total of 23 missiles were fired. They were fired from two United States ships, the U.S.S. *Peterson*, DD-969, a Spruance class destroyer in the Red Sea; the U.S.S. *Chancellorsville*, CG-62, a Ticonderoga class guided missile cruiser. Fourteen came from the *Peterson*, nine came from the *Chancellorsville*. One—it was originally planned to be 24. One did not align properly and was not fired. So 23 of the 24 missiles that were planned were launched, and the best information we have at this point is that those 23 all performed as they were supposed to. We do not have bomb damage assessment yet, but we have some preliminary indications that they are in the target area where they are supposed to be. I think you are all familiar with the TLAM sea missile, but we can go into that if you need any further details ....

—*From a media briefing by then-chairman of the Joint Chiefs of Staff Colin Powell*

The target referred to in the preceding excerpt was the building in central Baghdad that housed Iraq's intelligence service. The strike, which took place on June 6, 1993, was, according to Washington, in retaliation for the attempted assassination of George Bush in Kuwait by an Iraqi hit squad sent by Saddam Hussein. And *TLAM* (pronounced *tee-lam*) stands for Tomahawk Land Attack Missile, generally referred to in the media as "Tomahawks" or "Tomahawk missiles."

By any name the Tomahawk has become an icon of stealth warfare and surgically precise destruction. A reporter, seeing one glide past the window of his room in the Rasheed hotel during Desert Storm, remarked on the chilling embodiment of death presented by TLAM as it unerringly turned a corner and vanished from view on its silent mission of annihilation.

Curiously, the Tomahawk has been frequently used as a modern-day *Vergeltungswaffe*, or "vengeance weapon" which is what its predecessor, the V-1 flying bomb or "buzz" bomb was called, and the purpose for which it was used. In addition to the just-mentioned retaliatory attack on the Iraqi *mukhabarat* headquarters in 1993, a Tomahawk missile strike was ordered in an apparent assassination attempt against Osama bin Laden in the Sudan following the 1998 bombing of the USS *Cole* in Oman.

TLAMs were again used in tandem with B-2-delivered JDAMs in an attempt to kill Saddam Hussein and his sons. This took place in the March 19, 2003, air strikes against the bunker complex beneath the presidential palace in Baghdad on the opening night of the shock-and-awe campaign against Iraq in Gulf War II.

The Tomahawk has also become one of the primary weapons used for attacks on strategic targets of all kinds. In the opening phases of both Gulf wars, for example, TLAMs equipped with the Kit-2S antielectrical package were deployed against Iraqi targets. The Kit-2S package makes use of rope chaff, a silicon-based filament impregnated with particulate carbon, in order to disrupt the transmission of electrically based streams across wire-based transmission systems.

In the opening phase of Desert Wind, some 28 electrical targets were selected in an operation code-named "Poobah's Party," derived from the call sign of the USAF general responsible for electronic warfare operations against Iraq. As a stealth weapon, the Tomahawk could prove useful in paving the way for follow-on stealth forces including manned aircraft like the F-117A.

## STEALTH MISSILE LINEAGE

As already mentioned, the granddaddy of all cruise missiles is the infamous V-1 buzz bomb. There's also a connection between the V-1 and this book: The V-1 was assembled by slave labor that toiled in the bowels of the vast Mittelwerke rocket complex hollowed out of the Hartz mountains of central Bavaria. It's reported that Hitler was so intent on building up a strike force of 50,000 V-1s to be launched against England that the SS scoured the streets of European cities for slaves.

My father was among those kidnapped to work in the missile factories. He was also among many who silently worked in those tunnels who risked their lives to sabotage the V-1 and later the V-2 rockets without acknowledgment or thanks. The stories I heard as a boy about the V weapons sparked a lifelong fascination with the technical side of warfare and the weaponry of stealth, and they launched one of my main connections to this book.

The V-1 was crude but presented the possibility of a standoff weapon that could strike high-value targets from afar with precision either singly or in swarms. During the Cold War such a weapon, fitted with a thermonuclear warhead, was seen as a powerful deterrent to the growing Soviet stockpile of nuclear missiles with intercontinental range and multiple warheads.

The concept of the cruise missile was borne out of the need to strike strategic targets deep inside the Soviet heartland. A weapon that was small, agile, and surgically precise; that could slip between gaps in radar coverage or lose itself in ground clutter; and that, once launched, needed no further human control, was seen as an ideal fire-and-forget solution to the problems associated with fighting a nuclear war against Russia.

By the early 1970s development of cruise missiles was beginning to produce results. The AGM-86 series of air-launched cruise missiles (ALCM) was test-flown in 1975 and in production by 1980. The AGM-131 short range attack missile (SRAM) gave rise to variants that were to become the main standoff armament on the B-1A strategic bomber prior to its cancellation; in the SRAM II version the missile was developed for the B-1B Lancer.

The AGM-129 advanced cruise missile (ACM) marked the development of a cruise missile that was carefully planned to incorporate low-observable characteristics into the design of its airframe. These LO implementations included a sharply tapering nose cone to reduce the missile's frontal radar cross section, a fuselage that was chined like the SR-71's in order to reduce the lateral radar signature, a covering of special low-reflective paint to give it visual stealth qualities, and the application of RAM to wing roots and other high-reflective surfaces, including exhaust intakes and propellant nozzles to further defeat enemy radars.

(USAF)

*AGM-129 Advanced Cruise Missiles on a B-52 bomber.*

The nearly four-ton ACM, which could be launched from a variety of NATO strategic bomber aircraft, such as the B-52H, the B-1B, and the B-2, was designed to carry the W80 nuclear warhead, and was compatible with internal rotary launchers found in the B-2 Spirit of St. Louis.

It was intended to strike hardened, high-priority targets that were reachable only through heavily defended sectors of enemy airspace. The missile's enhanced stealth characteristics and guidance system made it worthy of its name. The ACM had longer range, higher accuracy, and lower RCS and IR signatures than preceding cruise missiles. It was intended as a one-shot, one-kill nuclear strike vehicle that was to function as a silver-bullet weapon in time of war.

TACIT RAINBOW was the code name for the AGM-136 air-launched cruise missile that was developed in the early 1980s and was one of the main forerunners of the Tomahawk land attack missile that followed. TACIT RAINBOW was essentially an antiradar missile cruise capability that meant it could be fired at targets at long range. It was relatively cheap and could be produced in large numbers.

The missile was intended to be fired in swarms, each vehicle's onboard guidance system having been preprogrammed to strike a designated target area. On launching, TACIT RAINBOW would fly a track to this designated target area and then go into loiter mode until it detected enemy radar emissions.

Virtually invisible to radar itself, the missile would home in on a detected enemy emitter and destroy it. Unlike previous antiradiation missiles, TACIT RAINBOW was highly resistant to electronic warfare countermeasures, such as jamming and spoofing. Its guidance system contained a library of false target signatures that it could compare against actual radar emission signatures (these would be collected by ECM or "ferret" aircraft prior to the mission and programmed into the missile prior to launch).

Since the missiles were to be deployed in deadly swarms, each missile could switch to acquire and home in on another radar target if its original target had already been destroyed by another AGM-136 in the missile swarm. As long as fuel remained TACIT RAINBOW could keep switching to new radars to kill.

## TOMAHAWK CRUISE MISSILES

Tomahawk cruise missiles, which were developed for a variety of launch systems including those used on ships, submarines, and planes, include many of the technological innovations in stealth and guidance systems pioneered in earlier cruise missile programs. The Tomahawk has also gone through a series of upgrades, known as blocks, to add further improvements to the system, with Block IV Tomahawks deployed in the second Gulf War.

It's fair to say that the missile represents a blend of stealth and accuracy in virtually every regard. The Tomahawk is not only stealthy in flight, being able to fly ground-hugging, nap-of-the-earth vectors toward remote inland targets, but is also stealthy because it can be launched from stealthy weapon platforms, like submarines, which can steal up close to the shore of a target undetected, launch their missiles, and quickly lose themselves under the waves right after launch.

The missile is so accurate that it can strike a specific individual building—or even a particular floor of that building—after a flight of more than 1,500 miles. As already noted, the Tomahawk can be fitted with a variety of warheads to suit differing tactical considerations and attack profiles.

The way a Tomahawk works can be shown by a hypothetical attack profile of a mission to destroy an inland target. In this mission, the TLAM is launched from a Seawolf attack submarine loitering a few hundred yards from the mainland in shallow coastal waters.

The Seawolf doesn't even have to surface to launch the missile. As it's launched, a solid-fuel booster rocket propels it up through the surface. Stub-wings and tail fins immediately pop out. On breaching the surface the booster stage drops away and the TLAM's air breathing turbofan jet engine fires up.

## INS and TERCOM

As the missile heels over onto a horizontal cruise trajectory, the TLAM's primary guidance system, its inertial navigation system (INS) kicks in, gathering course information and computing air speed, and heading from a complex of gyroscopes and sensors as it heads for the coast.

Once it's over land, its secondary TERCOM guidance system takes control. TERCOM, which stands for terrain contour matching, becomes necessary because even the most advanced INS system will produce small errors that will compound into a major target error after the 1,000-plus mile flight this TLAM will navigate to its target. TERCOM uses a digital contour map of the terrain over which the TLAM will fly to its target. The map is made up of grid squares.

At this point the missile has already descended to begin the first leg of its stealthy, ground-hugging flight to the target, guided by terrain following radar similar to that found in fighter planes and strategic bombers. The radar enables it to fly through canyons, around mountains, along rivers and highways, and close to the ground, where it will have the best chance of coming in under the curtain of enemy radars or slip between gaps in hostile radar coverage.

Because TERCOM works best with distinctive terrain features, the missile's approach to the target in this midcourse phase of its flight will zig and zag across the landscape, all the better to confuse ground observers, skirt SAM sites and avoid broad, flat, featureless terrain that might confuse TERCOM.

## DSMAC

As the missile approaches its target, TERCOM maps become smaller and more precise, and as the TLAM reaches its target—say a munitions factory over 1,000 miles inland from the coast—the tertiary navigational system, DSMAC activates to control the missile's terminal flight phase.

DSMAC, which stands for digital scene-matching area correlation, gathers real-time target data through a downward-scanning nose camera (which is illuminated with a strobe for night missions) and compares it with a library of actual images of the target and the area surrounding it. Once DSMAC matches the actual target with the library, Tomahawk arms its warhead, makes final course adjustments, and either detonates as an airburst or plows straight into the target.

So accurate is this terminal guidance system that the missile can be programmed not only to strike a particular building on a particular street, but a particular window on a particular floor of the target.

Warheads can likewise be purpose-designated, and ones that are conventional shaped charges as well as those that blow apart dispensing submunitions or splinter clouds of ball bearings can be used. Other warheads can be nuclear or equipped with specially hardened penetrator casings, such as those used against Saddam's bunker complex early in Gulf War II.

# JASSM

During the mid-1990s, in the years following Desert Storm, a new type of advanced cruise missile in support of new military doctrines emphasizing jointness of forces and a "system of systems" approach to warfighting was developed. This is AGM-158, the joint air-to-surface standoff missile, best known by its acronym JASSM (pronounced *jassum*). JASSM was planned to be a low-observable, highly survivable, precision air-launched cruise missile with advanced fire and forget capabilities.

JASSM is to be used against highly defended, high-value, time-sensitive targets. Almost the size of a small manned aircraft, JASSM is to be capable of carrying warheads with weights of up to 1,000 pounds. These can be either conventional or nuclear.

JASSM is to be integrated for carriage by a wide assortment of strike and bomber aircraft, including the B-1, B-2, F-15E, F-117, F/A-18C/D, and Joint Strike Fighter. Its main navigational improvements over preceding weapons, including existing Tomahawk block versions, are its use of a global positioning system (GPS) to augment its onboard INS system, and a general pattern match-autonomous target recognition system using infrared (IR) illumination of targets; this affords it a day-night and all-weather capability since IR imaging will enable it to see through rain, fog, and darkness much more efficiently than TLAM.

The GPS guidance system would make use of satellite-generated position data instead of the TERCOM map-grid technique to guide it toward its target; since GPS data are more accurate than the TERCOM approach, this would translate into the ability to make faster inbound flights along straighter vectors than previously possible.

JASSM has undergone testing since 2001 and in April 2002 entered its final preproduction phase. The missile is currently in initial production. It was too late for Gulf War II, but catch it in the next war—or better yet, be sure you don't.

# CHAPTER 12

# STEALTHY SUPERPLANES OF TOMORROW

In 1999 the U.S. Air Force announced its Future Strike Aircraft (FSA) program. The USAF's technology road map calls for next generation subsonic, supersonic, and hypersonic strike-reconnaissance aircraft with global range. These planes are intended to mesh with the projected requirements of the 2020–2030 war-fighting scenario.

Although their projected service will extend to 2040, according to the USAF, by around 2020 the first-line long-range strike and recce aircraft in the U.S. fleet, such as the B-1, B-2, and F-117 are assumed to have reached the end of their service life. The two aforementioned stealth aircraft were in any case designed to fight superpower-dominated World War III and were transitioned into the regional conflicts that marked the end of the Cold War. But they had never been intended to be used in such limited conflicts. All three aircraft were intended to strike deep inside the Soviet heartland with conventional and nuclear weapons. They were conceived to function within the tactical framework of how big wars had been previously fought—with forward-basing of strike aircraft, periods of buildup toward an offensive, extended logistics chains, and all the other stuff you saw in the movie *Patton* or read in the last 16 Clancy's Op Center novels.

Nobody was thinking about Baghdad or Bosnia at the time current U.S. first-line long-range strike and recce aircraft were produced. Nobody was thinking about flash wars that last mere weeks. Nobody was thinking about asymmetric warfare scenarios, in which war is waged by nations against nonstate actors, such as terrorist cells hidden in distant mountains, jungles, and deserts. But that's what happened. Next-generation warfare systems will have to meet the requirements posed by these new challenges.

Stealth warfare systems won't be any exception. Stealth technology, like nuclear and other technologies, has proliferated. Adversaries are devising ways to counter stealth so that stealthy military platforms can be detected and killed. In the FSA concept, the U.S. Air Force wants to build "stealthy, supersonic strike aircraft designed to penetrate heavily defended airspace in the initial phase of a conflict and deliver precision-guided munitions on time-sensitive and other high-value targets."

Obviously low-observable characteristics, multimach velocities, and high maneuverability will be among the qualities necessary for such aircraft. Maybe less obvious is that in next-generation warfighting scenarios it's projected that stealth itself, at least as far as current stealth implementation goes, might not be enough to ensure survivability of friendly strike aircraft. Innovations in stealth technology will prove necessary in order to maintain the stealthiness of stealth.

## THE SKUNK WORKS'S VISION

The Skunk Works's vision of a hypersonic delta-shaped lifting body with highly swept wings and large engines is typical of the designs presented by aerospace contractors. Capable of reaching sustained supercruise speeds of Mach 4 or better, carrying a crew of two consisting of pilot and weapon systems operator, with a combat range of some 3,000 miles without needing to refuel in the air, the FSA would also be capable of lifting a larger bomb load than its predecessors.

It would also be much faster, possibly using a wave-riding propulsion system powered by a liquid hydrogen-fueled pulse detonation engine, or by a ramjet or scramjet, both of which burn oxygen compressed by the forward speed of the aircraft itself. Ramjets, such as those powering the SR-71, operate from about Mach 2 to Mach 5. Scramjets, or supersonic combustion ramjets, in which airflow through the entire engine is supersonic, operate at speeds between Mach 5 and Mach 10. The FSA would be capable of reaching transatmospheric altitudes, enabling it to transit the globe at the edge of space and reach distant war zones within a two-hour period.

Northrop's design for such an aircraft resembles a giant inverted surfboard. The aerodynamic shape would enable the plane to ride the shock wave of compressed air created by an aircraft moving faster than the speed of sound. Most of the shock wave would be contained below the wing surfaces, allowing the aircraft to "ride" the wave with high lift and low drag. A hypersonic bomber would give the Air Force a fast reaction capability with a bomber fleet based safely in the continental United States and yet able to strike anywhere in the world with nuclear or conventional weapons.

The FSA would not only be more difficult to detect on radar but would also be harder to see by conventional photo-imaging systems, including thermal and infrared or by the spy cameras of orbital intelligence satellites. By the time the FSA would see active service, it's anticipated that rogue states like Iran would have observation satellite capability, or possibly even long-endurance UAVs that could loiter at high altitudes and scan the skies for approaching strike aircraft.

As has been noted earlier in this book, the Japanese Defense Agency has predicted that in future warfare the side that acquires the target first is the winner by default, or, to put it differently, that the first shot equals the first kill.

New stealth technologies that would render the plane very hard to see, or even invisible, in the visible light spectrum the way current stealth is to radar and thermal imagining, would enable the FSA to be used reliably on daylight as well as in night missions. Flexible, aeroelastic wings could enhance the plane's stealth by morphing their shape to deflect different radar frequencies encountered in flight as well as enhancing maneuverability.

## FSA'S TARGETING AND WEAPONS SYSTEMS

The ability to track and engage multiple, mobile targets is another important consideration for the FSA program. Future conflicts will present far more dynamic target sets than those of the past. Target acquisition systems onboard the plane would need to be more agile than present systems, which are geared to destroy fixed or stationary targets, and the munitions carried by the FSA would need to be smarter, faster, and more lethal than today's generation of missiles and bombs.

Instead of, or in addition to, more conventional types of air-to-air and air-to-ground munitions, it's been proposed that an FSA also carry outrider UAVs. These unmanned, remote-piloted aircraft would be under the control of the FSA's weapons systems officer. The HGV or hypersonic glide vehicle concept, developed in the 1980s by Lockheed from technologies transitioned from the much earlier Dyna-Soar, could yield the prototype for outrider munitions.

### FALCON

Contractors have begun work on the Force Application and Launch from the Continental United States (FALCON) program, a joint DARPA/USAF program to develop advanced long-range strike-reconnaissance aircraft. The program envisions an initial, or near-term FALCON deployment circa 2010, with a far-term deployment circa 2025. The program currently envisions three vehicles. The first is a reusable hypersonic cruise vehicle (HCV) capable of taking off from a conventional military runway and striking targets as far as 9,000 miles away in less than two hours. The second and third are conceived as a common aero vehicle (CAV) and an enhanced common aero vehicle (ECAV). The CAV would be an unpowered, maneuverable, hypersonic glide vehicle (HGV), capable of carrying about 1,000 pounds of munitions, with a range of about 3,000 nautical miles. The ECAV would offer greater range and improved maneuverability over the CAV.

Rocketing away from the mother ship at speeds approaching Mach 18, the HGV could then glide more than 5,000 miles to its target, reaching it only 30 minutes after launch. Its heat-resistant carbon-carbon hull would have withstood the blistering air friction of its journey. Using onboard guidance or with partial control from the FSA's wizzo, the HGV could strike mobile targets at speeds so high that even if detected it would strike them before they had a chance to move.

The HGV might be armed by a conventional or nuclear warhead, but wouldn't necessary need one—at the incredible multimach velocities it would act as a hyperkinetic-hypervelocity weapon, releasing the equivalent detonative force of a small nuclear explosion on impact with its target without using conventional or nuclear explosives. "At 6,000 feet per second, a pound of metal releases as much energy as a pound of TNT," according to Paul Czysz, professor of aerospace engineering at St. Louis University.

Czysz, an expert on hypersonics who has worked for a leading U.S. aerospace defense contractor added that a solid penetrator such as an HGV weighing 200 pounds would be enough to lift a 28,000-ton warship 10 feet out of the water (though in actual combat an HGV strike would probably vaporize a ground radar station or a cluster of tanks or APCs and leave a sizable crater behind).

An HGV could also be equipped with warheads of various types, from nuclear to something as exotic as a fléchette warhead, which would blow apart to release airbursts of tungsten-carbide darts. Three-pound fléchettes could turn concrete structures into Swiss cheese while one-pound fléchettes would let the daylight into tanks, APCs, and other heavy combat vehicles. Large FSA designs, the size of B-52s, could carry a massive payload of HGV-type unmanned kill vehicles, reconnaissance UAVs, cruise missiles, and GPS-guided gravity bombs. They could launch some of these weapons from extreme standoff ranges yet be stealthy enough to dance around SAM sites like Baryshnikov and drop more conventional ordnance on static and fixed targets deep in enemy territory unseen even in broad daylight missions.

In light of the FSA program requirements it's believed by defense watchers that certain clandestine aircraft development projects as well as other projects that were abruptly canceled are connected with the FSA, having functioned as secret test beds for advanced FSA technology in addition to whatever their open or officially avowed purposes might have been.

Project Aurora, which has never been acknowledged, is suspected by many to have been a hypersonic surveillance aircraft, either manned or unmanned, that possessed many of the design qualities of the proposed FSA. These include the characteristic delta-configuration of the lifting body design, which is characteristic of the FSA designs produced under the USAF's 1999 directive.

## BIRD OF PREY AND OTHER STEALTH CONCEPT DEMONSTRATORS

In October 2002, Boeing unveiled another ultrasecret advanced aircraft project, the Bird of Prey. This highly classified program produced what was dubbed a "technology demonstrator" at its unveiling at Boeing's giant St. Louis Phantom Works facility after a decade of covert research and development by Boeing, DARPA, and the USAF. According to Air Force officials, the program's purpose was to "test specific and breakthrough stealth technologies, along with rapid-prototyping techniques" developed by Phantom Works.

These stealth technologies went beyond enhancements to lower the RCS of the airframe. They also focused on visual, thermal, and even acoustic signature reduction. These latter enhancements, officials present admitted, were toward development of daylight stealth. The shape of the aircraft, with cranked, aft-set wings smoothly blended into the fuselage, with moveable control surfaces covered with flexible material that show no seams or joints, and an air inlet completely masked when viewed frontally, seems laid out to avoid shadows, for example.

### STEALTHY COMPARISONS

Just how stealthy are stealth aircraft? A good way to get an idea is by comparing the sizes of their respective radar cross sections or RCS. At one end of the spectrum, the B-2 stealth bomber has a frontal radar reflection of –40 dBsm (decision boundary scatter matrix), which is approximately the size of an aluminum marble. The RCS of the F-35 Joint Strike Fighter will be somewhat larger, but still respectively small, at around –30 dBsm, which is about the size of a golf ball. By comparison, the F/A-18E/F Super Hornet and the B-1B Lancer strategic bomber both have radar cross sections in the vicinity of +1 dBsm, or roughly the size of a three-foot sphere. At the other end of the spectrum, the RCS of the venerable B-52 at approximately +40 dBsm shows up on radar with a size equivalent to that of a sphere 170 feet in diameter.

(USAF)

*The Joint Strike Fighter (JSF) seen during a test flight. The bulge visible in front of the right air intake is one of the plane's shared sensor apertures, which also serves as a baffle for radar energies entering the engine duct. Although subtle, the curvature of the upper fuselage has been computer designed to maximize the aircraft's low-observable properties. Also note that pilot and WSO are seated side-by-side in the cockpit compartment, a departure from conventional fighter plane design.*

A conspicuous white patch set in front of the air intake appears to be part of an active visual camouflage system. It's possible that this was augmented by clusters of lamps or glow panels during tests to eliminate shadows and make the plane harder to see from the air or the ground. Whatever the program's accomplishments in more exotic stealth applications, it's hypothesized that the Bird of Prey achieved an RCS reduction level that would make it show up as smaller than a mosquito on radar scopes.

Stealth morphing, referred to earlier, has been pioneered by NASA, which unveiled a computer-simulated technology demonstrator in April 2001. The aircraft was equipped with active aerostatic wings that bent and flexed in birdlike movements giving the virtual aircraft the appearance of a hawk as it flew at low speeds, and then morphed into a conventional swept-wing configuration for high-speed, high-altitude flight. Wings made of new lightweight "smart" materials, containing embedded sensors and actuators would enable future aircraft to morph into various shapes to suit various flight envelopes.

The morphing quality could, according to experts, also afford a high degree of stealthiness by changing shape in response to changing conditions in the electronic and visual environment. The wings would sweep back and change shape for high-speed drag reduction and low sonic boom. The engine inlets and nozzles would morph, too. Small jets of air and feather-like control surfaces would provide additional control forces for extreme maneuvers and added safety.

In the low-speed configuration, the wings upsweep and increase in thickness and span to improve efficiency. Instead of a vertical tail, the aircraft would use thrust-vectoring. The adaptable wings would have controllable, bone-like support structures covered by a flexible membrane with embedded muscle-like actuators.

Two canceled projects of the mid-1990s also hint at future stealth aircraft designs. The Navy's A-12 AX program was intended to produce a strike-attack aircraft that was to replace the aging F-111 swing-wing fighter. The General Dynamics/Lockheed design team that set to work on the project produced a technology demonstrator mockup of the aircraft prior to the axing of AX in 1994.

The mockup is an all-delta wing-shaped aircraft with a bubble cockpit and single-pilot cabin with conformal bays for weapons carriage. The asymmetric air-scoops, engine nacelles buried deep in the fuselage, blended control surfaces, pointed nose, and groove channels on the upper wing surface to deflect and diffuse radar energies point to an extremely stealthy aircraft design. Here again is an aircraft that bears a striking resemblance to proposed plans for an FSA.

Yet another mockup of an advanced-design stealth airframe was the Technology Demonstrator for Enhancement and Future Systems (TDEFS) built by DASA, the German-based Daimler-Chrysler Aerospace Company. TDEFS also displays a triangular shape, swept back wings, and undermounted air scoop similar to FSA designs. This stealth project also never made it off the ground, due to a combination of factors that included the lessening of the threat of Soviet invasion of Western Europe by the mid-1990s and lack of funding.

The FSA project, which is still in its infancy, will need to develop a raft of new technologies and radically miniaturize existing ones, before the first advanced long-range strike aircraft of the series get off the ground. In the meantime the B-2 and F-117 will continue to own the night skies.

# CHAPTER 13

# STEALTH IN SPACE OPERATIONS

Space has so far been a supporting arena for combat on earth. It will soon become a primary theater of operations. The United States today enjoys space dominance. Maintaining dominance in orbital space is viewed as key to continuing to prevail in all other sectors of military operations.

Gulf War I brought home how important space could be for combat operations to the U.S. military and its NATO partners. Potential aggressors also learned a number of lessons about the military value of space. One of these was that asymmetric warfare could be highly effective when space-based assets were targeted. As then-CINC of SpaceCom, General Joseph Ashy, stated in 1996, "It's politically sensitive, but it's going to happen. Some people don't want to hear this and it sure isn't in vogue, but absolutely we're going to fight in space. We're going to fight from space and we're going to fight into space."

Satellites—vital to military command, control, and communications—are vital to space dominance. They transmit voice, tactical imagery, global positioning information, targeting data, and an assortment of other vital information. Obviously a modern military force could not effectively function without these space-based assets. This makes them a priority target for asymmetric attack. Disrupting information operations on the digital battlefield by destroying or crippling satellite networks is an effective form of information attack. It can create havoc on military forces that depend on digital information systems to plan and carry out operations and to assess post-strike battle damage.

> One of the best ways to disrupt a future regional offensive might be to jam the satellites on which friendly coalitions rely or to blow up ground stations that control the satellites transmitting targeting data, such as those in the United States or United Kingdom.

Space-based assets have been relatively safe from attack so far but will become increasingly vulnerable to peer antagonists and asymmetric threats such as terrorists, who can strike at them by physically attacking ground-based control stations or infecting either ground stations or onboard computers with viruses. More sophisticated adversaries could jam satellite transmissions, use airborne or ground-based lasers to temporarily dazzle or permanently blind satellite optics, fry their electronics with radiation, blow them up with maneuverable killer satellites, or inject viruses at long range using electromagnetic transmission sources.

Friendly space systems will not only have to be defended, but they'll have to be made harder to detect. This, of course, means that they will need to be made stealthier than the present generation of orbital defense platforms. Other systems that attack unfriendly space assets will also have to be made stealthier. They will need to counter the stealth of their targets and be stealthy themselves in order to avoid detection.

The Reagan-era plan for Strategic Defense Initiative (SDI), otherwise called Star Wars, envisioned an elaborate network of orbital weapons in space that would detect and destroy incoming Soviet nuclear missiles using high-energy lasers and a Rube Goldbergesque array of exotic strike systems. That SDI may have been as much a political disinformation strategy as an actual defense program is evident from the fact that it never materialized.

# CHAPTER 13: STEALTH IN SPACE OPERATIONS

> Laser weapons pose a threat to space-based military assets including satellites. Despite the failure of Strategic Defense Initiative (SDI) to build a viable space-based antimissile shield in part based on laser weapons, ground and airborne lasers are capable of blinding satellite sensors and disabling critical components of orbital surveillance and reconnaissance platforms. One such system, the airborne laser (ABL), has already been developed by the U.S. Air Force.

The reality of military operations in space, at least for the near future, appears to be centered around attack and defense of tactical command, control, communications, intelligence surveillance, and reconnaissance (C4ISR) systems in orbit. This is much closer to the 1950s and 1960s vision of military operations in space than it is to Star Wars.

Satellites will attack other satellites. Manned and unmanned trans-atmospheric vehicles, capable of flying into orbit and returning to earth, will, like the Space Shuttle, put satellites into orbit, service and refuel those already in place, and search out and destroy enemy satellites. Given this, next-generation space planes would have to be low-observable, both in order to effectively attack orbital targets and avoid attack themselves.

The Pentagon assumes that by 2017 space will be highly weaponized. This has led to the establishment of a USAF Space Operations Directorate and the creation of new units in 2001. These were the 76th Space Control Squadron and the 527th Space Aggressor Squadron. The mission of the 76th Space Control Squadron, part of the 21st Space Wing at Peterson AFB, Colorado, is to explore future space control technologies by testing models and prototypes of counterspace systems for rapid achievement of space superiority. The 527th Space Aggressor Squadron, also at Peterson AFB, looks at possible enemy capabilities in space and how to counteract them. War-gaming scenarios conducted since the late stages of the Cold War have predicted that adversaries would try to knock out U.S. space assets in the early stages of a conflict.

During the Cold War the Soviets had developed an array of antisatellite weapons to attack U.S. satellites if war broke out, including the only then-deployable antisatellite missile system. More recently China's senior military policymakers have viewed asymmetric attack as key to prevailing against a technologically superior enemy like the United States in a future confrontation.

Likening this new strategy to that of the ancient martial arts form Dim Mak, where a master practitioner with a knowledge of vital body parts can kill an opponent with a minimum of movement and in absolute stealth, Chinese policymakers have called for the rapid technology development of information, stealth, and long-range precision strike weapons with a focus on combat in space and computer combat, both of which would target U.S. orbital assets as well as destroying or disrupting battlefield sensor and tactical communications grids.

Missiles equipped with radio frequency microwave warheads or warheads capable of generating powerful electromagnetic pulses (EMP) that can cripple or destroy electrical and electronic systems are some projected weapons. Depending on their state of development, such weapons could be used on the ground, in the air, or in space against friendly space systems.

Satellites could be rendered ineffective by attacking AWACS or JSTARS aircraft that rely on orbital surveillance data in order to direct aircraft and control land warfare forces. Exotic weapons using ultrahigh and subsonic waves, plasma jets, high-energy pulses, and information attack could be used to stealthily assault the vital points in digital battlefield networks to sow discord on an enormous scale comparable to the size of the initial attack.

At the opposite extreme, the Chinese contemplate the development of the submarine and stealthy naval vessels as platforms to attack the space assets of an advanced enemy, which could presumably only be the United States or Russia. Recent thinking by the Chinese military projects the development not only of underwater arsenal ships and mine-laying robots, but of "a naval force equipped to destroy reconnaissance satellites and other space systems" using tactical laser weapons and, presumably, anti-satellite missiles of various types.

Stealth warfare in space will therefore not be limited to orbital weapons. Land-based, naval, and atmospheric systems would also figure into space-based military operations. The digital battlefield is a network-centric theater of operations. As such it's a multidimensional battle space that combines simultaneous operations on land, sea, air, space, cyberspace, and the electromagnetic spectrum. An attack on any one of these areas will have effects in all other zones of the combat theater.

The nature of space warfare gives rise to entirely new aspects of stealth applications beyond the conventional forms of stealth. Destroying a satellite in orbital space wouldn't necessarily require surgical precision. An attacker might only need to have a general idea of where the satellite was located and then take it out with a warhead that detonated into a lethal cloud of steel fléchettes.

In orbit, with extremes of heat and cold unlike those found on earth, thermal and infrared detection systems could prove more effective than radar, so that conventional radar-evading stealth might not be enough. Visual, thermal, and radiation stealth would be the answer.

Space systems that could change their visual and thermal signatures to make themselves blend into the star-flecked blackness of outer space by bending visible light and keeping their surfaces at ambient temperatures would be more survivable than those that were only resistant to radar detection. Satellites could generate a radiation signature that would make them blend into the background noise of outer space to enhance their stealthiness. They could also be equipped with electronic warfare capabilities to be used to jam or deceive enemy attempts to detect and destroy them.

Manned vehicles operating in space would rely on speed as one means of protection from attack. Transatmospheric vehicles (TAVs) such as manned space planes would need to achieve extremely high speeds in order to reach the velocities needed to place them into orbital trajectories.

Those same high speeds would be an effective defense against interception because at hypermach velocities even a small change in course would in a second put a TAV miles from the point where an incoming cruise missile had acquired a lock on it. The TAV would be long gone before the missile could reacquire its fleeing target.

Speed in itself wouldn't be enough of a defense to ensure survivability against all conceivable threats and warfare contingencies for orbital spacecraft, however. The same stealth strategies discussed for satellites would be useful in protecting TAVs from detection as well as making them harder to spot when they played offensive roles.

Because cyberwarfare will also be a key battlefield in the arena of space warfare, stealth will have to play a role here, as well as assume unconventional forms. Stealth computer programs able to conceal themselves from viral code injected into computer systems and then attack and destroy the invader programs might prove necessary to preserve space-based systems from asymmetric attack.

For all the projection and hypothesis concerning the future of space operations, and the obvious fact that space operations are critical to the digital battlefield of the twenty-first century, space warfare is still in its infancy. In the view of many, greater militarization of space will produce a new arms race that poses a greater threat to the United States and its allies than it does to their adversaries.

The argument goes that because the United States is the country most highly dependent on a vulnerable grid of satellites in orbital space and the one most heavily invested in a high-technology military force dependent on space-based assets, that it sets up the United States, and by extension its coalition partners, as vulnerable targets for asymmetric assault.

On the other hand, because potential adversaries such as China are already aware of the vulnerability of U.S. space systems and are developing war plans and technologies to attack those systems, the United States has no choice but to develop its space capabilities even if this does translate into a new arms race in space.

Regardless of the outcome, it's clear that stealth technologies will prove as vital to military operations in space as they have proven to every other sphere of warfare. You might even say it's written in the stars.

# PART 3

# NAVAL OPERATIONS

By now it should be evident that stealth has transformed warfare to the point where it would not be an exaggeration to say that all warfare is stealth warfare. Regardless of whether a weapon system cruises on or under the sea, flies through the air, or moves across the land, stealth will enhance its survivability and effectiveness in combat. Naval operations will need to take full advantage of stealth technologies both to remain survivable and to continue to effectively project sea power onto engagements on land.

Mastery of the oceans is absolutely necessary in order for the United States to project military power across the globe in the twenty-first century. With the era of bipolar superpower confrontation having given way to global regional conflicts in far-flung corners of the world, U.S. naval forces have shifted their focus from ocean-going (or blue water) operations to operations in the littorals—those parts of the oceans close to the shorelines—to which they can rapidly bring precision firepower, supporting infrastructure and combat personnel.

Under the seas, on the ocean, and in waters close to foreign shores, stealth remains a key to success in battle for modern naval forces.

# CHAPTER 14

# NUCLEAR SUBMARINES: STEALTH BENEATH THE SEA

Submarines have been around for a long time. The concept of a ship or vessel that could cruise silently and swiftly underwater as ordinary ships do on the seas dates back at least to Renaissance times, and probably earlier. In the 1860s, Jules Verne wrote *20,000 Leagues Under the Sea*, a novel predicting the effectiveness by which submarines could be used against surface ships, albeit arming Captain Nemo's *Nautilus* with a battering ram instead of torpedoes.

Regardless of how submarine warfare was depicted or actually conducted, the appeal of such an invention has always been its stealthiness. Because the ocean's depths form a natural concealing medium, it was evident from the first that any military force able to cruise those depths could strike without warning and vanish before the enemy could retaliate.

This has been the guiding principle of submarine warfare all along. During the Civil War submersibles figured in maritime battles, attacking surface shipping on the Great Lakes. When true submarines were developed and used extensively in combat during the First and Second World Wars, the principle remained largely unchanged. These early submarines of the twentieth century were mostly sent out to prey on surface shipping.

During World War II, German U-boats sent millions of tons of Allied shipping to the bottom of the Atlantic. Until the threat they posed was finally stamped out in the latter years of the war, Germany's submarine force had exacted a tremendous toll on the ability of the Allies to transport critical supplies and troops overseas.

## MIDGET SUBMARINES VERSUS UNMANNED UNDERWATER VEHICLES

Midget submarines first made their modern appearance during World War II, principally by the British and Italians. The British called theirs "chariots"; the Italians dubbed theirs "pigs."

They were used mainly to destroy warships in enemy harbors, either by bringing divers in close enough to lay mines, or by launching torpedoes. In the case of the Imperial Japanese Navy, most of the sneak craft were designed for one-way travel only. They were essentially manned torpedoes that would be piloted to their targets and then detonated by suicide riders.

Minisubmersibles can be classed as three different types: chariots, human torpedoes, and true midget submarines. While unmanned underwater vehicles (UUV) are today being developed by the United States and other countries to do what midget submarines have done in the past, there are roles that manned mini-submersibles can play, such as deploying divers to cut through antisubmarine netting or to conduct surveillance and reconnaissance activities, that still make them useful tools of stealth warfare.

# POST-WW II ROLE

It was not until after World War II that the role of submarines, and the nature of submarine warfare, evolved into a new form. The onset of the Cold War saw the United States and Soviet Union squaring off like heavyweights in a boxing ring, each armed with a devastating nuclear punch. While submarines would still be built and armed to send shipping to the bottom, this traditional role was superseded by a new use: nuclear missile launch platforms.

Nuclear-powered ballistic missile submarines (SSBN) are called "boomers." They're called this for good reason, but it has nothing to do with the sound they make as they ply the ocean's depths. On the contrary, silence is the watchword when it comes to submarines of all types today, be they boomers, attack subs, or non-nuclear diesel-electric boats (submarines are always called "boats," never ships, by the way).

The term "boomer" refers to the effects of the nuclear missiles carried by the boats—their thermonuclear concussions, up to 5,000 miles from the point of launch, would produce some pretty loud booms indeed. But there, in the sea, even as distant cities went up in mushroom clouds, the emphasis would continue to be on silence ... and stealth.

Carrying a contingent of nuclear-tipped ICBMs, in some cases with MIRVed warheads (MIRV stands for multiple independently targetable reentry vehicles), nuclear boats were seen as the key to credible deterrence against nuclear attack by Cold War antagonists. Subs formed the third leg of the so-called nuclear triad made up of land-, air-, and sea-based nuclear forces.

As such they were a formidable factor in the geopolitical and military dynamics of global superpower confrontation. Because of the stealthiness and global range that enabled nuclear subs to operate in all regions of the world's oceans, including frigid arctic seas beneath the polar ice caps, no side could be certain of destroying enough nuclear boats to reasonably ensure its own survival.

This made the nuclear missile submarine the key to the policy of deterrence practiced by successive presidential administrations. Deterrence was based on the concept of mutual assured destruction, abbreviated as MAD, formulated in the early 1960s. MAD, which was applied by both superpowers throughout the Cold War, essentially meant that any nuclear attack would prove suicidal, since enough of the enemy's nuclear forces would survive to enable it to deal the other side a lethal counterblow.

Even in the wake of a surprise BOOB or "bolt out of the blue" salvo of ICBMs that would reduce the target nation to a radioactive wasteland, U.S. and Soviet nuclear boomers would still be out there, packing more than enough megatonnage to ensure that the surviving nuclear power was itself wiped out. It was a doomsday scenario straight out of the movie

*Dr. Strangelove*, but it was so terrifying that it worked. The world did sometimes approach the brink of nuclear conflict, such as during the Cuban Missile Crisis, but never crossed the line.

It could be said that the master key to SSBN stealth is the ability of nuclear boats to remain submerged for extended periods, only limited by crew endurance and food supply, if necessary—unlike the diesel-electric boats that preceded them, nuclear subs aren't impeded by the need to periodically surface for extended periods to recharge batteries, replenish their air supplies, or run communications. This ability is made possible by the use of a nuclear reactor instead of a conventional diesel engine to drive the boats. The reactor core lasts for years, and modern nuclear boats have a mean time between failure of critical components of equally long duration.

While on station, nuclear boats operate rarely at surface level and only for brief periods when they do. Even when using the periscope, a boomer's skipper will only expose a small portion of the periscope mast above the waterline for a few seconds at most. While there are some things that only visual inspection can tell a sub's commander, any sub captain worth his salt will keep those look-sees as short as possible.

Some skippers even use the technique of closing their eyes as the periscope mast is lowered to preserve the fleeting impression of what they've seen, while immediately issuing orders based on what they've mentally recorded. For a nuclear submariner stealth is the first commandment. The boat is always in hiding, on the hunt for submerged or surface prey, secretly gathering intelligence, or preparing to launch equally stealthy missiles, torpedoes, or advanced undersea or surface mines, to say nothing of deploying various countermeasures to thwart hostile detection.

The nuclear boomer's ability to remain submerged for incredibly long periods of time would not in itself be enough to preserve the sub from attack or allow it to carry out its mission. Silence and speed are other things in a submariner's bag of tricks. In fact, the same nuclear propulsion system that enables boomers to remain submerged so long was a major detriment to the stealthiness of nuclear boats.

# THE U.S. THRESHER, PERMIT, AND STURGEON CLASSES

It was realized from the outset that nuclear power plants would tend to be far noisier than diesel-electric engines. The nuclear power train is a compendium of pumps that push superheated reactor water (or in the case of Soviet subs a slurry of lead and bismuth) through a network of pipes, a steam generator that powers the propeller shaft turbine, the rotating propeller blades themselves, and an assortment of reduction gears that maintain and control the speed of the boat, all in constant, furious motion. Its noise signature, by comparison to the far simpler propulsion system of diesel-electric boats, made nuclear power plants a nightmare for planners of the world's emerging nuclear submarine fleets.

A high-power train-noise signature plagued the early Skipjack-class nuclear boats, which, though fast and agile, were also about as noisy as a German oompah band in a Munich beer hall. Simultaneous improvements in sonar made the Skipjacks virtually useless as both ICBM launch platforms and in the antisubmarine warfare role.

As a result, the next generation of subs, the Thresher, Permit, and Sturgeon classes, were designed with the lowering of acoustic signatures as a primary concern. Despite the loss of the ill-fated Thresher on a sea trial on April 10, 1963—probably due to a defect in the sub's outer hull (called a pressure hull) that caused it to sink to below the point beyond which the pressure hull would hold (its crush depth)—the redesigns proved successful in drastically reducing the acoustic signatures of next-generation nuclear boats.

The main innovation used to accomplish this was the mounting of the noisy power train on a so-called raft. The raft, a padded frame for the power train, was isolated from the sub's inner hull. Its use greatly reduced the amount of power train noise that reached the sub's pressure hull and radiated out into the surrounding water. Its use meant increasing the sub's overall bulk and therefore a subsequent enlargement of the hull that increased drag on the hull as the sub moved through the ocean—what submariners call skin drag—but the tradeoff was minimal compared to the benefits of the reduction in acoustic signature afforded by the redesign.

The use of new hulls, made of lightweight high-tensile steel cocooning a tubular midsection, was another innovation introduced in these new generations of nuclear boats. This, too, increased the stealthiness of nuclear submarines by allowing them to dive to ever-increasing depths, making it far harder for surface ships, aircraft, and satellites to detect their presence. The increased depth capabilities also gave sub skippers critical extra seconds to crash dive in the event the sub was detected and offered added insurance against the kind of disaster that claimed Thresher if the sub dived at too steep an angle due to mechanical or human error in the course of operations or while evading pursuit.

## THE SOVIET ALFA, VICTOR, AKULA, AND SIERRA CLASSES

The Soviets had not been lax in their own efforts to close the gap between their own submarine fleet and that of the United States. Early in the Cold War their Alfa-class nuclear boats posed many of the same drawbacks as U.S. Skipjacks; though Alfas arguably still hold submarine depth and speed records, they're also among the noisiest subs ever built, especially when running at high speeds. Well aware of the innovations by which the United States was silencing its nuclear boats, the Kremlin pursued a mix of Western silencing approaches and novel native technical discoveries.

The result was the Victor-class boats that began appearing in the late 1960s. The Victors were by far the most silent undersea boats built by the Soviets. With the appearance of the Victor III in 1978, the Soviets had reached a state of rough parity with the preceding generation of U.S. Sturgeon-class boats in quieting technologies and were approaching the stealthiness of the new Los Angeles class boomers then entering service as the standard-bearers of the American nuclear fleet.

The Victor III used the same approach of raft-mounting the nuclear power train to reduce the transmission of vibrations and noises to the sub's pressure hull, but intelligence photographs of the new submarines also revealed a puzzling feature of the hull that the United States knew nothing about. This was a vine-like network of tubular capillaries winding and twisting around the hull.

This piping, which would normally have been detrimental to the operation of the sub because it would increase drag forces on the hull, was thought to secrete lubricating polymers or discharge a noise-absorbing buffer of air bubbles between the hull and the ocean. The exact purpose of the Soviet capillary system has never been officially revealed, but the fact that the USSR began retrofitting many of its older subs with the same system strongly indicates that these strange contrivances represented a technology that increased the stealthiness of Russian boats.

Another mysterious feature of the Victors was a pod mounted atop the tailfin. It was originally thought to house a towed sonar array but was later believed to actually contain an auxiliary magneto-hydrodynamic (MHD) propulsion system to augment or replace the nuclear engine for spurts of ultrasilent running or during emergencies. An MHD system produces a powerful magnetic field in an outer sleeve containing a liquid electrolyte, which encircles an inner propulsion tube, causing the sleeve to pulsate. The pulsations make the inner tube undulate, drawing seawater in through the front and expelling it from the rear in a jet powerful enough to propel a submarine through the sea. Like the mysterious tubing network, the purpose of the Soviet tailfin pod has never been officially revealed.

The Akula- and Sierra-class boats that succeeded the Russian Victors were quieter still and also capable of crash-diving to depths thought to exceed even those that U.S. boats were able to reach. The new Soviet boats were fast closing the gap between the ultrasilent Los Angeles–class boats fielded by the United States and the front-line vessels of the Russian undersea fleet. This meant that the critical edge of superiority held by the United States in early detection of Russian subs was being eroded bit by bit.

## BLOWS TO U.S. UNDERSEA STEALTH SUPREMACY

By the late 1980s at least one incident revealed how much of an edge the United States had lost. While tracking an Akula in Soviet waters the skipper of a still officially unidentified U.S. submarine heard the ping of active sonar. With a shock he realized that the Akula had detected his sub first and that in actual combat the Soviet sub would have been mere seconds away from launching a torpedo. The experience was like a fencing master being touched on the heart by the point of a backward student's sword—a completely unexpected development. More points in the contest of undersea stealth were given to the Russian side as a U.S. spy ring, led by

John Walker, fed secret U.S. intelligence on submarine warfare to the Soviets over the course of 15 years.

Yet another blow to the supremacy in undersea stealth was dealt the United States in the late 1980s when the Kremlin received advanced, computerized lathes necessary to mill submarine propellers with grooved blades precision-machined to reduce cavitation and propeller noise. Cavitation is the propensity for spinning blades to form bubbles at certain speeds and depths; as the bubbles pop it's as telltale a sound as seltzer fizzing in a glass to eavesdropping sonar.

With the anti-cavitation propellers of U.S. boats now duplicated by the Soviets and installed on their newest Typhoon-class (the NATO name for Akula) boats, the Russian navy was steadily closing the undersea noise gap. Of equal if not greater importance, the keys to decrypting U.S. submarine communications sold to the Russians by the Walker ring enabled Soviet ASW forces to track U.S. subs and build a database of acoustic profiles that could help them locate and track the U.S. fleet.

Though the Cold War saw the erosion of the U.S. lead in undersea stealth by the Soviets, it didn't necessarily mean that the Kremlin had reached parity with the West. On the contrary, with every improvement in Soviet boats, successive upgrades of U.S. nuclear boomers and attack boats fielded by the U.S. Navy (USN) kept the edge—if sometimes dulled—with the American fleet.

The mainstays of the USN's boomer fleet today are its Trident-class submarines. Tridents, first introduced in the 1960s, have been retrofitted with advanced sonars and fire control systems, extending their service lives well into the first decades of the twenty-first century. Typhoon-class boats are the Russian boomer fleet's mainstay; these, too, have been retrofitted by the Russian navy to extend their service lives. We'll take a closer look at nuclear boomers and attack submarines in the following chapter.

# CHAPTER 15

# NUCLEAR BOOMERS AND ATTACK SUBMARINES

There are two main differences between SSBNs and SSNs (attack submarines). The first has to do with the operational roles performed by the two classes of boats. SSBNs are first and foremost undersea launch pads for nuclear missiles with intercontinental range (called sea-launched ballistic missiles or SLBMs). They can be thought of as the strategic bombers of the ocean, kind of undersea B-52s.

Attack subs are more like fighter planes, a not very farfetched analogy since Los Angeles–class boats are said to handle very much like fast aircraft, except for the lack of G-forces that normally press pilots into their seats. (This can make for a rough ride during dives and turns, which is why Los Angeles–class SSNs are equipped with handholds resembling those found on subway cars.) While attack submarines also fire SLBMs, theirs are generally medium-range or theater missiles, which have a more limited range, such as Tomahawks carrying nuclear warheads.

Another distinction that can be made between boomers and attack boats is that while all strategic missile submarines currently in service are nuclear submarines, this isn't the case for all attack submarines. Russia's diesel-electric Kilo-class boats, for example, are among the world's first-line attack subs. The SSN designation actually refers only to U.S. attack submarines, all of which are nuclear-powered.

## NUCLEAR BOOMERS

Strategic nuclear submarines, with their contingents of missiles (12 in the case of all U.S. boats, save one, which has 24 in its "Christmas Tree Farm," and 20 being standard for Russian strategic subs) are man-made leviathans of the deep. They're the largest and most powerful undersea warships ever built.

As already mentioned, the mainstay of the U.S. strategic nuclear fleet is its 18 Trident nuclear subs, the last of which, the USS *Louisiana*, was commissioned on July 27, 1996. Of those 18 boats, at least 10 carry the improved D-5 variant of the Trident missile, otherwise known as the Trident II, which is a MIRVed version with eight independently targetable nuclear warheads.

Even after reductions in strategic warheads negotiated under START-II and other nuclear reduction treaties between the United States and Russia, this still leaves thousands of nuclear warheads capable of being fired from U.S. submarines in the event of nuclear war. In fact the higher ratio of sea-based to land-based warheads will likely continue to hold sway because Trident SLBMs, comprising the bulk of the U.S. sea-based nuclear force, are considered highly survivable and essentially immune to preemptive attack. As already noted, this is considered a key "leg" of the nuclear deterrence triad.

For this reason it's on nuclear boats that the last MIRVed warheads will likely to be found even if all land-based ICBMs are downloaded to single-warhead versions. It could be said that stealthy nuclear boomers are the ultimate *Vergeltungswaffe*—the so-called vengeance weapon that Hitler believed he had created in the V-missiles of World War II. As such they were the hole cards in the global poker game between the United States and Russia that was played out during the Cold War. Because the Cold War is over, the SSBN is something of a holdover from a previous era of bipolar superpower conflict. Submarine operations have become refocused on operations supporting warfare in regional conflicts. The world's boomer fleets have been retasked to perform new roles consonant with war's changing face in the twenty-first century, but like the dinosaurs they resemble they're suited to a limited role.

Both the Trident and Typhoon submarines were built with a single purpose—to deal a countervailing nuclear death blow against the opposing superpower when global showdown destabilized from stalemate to shooting war. The nuclear warheads they would have fired were "city-busters" paying back megadeaths for megadeaths.

In the Second Cold War, as some have begun to call the war against global terrorism and transnational, asymmetric threats, the boomer's awesome nuclear striking power looks increasingly obsolescent. Like a Cyclops, one-eyed and hunting for pygmy prey, its power would be defeated. Surgical accuracy rather than brute nuclear force is necessary to combat these new and far more amorphous threats to the established Western nation-states.

That the boomer will certainly survive into the foreseeable future is testament to the uncertain ground that still exists between the United States and Russia, and the looming threat of a rapidly arming China and bellicose North Korea (whose nuclear missiles at this writing are more wishful thinking on the part of its leader than operational weapons). Russia, while today an ally, continues efforts to rebuild its decimated military forces and develop new generations of stealth weaponry, including its own formidable nuclear submarine fleet.

As we'll see, it's also one of the prime exporters of stealthy non-nuclear submarines to potential future adversaries. Apart from being one of Russia's most lucrative customers for naval armament, such as the recently delivered stealthy Sovremenny-class guided missile destroyers, China is also engaged in indigenous weapon development programs with strategic implications for the United States which must retain unfettered use of the Pacific Ocean in order to remain a global superpower.

For these reasons it's clear that the nuclear boomer will continue to be a deadly, if stealthy, presence in the world's oceans for quite some time to come.

# TRIDENT SUBMARINES

Trident submarines are the largest and most powerful undersea warships ever built in the free world. At 560 feet and 18,750 tons, they are the nation's first line of defense. Each sub is powered by a nuclear reactor and carries 24 ballistic missiles. Trident submarines are noted for their long-range missile capability and extremely quick operations.

Trident submarines are manned by two alternating crews, one called the Gold crew and the other called the Blue crew. Each crew is composed of about 165 officers and men. While one crew is at sea, the other crew is in training at Kings Bay, Georgia. At the training facility, there is a mockup of all equipment (except the nuclear reactor) aboard the sub, and the crew is trained in all aspects of the sub's operation. After about 100 days, the crews exchange places, maximizing the submarine's at-sea time.

# ATTACK SUBMARINES

If, as already mentioned, the boomer can be thought of as a kind of underwater strategic bomber, the attack sub can be likened to a fighter plane. But also, if boomers are dinosaurs, then attack subs are sharks. Dinosaurs may lumber along with the power to make the earth shake underfoot, but sharks are swift and deadly predators of the sea.

Silent, swift, stealthy; sensing prey at long range and able to strike with cold malevolence, attack submarines are man-made ocean predators. Unlike boomers, their first mission priority is the ASW role. Attack subs are engineered and built to seek out and destroy enemy submarines. Indeed the attack sub evolved with the main purpose of hunting for a specific species of prey.

This prey was Soviet strategic missile boats. The attack submarine evolved as a weapon to be used against Russia's undersea fleet in the event of nuclear war, both to destroy or decimate the third leg of the USSR's nuclear triad, and also to prevent Soviet attack submarines and surface vessels from killing U.S. SSBNs before they could launch a nuclear salvo against the Soviet Union.

Although the end of the Cold War also put an end to the original mission for which the SSN was conceived, attack submarines were easily recast into strategic roles consonant with the emerging world order. Because they are small, highly maneuverable, extremely stealthy, and able to fire sea-launched cruise missiles such as the TLAM, attack submarines emerged as a versatile multimission platform for combined arms naval operations in the world's littorals. Attack submarines are not only suited to project sea power into the land battle by means of Tomahawk strikes, but they are also an effective means to stealthily insert commando teams into the field to conduct special operations missions.

To deploy special ops forces, boats can be outfitted with dry deck shelters (DDS). These cylindrical steel storage containers can accommodate SOF teams with full gear as well as swimmer delivery vehicles (SDV) that enable SOF personnel to stealthily negotiate the distance between sub and beach landing zone. Storage containers enable commando teams to "lock in" from inside the submarine and "lock out" again into open water where they can retrieve gear and weapons and deploy SDVs to take them the rest of the way in.

SDVs come in all shapes and sizes, from rubber Zodiacs to minisubmarines. Different SDV types can operate either on or below the surface, and some types are capable of being used under both sets of circumstances.

Special forces teams lock in to the containers while the sub hovers at or just below periscope depth (about 30 feet) from inside the boat via an inner hatch. When ready to deploy, the team undogs the hatch of the SDV and emerges in full SCUBA gear. Weapons and gear are generally retrieved from separate lockers either carried topside or conformally fitted into the hull of the submarine. Larger SDVs are carried in topside hangars from which they can be retrieved when a team locks out.

Several versions of Los Angeles–class boats are equipped with integrated lock in/lock out facilities. One such is called an escape trunk. These take the form of chambers located forward of the submarine sail, topside on the hull. Divers enter through the bottom hatch, seal it, and open the flood valve to fill the escape trunk from an internal water reservoir.

Once acclimated to outside water pressure, divers can then swim from the submarine through either a top or forward escape hatch located to one side of the chamber, retrieving SDV and gear in the same way previously described. Although this system doesn't impact on the submarine's sonar signature by generating drag forces on the hull like hull-mounted DDSes, it has the limitation of being able to accommodate only some five divers at a time who must endure close quarters after assembling in the escape trunk.

# THE NEW ATTACK SUBMARINE

The New Attack Submarine (NSSN) which is being built as a successor to the Los Angeles–class boats, as well as the sole three Seawolf (Centurion-class) submarines in service, is to be equipped with a far more spacious and elaborate internal lock in/lock out system for swimmers. These new Virginia-class attack boats will be equipped with a range of facilities for covert and special warfare missions, including search and rescue, reconnaissance, sabotage and diversionary attacks, forward observation for fire direction, and direct strikes against enemy objectives.

To support special forces operations NSSN subs are to be equipped with an internal nine-man lock in/lock-out chamber. It will also have mating surfaces compatible with either the advanced SEAL delivery system (ASDS)—which is essentially a 55-ton mini-sub—or a conventional DDS.

In addition, the torpedo rooms of Virginia-class boats will be reconfigurable to allow the center weapons and their stowage structures to be removed so that greater numbers of SOF personnel can be carried by the boat. The NSSN's optimization for operations in shallow-water, littoral environments, which include advanced mine and shallow-water hazards detection, make it further suited to supporting special warfare operations of many kinds.

Though increasingly being used for unconventional operations, including domination of the littorals in pursuit of a "from the sea" strategy to influence events ashore, attack submarines will continue to pursue their original mission—for direct support of carrier battle groups and deep-water antisubmarine warfare against strategic nuclear submarines and enemy attack submarines. As such, their acoustic stealth characteristics and high speeds will make attack subs weapons of choice in more conventional applications.

In the ASW role, attack submarines need to rely on speed and stealth to attack and evade pursuit of their prey. In the deadly game of undersea hide-and-seek that epitomizes submarine combat, the submarine that can detect another submarine or submarines first is the one that will most often win the duel.

Sonar is the main underwater system in use today and despite new non-acoustic technologies that are planned for the NSSN and the Future Attack Submarine (FSSN) that is to follow circa 2020, sonar remains the primary system for undersea navigation and combat. Because submarines essentially hear rather than see their environment, sonar has to defeat quieting technologies designed to make subs hard to detect.

## MORE THAN MEETS THE EAR

We've already discussed some of the technological aspects of acoustic stealth in the previous chapter, but there is considerably more to the acoustic stealth of a submarine than technology. Submarine maneuver tactics make all the difference between success and failure, life and death in submarine combat. Without an able commander and crew well versed in submarine operations all the stealth technology in the world won't guarantee success—or survival.

The path of sound traveling underwater is deflected and amplified by the path it travels through the depths. Ocean water is made up of several layers of water divided by temperature gradients. These layers make sound behave in different ways as it passes through them.

At the upper depths lies the surface layer. Just below it is the main thermocline layer and below this the isothermal layer. Sounds under the ocean can travel in two ways, firstly by direct propagation within a layer, and secondly by moving through the layers. In the second mode, underwater sound waves bend into a snakelike pattern referred to by submariners as a convergence zone (CZ).

The CZ path behaves in different ways depending on the position of the submarine in any individual layer and its position relative to other submarines in the same or other layers. Sounds moving along convergence zone paths through the layers can be heard for miles through reflection and refraction through the ocean's thermal layers. But the large, sinuous waves formed by CZ propagation can also mask the presence of another submarine lurking below the layer of the first sub if it lies between the peaks and troughs of these elongated sound waves. The acoustic stealth properties of submarines and the keen hearing of sonar operators are the determining factors in these battles.

As quieting technologies produce subs that are increasingly stealthy to acoustic detection, sonar systems have been married up with digital processors to enhance their capabilities in the game of underwater hide-and-seek. Los Angeles attack subs of the Improved-688 class were commissioned with BSY-1 integrated sonar and fire control systems, known to submariners as "The Busy One." With BSY-1 sonar, operators for the first time relied more on visual indications rather than the audile data of earlier generations of sonar gear.

A major innovation was the use of monitors in which sonar data was displayed as cascading lines. These so-called cascade displays were augmented by an extensive database of sonar signatures belonging to known sources of undersea and surface radiating sound, from ships to subs to pods of whales.

The system could automatically cross-reference new sonar signatures with this database in order to match them with its signature library. It could also scan hundreds of individual sonar contacts simultaneously and perform other computations that no human operator could duplicate, let alone approach. Advanced attack submarines, such as the NSSN, will be sent to sea with still more elaborate sonar and threat detection systems.

For all of this the job of detecting stealthy submarines continues to get harder instead of easier. One of the reasons is the proliferation of inexpensive diesel-electric boats, with power trains that are inherently quieter than nuclear systems, but in addition are equipped with advanced acoustic stealth characteristics rivaling those of the most advanced U.S. subs.

Such attack submarines are high on the wish list of rogue states. The most advanced of these submarines are Russian-manufactured Kilo-class boats (known as the Amur class in Russia). The most advanced Kilos are the 636 types (Amur 1850), which, declares Russia's Rubin Maritime Design bureau, is eight to ten times quieter than the preceding generation of Kilo submarines.

*(Department of Defense)*

*A Russian-built, Kilo-class diesel submarine purchased by Iran is towed by a support vessel in this photograph taken in the central Mediterranean Sea during the week of December 23, 1995. Ships and aircraft from the U.S. Navy's Sixth Fleet tracked the sub as it crossed on the surface. This was the third Kilo-class submarine the Iranians bought from Moscow.*

Rubin, which designs export versions of Kilo attack boats to the specifications of individual customers, also declares that the most advanced Kilos have "a highly efficient sonar system, coupled with the low level of noise of the submarine proper, guarantees early detection of enemy ships, including super-low-noise submarines, at large distances," adding, "Consequently the most favorable conditions are created for deciding when to attack."

## FUTURE THREATS

While U.S. and coalition forces have so far had little difficulty in projecting power into the Persian Gulf, future maritime contests against hostile powers equipped with first-line Kilos could have different outcomes. Kilo submarines could also be deadly stealth weapons if procured by transnational or terrorist threats. Stealthy, small, fast, and highly maneuverable, they can be equipped with an array of third-party cruise missiles capable of reaching targets inland.

Clearly, the story of undersea stealth is far from written. Yet one thing is certain: as advances in submarine technology continue to produce faster, stealthier, and more lethal boats, the oceans and land masses of the world will continue to be vulnerable to this stealthy man-made predator of the seas.

# CHAPTER 16

# STEALTH ON THE SURFACE

It's not only in undersea naval systems that the battle will go to the swiftest, strongest … and stealthiest. On the surface of the world's oceans, stealth continues to become increasingly vital to success and survivability in combat and key to global power projection for maritime forces.

In the blue water operations characteristic of sea battles of World War II, and those that had been projected for the U.S.–Soviet World War III by Cold War military strategists, stealth was not as much of a consideration for surface vessels as raw firepower and maneuverability. In this scenario sea power would be projected via the modern aircraft carrier via fighter planes while lighter, more agile vessels, such as frigates and battle cruisers, defended the carrier as well as directed and prosecuted attacks against enemy formations on the sea.

In the aftermath of the Cold War, littoral operations changed the equation. Joint Vision 2020 called for a "From the Sea" strategy for U.S. naval forces based on global reach, regional attack from the shallow offshore waters, and a network-centric approach to battle group operations where scattered and diversified forces were all linked together into a coordinated effort. In the new joint and combined arms battlespace environment, stealthiness was as important as it was to other systems that had used it to advantage. Obviously naval aviation would need to invest in next-generation stealth aircraft to prosecute strikes on land-based targets and unfriendly maritime assets alike, but more than this the carrier battle group itself would need to become far stealthier than it had been or risk obsolescence.

## ONE SHOT, ONE KILL

A wake-up call was given in two conflicts late in the twentieth century. The first was the Falklands War. Britain's military commanders saw little to prevent a quick, sweeping victory in taking back the Falkland Islands. Lying off the Atlantic coast of Argentina, the islands had been unilaterally reclaimed by the Argentinean government. A naval fleet soon steamed for the South Atlantic, confident of easy victory. Instead Britain found that it had flung its forces into the teeth of bloody fighting on land and on the sea.

Possibly the greatest shock not only to the British Ministry of Defense, but to the Pentagon as well, which was closely following the action (the Thatcher government was being provided with high-resolution satellite imagery from Defense satellites; the U.S.–UK "special relationship" transcended mutual defense treaties the United States had with Argentina), came when an Exocet antiship missile was fired at a British aircraft carrier by an Argentinean cruiser. The French-made Exocet, skimming low above the waves, was a stealthy target. The destroyer HMS *Glamorgan* was the opposite—large and highly observable. In a matter of seconds the contest between stealth and raw firepower was decided in favor of stealth. The single Exocet strike severely damaged the British ship, taking it out of the fighting. A second strike could have easily sunk the vessel. The *Sheffield*, and later the *Coventry* and *Atlantic Conveyor*, were not as fortunate. Exocets fired by Argentinean attack vessels in separate engagements hit them broadside, immediately sinking the *Sheffield* and *Coventry*, and sending the *Atlantic Conveyor* to the bottom of the sea after crippling her with direct, high-explosive hits.

Not long after this event it was the turn of a U.S. naval vessel to have a deadly run-in with an Exocet missile. During the so-called Tanker War, which took place in the Persian Gulf between 1984 and 1988, U.S. naval forces protected reflagged vessels passing through the Straits of Hormuz at the mouth of the Gulf from the threat of Iranian shelling and seizure. In 1988, during an action in the Gulf, two Iraqi Exocet missiles struck the USS *Stark* broadside. Like the HMS *Glamorgan*, the *Stark* survived both hits, but that's not the point.

What was a matter of grave concern was that the *Stark* was a Ticonderoga-class Aegis battle cruiser equipped with advanced SPY-1 radars and bristling with missiles and deck guns. The *Stark* was a ship designed to track, locate, and deal with multiple threats from aircraft, missiles, other ships, and from land. Yet Exocet's stealth characteristics penetrated the defenses of possibly the most advanced cruiser of its kind in the world.

Exocet antiship missiles were used by Argentina against British warships during the Falklands campaign in which they caused heavy damage to the British fleet. Exocets are sea-skimming missiles that streak toward their targets only a few feet from the waterline. Guided by active homing radar, an Exocet penetrates the hull of the ship before a delay-action fuse detonates its high-explosive warhead. In addition to production variants that can be fired from ships or launched from aircraft, Exocet is available as a land-based, coastal defense missile system.

These two incidents drove home a sobering lesson to the world's great naval powers and an encouraging lesson to their more poorly equipped antagonists: A single missile, if stealthy, can do enormous damage to first-line naval vessels.

To put it another way, stealth weaponry proved itself as a powerful enabler for asymmetric attack. It was now clear that not only submarines needed to be stealthy but surface vessels, too. It was also becoming clear to potential adversaries of the world's big powers that an investment in inexpensive stealthy naval warfare systems, be they Exocet missiles or Kilo-class submarines, could pay sizable dividends in future confrontations.

These and subsequent military developments, such as those in the Gulf War, led to the development of stealthy surface vessel concepts, prototypes, and production models. Accordingly, naval doctrine, strategy and tactics were revised to put a far higher emphasis on stealth warfare operations than at any time in the past.

The U.S. Navy's "From the Sea" vision for transformation of the fleet to meet twenty-first century global challenges under the Defense Department's JV 2020 roadmap emphasizes stealth along with jointness of forces. Under JV 2020, naval surface forces would not only become stealthier themselves but field an enhanced ability to detect and defend against stealthy oppositional forces. These abilities are seen as the key to surviving and prevailing in operations in the world's littoral areas, where carrier battle groups (CBGs) would be called on to project sea power onto the land battle.

In littoral combat operations the CBG is perilously close to the enemy's military centers of gravity and is therefore most vulnerable to attack by all sectors of the enemy's forces, seaborne, airborne, or land-based. At the same time an important part of the CBG's task would be to land amphibious forces to establish control of beachheads and resupply those landed forces.

The need to maintain a presence offshore in the face of threats to the force like Exocet, Chinese Silkworm missiles, or other asymmetric assets means that friendly assets must be stealthy on the one hand and on the other prepared to counter the stealthiness of attacking forces.

During the Gulf War and the War in Iraq, coalition naval forces proved key to success in the land battle. They not only were the most speedy and efficient method of transporting large numbers of troops, weapons, armor, and supplies to the Persian Gulf and landing those forces and materials, but they were also key to projecting military power on land—aircraft carriers served as floating airstrips for fighter planes and launch platforms for cruise missiles like Tomahawk. During these last two major regional engagements, Western forces were able to operate in the littoral virtually unopposed. Yet the time may be fast approaching when the United States and coalition allies may face tough opposition from forces equipped with advanced and stealthy naval weaponry.

## NEW STEALTH WARSHIPS

China's recent purchase of sophisticated new surface vessels and submarines and the development of lethally stealthy shipborne missiles pose an escalating threat. The Chinese People's Liberation Army Navy (PLAN) views high technology forces critical to building a capability to military pressure on Taiwan and to deny U.S. forces the ability to rush to the aid of its ally and principal trading partner in the South China Sea.

China's expenditures for its military buildup totaled about $20,000,000,000 in 2002, according to Pentagon figures; its annual expenditures could increase fourfold by 2020 according to current projections. Beijing has purchased four advanced Kilo submarines, among the quietest in the world. It has also modernized its existing diesel-electric and nuclear submarine fleet; its diesel-electric SONG submarines can launch antiship cruise missiles while submerged. PLA and PLAN are also improving the accuracy and stealth of land-based and seaborne ballistic missiles and investing in long-range strike aircraft.

While China is clearly intent on preparing its forces to keep the United States out of the South China Sea in the event of confrontation with Taiwan, it may also be trying to establish a presence in the Indian Ocean. In the latter it has built signal intelligence facilities and installed radar equipment to monitor Indian naval communications in the Cocos Islands, belonging to nearby Myanmar, and modernized an existing naval base there. These moves worry India, a U.S. ally and regional power, which has invested in advanced naval technologies of its own.

India sees stealth as critical to its defense. India has not only been acquiring stealth technology for naval defense from other nations, such as Russia, but has been developing an indigenous stealth frigate as well (the Indian navy has a goal of 70 percent indigenization by the end of the decade) under the innocuous-sounding Project 17 program. The Shivalik, currently undergoing sea trials, is the first of 12 planned stealth warships to be acquired by the Indian navy.

The Shivalik is entirely constructed of carbon fiber reinforced plastic (CFRP), which, aside from being extremely lightweight and highly shock-resistant, also has strong radar-absorbent qualities. The Shivalik's hull is nonmagnetic to afford protection against mines, and is contoured to deflect and dissipate radar echoes. Like stealth aircraft, gas turbines and exhausts are concealed in hidden outlets on the stern close to the waterline; visual signatures are reduced by hiding glinting surfaces, such as rotating search radars, under special radomes.

Quieting and cooling technologies have been incorporated into the frigate to defeat sonar and thermal detection. The Shivalik uses low-noise propellers, its diesel engines are double-mounted to cut hydroelectric signatures and covered by a sound suppression hood, and there are other special mountings for noise-critical machinery. Water is injected into engine exhaust to reduce its magnetic and heat signatures. The ship's stealth design is intended to cut the radar signature of the ship by 1–1½ percent. It's armed with an array of offensive weapons including seaborne missiles and ship-launchable torpedoes, which also have special stealth mountings.

India has also incorporated low-observable characteristics into the Talwar frigates it has commissioned from Russia (which is doing well in the region by at the same time supplying China with advanced Sovremenny-class destroyers). As already mentioned, Russia is ready to tailor exportable military systems to the purchaser's requirements. The Talwar is no exception. India received its first Russian-built Talwar as this book was being written in August 2003. These frigates have incorporated stealth technology in their design and construction.

These include hull construction aimed at giving the frigates a low radar cross section and the application of RAM or radar-absorbent materials to strong radar reflective points on the ship. To defeat sonars, the Talwars are also designed with a sound isolation system on the power train similar to those used in submarines.

The Talwar class is intended to be used to patrol the littorals around India; using a phased-array radar system similar to that found on U.S. Aegis cruisers, it's intended to present a stealthy, low-observable profile to enemy ships, missiles, and submarines while being able to target the opposition first. India is also studying the acquisition of Visby-class stealth corvettes.

The Visbys are similar in concept and design to the Shivaliks but are arguably more technologically advanced and were the first stealth vessels to be launched, in June 2000. The Visby is currently undergoing combat system trials with a planned entry into service in January 2005. The second Visby-class cruiser was launched as this book was being written, in June 2003. Its manufacturer, Kockums (a subsidiary of the German defense contractor HDW) has signed a partnership agreement with

Northrop Grumman Ship Systems toward the development of the USN Littoral Combat Ship (LCS), an element of the DD(X) family of stealthy surface vessels under development by the United States. Northrop Grumman plans to use the Visby as the baseline design for its LCS proposal.

*(Kockums-HDW)*

*The Visby stealth corvette churns up spray while undergoing sea trials. Its hull, made of composite materials, is angled to return a small cross section to probing enemy radars. The ship is also acoustically stealthy to defeat sonar. The hull is painted in flat gray tones to afford visible stealth.*

It's obvious that the asymmetric advantage of naval stealth warfare systems is one of the reasons why stealth development has been pursued by developing and smaller nations while the United States has lagged behind. The United States views its current naval forces as adequate for ocean and littoral dominance through 2020, but is preparing to overhaul its surface forces by then to counter increasingly stealthy systems of potential adversaries.

The DD(X) multimission destroyer—previously known as the DD-21 Zumwalt-class land attack vessel—is, as already mentioned, to be the first of a family of stealthy surface vessels designed for littoral warfare by the U.S. Navy that is to include the CG (X) cruiser and the smaller LCS.

The DD(X) is to replace Oliver Hazard Perry–class frigates (FFG 7) and Spruance-class destroyers (DD 963) starting in 2012.

The stealth ship's main mission would be to provide land attack support for ground forces and also carry out traditional destroyer missions of anti-air, antisurface, and undersea warfare. Its design is to be similar to those of other stealth ships, but it will feature a "tumblehome" hull form, in which the hull slopes inward from above the waterline, and which reduces the vessel's RCS since such a slope returns a much less defined radar image than a more hard-edged hull form.

## STEALTHY FUTURE AIRCRAFT CARRIERS

The aircraft carrier is to become far stealthier, too, in the world's two largest navies. Both the U.S. and Royal navies have plans underway to build a Future Aircraft Carrier (FAC). The U.S. program calls for planned delivery of the first FAC in 2014. The UK program calls for constructing two carriers to enter service between 2012 and 2015. Both carriers are to be optimized for stealthy blue-water and littoral operations.

The U.S. carrier, designated CVN-21, formerly CVN(X), and the British future carrier, CVF RN, share similar design features, including large decks, hulls designed to produce small radar cross-sections, visible stealth features, and nuclear power train quieting for acoustic stealth. They will also share integrated facilities for naval variants of the F-35 Joint Strike Fighter, which both navies will also acquire to replace the aging Sea Harrier STOVL, as well as for carrier launchable and retriev-able UAVs and UCAVs.

In the interim, construction is to start in 2007 on a tenth and final nuclear carrier of the Nimitz class now servicing the U.S. fleet; it's sched-uled to enter service in 2009. This last Nimitz carrier, the USS *George H. W. Bush* (CVN 77) will incorporate new technologies geared to network-centric warfare and reduction of radar, visual, acoustic, and ther-mal signatures.

# CHAPTER 17

# STEALTH IN NAVAL AVIATION

The fact that the U.S. Air Force flies the stealthiest military aircraft in the world and the Navy doesn't isn't for lack of trying. The Navy has engaged in stealth aircraft development projects since the end of the Second World War. The most recent of these, the AX, would have seen the production of an ultra-stealthy delta-shaped aircraft to replace the F/A-18 Hornet. There were other navy stealth projects before AX, including its immediate predecessor the A-12 Avenger and a carrier-transportable variant of the F-117A Stealth Fighter.

That stealth fighters haven't lifted off the decks of Nimitz carriers is testament to the same types of political boondoggling and fiscal mismanagement that have canceled other big-ticket weapon systems, such as the Army's super-howitzer, Crusader. It may not be until the first Future Aircraft Carriers are launched that true stealth fighter aircraft scream off U.S. and British carrier decks.

In fact it's currently only France that has deployed a completely new next-generation strike aircraft on its carriers. This is the Rafale multirole combat fighter in its single-seater M version. Lacking key stealth features such as conformal weapons carriage, the Rafale couldn't be described as a stealth aircraft per se. But it could certainly be considered highly stealthy. The Rafale was constructed to have a low radar cross section compared with preceding generations of Mistral and Mirage fighters. Composite, radar-absorbing materials comprise up to 50 percent of Rafale's gross weight. It's estimated that stealth characteristics built into the Rafale will make it only about 30 percent less stealthy than the F-22 Raptor flown by the United States. Indeed, the "D" designation of Rafale D air force versions of the plane stands for *Discret*, the French term for stealthiness.

While giving away advantages in stealth to the far more costly U.S. air-dominance fighter, Rafale is slightly faster. It's an agile, highly maneuverable plane (the Rafale can snap a 180° turn in less space than any other fighter) that can launch a large variety of missiles from standoff range at distant targets or engage in terrain-following flight to evade enemy ground radars.

Rafale's stealth is also enhanced by its SPECTRA system (*système pour la protection électronique contra tous les rayonnements adverses*)—a digitized electronic protection suite including advanced radar and infrared warning sensors, radar jammers, and chaff and flare dispensers. There are currently seven single-seat Rafale M versions, which entered service in 2001, aboard the *Charles de Gaulle* aircraft carrier. A two-seater N version is being developed for the French navy with delivery scheduled for 2008.

# U.S. NAVAL STEALTH PROGRAMS—THE STEALTH THAT FAILED

U.S. naval aviation has experienced problems in delivering true stealth aircraft to its forces, though not for want of trying. Since the difference between tragedy and comedy is a happy ending, the curtain will fall on the drama when the fat lady sings. In this scenario the "fat lady" is the Joint Strike Fighter. Following is the play's synopsis.

## Sea Dart

U.S. Navy stealth programs trace their origin to the XF2Y Sea Dart. This aircraft was flown as a prototype on May 9, 1953. The Sea Dart was to be a water-based fighter. It would have been able to take off from the surface of the ocean and transition to flight by powering over the water on a hydrofoil system, dubbed "hydroskis" by the Navy, until it gained enough lift to take off. The reason the XF2Y's hydrofoil system was called by this name was because the Sea Dart skimmed across the surface like a water-skier as hydrodynamic forces pushed the hydrofoil down on the surface. The concept behind Sea Dart was to provide the Navy with a versatile aircraft that could operate from any reasonably clear stretch of water without needing a runway, virtually anywhere in the world. By the standards of the 1950s the plane would have carried an effective weapon load, initially two of the newly developed AIM-4 Falcon missiles and the later AIM-9 Sidewinders.

The most important aspect of the XF2Y to this book, though, is the aircraft's futuristic design—a design that would have made it far stealthier than the jet fighter aircraft of the era. Once it cleared the water and its hydroskis retracted into the underside of the fuselage, the Sea Dart presented a sleek, delta-wing profile that would have given it a small radar cross section, much like a similar delta-wing design did for the SR-71. Like other stealthy aircraft designs, its engines were cocooned inside two nacelles mounted at the top of the fuselage, as were the main engine air intakes.

Although the Sea Dart's cancellation—largely due to continuing engine and vibration problems on takeoff—came before new versions with more powerful engines could be built, there's no reason to doubt that the Sea Dart could have achieved speeds rivaling or exceeding those of first line fighters of the era. As it was the Sea Dart reached supersonic speeds, giving it the distinction of being the first and only supersonic flying boat ever built.

## The AX

The AX (which stood for advanced attack aircraft experimental) was inauspiciously named—an ambitious aircraft project that redesigned stealth from the ground up—hardly had the paint dried on the first mockup than the multibillion dollar project was itself axed by Congress, following Pentagon reassessment of the need for the new plane. In September 1992, acting Secretary of the Navy Sean O'Keefe told the press, "What we are looking at here is the requirement for deep strike interdiction [which] is now a tertiary kind of mission." O'Keefe echoed the prior assessment of then-General Colin Powell, Chairman of the Joint Chiefs of Staff, that airborne deep strike missions could be better performed by Air Force bombers than by carrier-based attack aircraft.

In short, in the immediate aftermath of the Cold War, with shrinking military budgets, spending a projected $14,000,000,000 to build a new hot-dog stealth fighter didn't seem like such a great idea after all. With the downsizing of the U.S. military force for major regional conflict rather than World War III, the AX's reason for existence was overtaken by events. It was deemed unlikely that any air defense threat in the post–Cold War order would be as dense as SAM fields anticipated in Central Europe nor as deep and multilayered as the Soviet homeland air defense system. By the fall of 1993, the AX was history, especially with the advanced tactical fighter (ATF) development project that eventually was to produce the F-22 and F-35 fighters already under way (it was begun in 1990).

At least that's the official story—in fact there are a number of mysteries surrounding the AX project, such as why the Navy, which had no stealth aircraft of its own and badly wanted one, was so willing to drop the program.

AX was a revolutionary aircraft concept. Another product of the Lockheed Skunk Works, it was intended to provide the USN and USAF with a common multimission strike aircraft. Naval variants of AX would have replaced the F-14 and A-6. Air Force versions would have superseded the F-111, F-15, and F-117 stealth fighters. With an all-delta lifting body and a bubble-shaped low-observable compatible all-round-vision pilot canopy, AX resembled no other aircraft ever flown. It was a simple triangle, far different in shape and far more futuristic looking than the B-2 and F-117 then just coming into service.

Officially only a nonfunctional full-scale mockup of AX was produced for wind-tunnel testing. Unofficially it is believed that a functional prototype of AX, possibly a half-scale remotely-piloted version, was built and tested at the secret government installation known as Area 51. In this scenario, the technology of AX was used to build a stealthy all-wing uninhabited combat vehicle or UCAV using clandestine funding, some of which may have been siphoned off from the F-117 and other stealth budgets. The UCAV would have been used in the SEAD (suppression of enemy air defenses) role, as an unmanned SAM-buster and antiradar weapon. As we've seen earlier, some Cold War UCAV plans called for the use of swarms of highly stealthy remote piloted vehicles that would automatically lock on to radar-emitting targets.

AX, now in the form of the F-24 Delta UCAV, would also be controllable by the weapon system officers of combat aircraft operating in the vicinity and also be linked to other command and control and surveillance aircraft such as AWACS and JSTARS. It's been theorized that the UCAV version of AX was in fact produced and tested, and that reported sightings of delta-winged aircraft in the early 1990s may have been attributable to the secret development program that came after the official cancellation of AX.

## The F/A-18E/F Super Hornet

In the wake of the AX's demise, a new version of the F/A-18 was developed. The F/A-18E/F Super Hornet was designed to provide an interim deep-strike aircraft that would bridge the approximate eight- to ten-year gap between the extant F/A-18C/D version and the F-35C, scheduled for 2010 delivery. At first glance the Super Hornet resembles its predecessor as closely as identical twins. But appearances can be deceptive.

The Super Hornet in many ways represents a thorough redesign of the aircraft, constructed largely of the same composite materials as true stealth planes. The F/A-18E/F has air intakes that have been reshaped to help make the aircraft stealthier to head-on radar coverage.

The sides of the fuselage have been canted and all leading edges, including those of the wings, have been aligned with the fuselage in order to reflect radar energies away from the front of the plane. These surfaces have been treated with radar-absorbent material as have weapons pylons and other key reflective areas, including some of the missiles fired by the plane. The wings, which have 25 percent more surface area than those of its predecessor, incorporate a leading-edge hound's tooth design to further enhance stealth.

In addition, the Super Hornet is equipped with a newly designed radial baffle system that masks engine air intakes and exhaust outlets from radar with a relatively small aerodynamic penalty. The plane's turbofan engine also represents an almost complete redesign over previous power plants, and is designed for speed and stealth with a higher thrust-to-weight ratio and lower infrared and radar signatures. With today's technology, the Hornet's conventional circular exhaust nozzles can be made stealthy without needing to configure added "platypus" exhaust baffles or other thermal reduction schemes characteristic of earlier stealth designs.

Active stealth characteristics of the Super Hornet include a low probability of intercept (LPI) radar and an ALQ-165 self-protection jammer; the plane can also deploy three towed decoys to defeat tracking and interception by hostile aircraft. While the Super Hornet is not generally considered a stealth aircraft, it certainly passes the test of stealth: The plane's RCS is said to be about 0 dBsm, which translates to about the size of an aluminum ball 3 feet in diameter. For a conventional airframe design, that's very stealthy; indeed it makes the Super Hornet stealthier than any conventional aircraft in the world.

## CAN WE TRACK OUR OWN STEALTH PLANES?

Are we able to track our own stealth aircraft? The official answer is, "If we told you we'd have to shoot you." The unofficial answer is a qualified yes. Sensitive radars in AWACS aircraft and even orbital satellites whose output is processed by powerful computers could theoretically detect and track stealth aircraft.

### The F-35 Joint Strike Fighter

Regardless of the truth or falsehood of its fate, there's no doubt that lessons learned about stealth from the AX program were transitioned into other ongoing aircraft programs. The ATF program, which was created to develop successors to the F-15 and F-16 for the USAF and the F/A-18 and Sea Harrier for the USN was already underway as AX bit the dust. Unlike AX the ATF program survived. The F-22 Raptor, now in production, and the F-35 Joint Strike Fighter (JSF), now in the prototype, or concept demonstration stage, are the end results.

The JSF is a stealthy multirole supersonic fighter. It's being built in three variants: a conventional takeoff and landing aircraft (CTOL) to be called the F-35A, a carrier-based variant (CV), to be called the F-35C and a STOVL or short takeoff and vertical landing version (the F-35B).

The F-35A variant will replace the F-16 for the USAF and the F-35C variant the F/A-18 for the USN; the F-35B variant will be the successor to the Sea Harrier for the Royal Navy and the U.S. Marine Corps.

In its two naval variants the JSF will be carrier-deployable. The F-35C will have larger wing and tail control surfaces for improved control of the aircraft during carrier landing. It will also feature a stronger internal structure designed to withstand catapult-assisted launches and tailhook-arrested carrier landings.

The F-35C will also have a somewhat larger wing than the A or B versions to give the naval warplane increased range and payload capacity. The F-35C STOVL version will utilize a shaft-driven lift fan to enable the JSF to lift vertically off the decks of carriers and other ships as Harriers currently do. It will also be capable of takeoff from extremely small or confined landing areas.

## STEALTH ON THE CHEAP

Although we've already covered the JSF in Part 2, we'll go into somewhat more detail now on the F-35's stealth qualities, especially as they pertain to naval aviation variants. The JSF is in many ways a departure from U.S. military aircraft design philosophy, which emphasized features over cost. Unlike virtually all other military aircraft, the JSF is intended to be inexpensive to manufacture and maintain, therefore producible in large numbers. This is much more like the design philosophy traditionally behind Russian military aircraft programs, one in which large numbers of planes are produced at low cost, consistent with Russian military doctrine of hitting the enemy with massive, overwhelming force.

One reason that stealth can be had on the cheap in the JSF is because of the radical advances in CAD or computer-aided design, as well as the raw processing power of supercomputers, that have been made since the planning and design of the first stealth aircraft. The F-117 was designed by conventional methods and its angular design was a result. The plane was stealthy but hard to fly as a result. The B-2 could be stealthy and more maneuverable because new computers and software enabled the design and greater use of curvilinear surfaces on the airframe.

The Lockheed-Martin JSF prototype acquired by the Department of Defense was the first aircraft completely designed on supercomputers. As such the stealth characteristics of the airframe could be tested in virtual reality at every stage of the design and testing process, predicting how the actual plane would perform in the real world with a high degree of accuracy.

As noted earlier in this book, the JSF also uses commonly available parts wherever possible; it has a requirement of between 70 and 90 percent commonality for all variants. This means that parts are cheaply acquirable for construction and replaceable in the field.

On another level, a "shared apertures" approach to airframe design places radar, infrared, missile warning, and passive electronic sensors into multipurpose compartments on the aircraft's skin. Advances in the production of radar-absorbent materials also mean that RAM applied to the airframe will last longer with less maintenance than has been the case with earlier stealth planes.

## NAVAL VARIANTS OF THE F-35

The JSF's two naval variants will be compatible with the Air Force's "A" version of the plane. As already mentioned, the USMC will fly the "B" variant. While the F-35B's overall shape, size, stealth properties, and avionics are identical to the F-35A, the power plant and airframe have been modified for the STOVL role.

The Marines will replace their aging fleet of F/A-18C/D Hornets and British-designed Sea Harrier jump jets with the new F-35B. These STOVL variants of the Joint Strike Fighter would be deployed with Marine Expeditionary Units (MEU). They would be capable of operating from either carriers or smaller ships with short or confined runways. The STOVL versions feature a shaft-driven lift fan propulsion system with a thrust-vectoring nozzle and wing-mounted "roll post" ducts to give the plane lateral stability on vertical takeoff and landing. The system is said not only to multiply the engine's lifting force, but to also deliver a much cooler thrust than that of the Sea Harrier, allowing ground crew to work closer to the planes.

Unlike other variants, the "B" version would not carry an internal gun but could be equipped with an externally mounted gun if a mission called for it; stealthy missiles and air-to-ground munitions would be its main form of armament. The USMC plans to acquire a total of 609 F-35Bs between 2010 and 2020.

The F-35C, which will be flown by the U.S. Navy, will be the most tweaked variant in the JSF aircraft family. Although the "C" version will share the same airframe, engine, and avionics suite as the variants flown by USAF and USMC, it will have a visibly different look, with larger wing and tail surfaces. These modifications to the airframe are necessary because of the slow speeds the plane must maintain to remain stable during carrier landing approaches. Wingtip sections of the F-35C will also be foldable, characteristic of carrier-deployable aircraft. The wing assemblies and airframe will be strengthened to absorb the shock of catapult launches and tailhook-arrested landings. The larger surface area of the F-35C's wings will also permit the plane to carry more fuel than the two other JSF variants, and this will translate into greater range and higher weapons capacity.

The USN plans to acquire 480 JSF Cs to replace its aging Hornet fleet; F/A-18E/F Super Hornets continue in operation until at least 2030. In tomorrow's air battle, F-35Cs would work the airspace in tandem with Super Hornets to project naval air power onto sea and land battles. The first production batch calls for a rollout of 22 F-35s in 2010. Of these the USAF and USMC will each get five fighters; the USN is to acquire four. The remaining eight aircraft will be used for various experimental programs and wind-tunnel testing.

# OTHER COUNTRIES AND JOINT STRIKE FIGHTERS

Other countries in addition to the United States and UK will be acquiring Joint Strike Fighter aircraft. Canada, The Netherlands, Denmark, Norway, Italy, and Australia are among those nations that have signed MOUs (memorandum of understanding documents) with the Defense Department to participate in the JSF development program and acquire their own variants of the F-35 following the projected rollout of the aircraft in 2010.

# CHAPTER 18

# REMOTE-CONTROLLED NAVAL WARFARE SYSTEMS

Naval forces, like all other armed services, will continue to integrate remote-controlled and autonomous systems into the order of battle. These are and will continue to be naval variants of UAVs already discussed in previous chapters, such as Predator, Darkstar, and Global Hawk. Ship-deployable airborne systems can be used for surveillance and reconnaissance on the sea and on land and to perform the same jobs they do for other branches of the military.

At the same time the Navy will also field remote warfare systems that are unique to the maritime warfare mission. Under this heading will be found unmanned underwater vehicles (UUVs) and remotely operated vehicles (ROVs). UUVs and ROVs are essentially the underwater equivalent of UAVs. They can be tethered or untethered, remotely piloted or autonomous. One of their main missions is in the deployment of mine-hunting sonar systems for mine reconnaissance (MR) and naval mine countermeasures (MCM) operations; another is antisubmarine warfare.

AUV, autonomous underwater vehicle, was an earlier military term for UUV. Today AUV generally refers to commercially built and operated unmanned underwater vehicles. UUVs are sometimes also known as unmanned undersea vehicles. Also, the distinctions between UUVs and ROVs are often blurry. The terms, as used here, are interchangeable, to reflect the fact that so far no one has agreed on a universally accepted terminology.

As already noted, optimizing naval forces for operations in the world's littoral regions is necessary to a global reach doctrine which has the projection of military power to distant trouble spots as its central premise. Operating in the littorals poses special risks, among which is the hazard of sea mines. In thinking about mines, the image of a spiky black ball bobbing in the waves at the end of a chain needs to be relegated to black-and-white action films starring Dana Andrews. Mines don't look that way anymore. Like all other systems used in warfare, mines have become upgraded, improved, streamlined, and digitized. They have also become extremely stealthy. So, before going on, a few words about mines.

## STEALTH MINES

Sea mines are an effective and inexpensive way to destroy big-ticket enemy naval hardware, such as aircraft carriers and submarines. They are also highly effective in area denial and interdiction operations, such as in closing off choke points in sea lanes and blocking access to harbors. Remember the flap over the U.S. mining of Nicaragua's harbor during the Reagan administration? Using mines to prevent shipping from breaking an embargo is a good way to help enforce a naval blockade, or just show the enemy that your side means business.

Today's high-technology mines are stealthy, smart, and deadly. They can almost be considered as stationary stealth missiles that anchor themselves to the sea bottom and lurk undetected in the depths until their prey comes rambling along. Then, like some underwater predator, they strike and destroy their hapless victim—"as the spider kills the unvay-ree fly," to use the words of Bela Lugosi, who portrayed a very stealthy dude in another old black-and-white film.

Although the principal U.S. means of mine laying is by aircraft, under-sea mines are frequently delivered by submarines, generally by being fired through a sub's torpedo tubes. The reason planes continue to fulfill the primary mine-laying mission is because subs can carry and deploy mines only at the expense of torpedoes, missiles, or other internally stowed weapons. For major mine-laying operations this means that submarines have to either be specially loaded before setting out to sea or return to port to offload previously berthed weapons, take on mines, and then make for the mine-laying area. Submarines are generally used as mine-laying vessels only when aircraft can't perform the mission. (Nevertheless some subs will carry a load-out of mines in order to be ready to deploy them on short notice.)

Note that I didn't add *ships*. No U.S. ships are currently used to lay mines, except during naval exercises. One of the reasons for this is that aircraft, such as the F/A-18 Hornet, are effective mine-laying assets; ship-board mine-deployment capabilities aren't all that vital in today's Navy.

Maritime mines used by the United States come in three basic types. One is a mobile antiship mine, known as SLMM for submarine-launched mobile mine. Another is CAPTOR for encapsulated torpedo mine. The third type is the Quickstrike and Destructor series of aircraft bombs modi-fied for use as shallow-water mines.

Most naval mines can be set to detonate under a variety of influences, such as magnetic, seismic, or acoustic. Counters can also be installed that will permit a specified number of ships or subs to pass by without causing the mine to detonate. Time-delay can also be programmed into most naval mines; this allows a submarine to safely leave the minefield it has planted or enable it to deactivate the mines after a specific period of time has elapsed.

SLMM and CAPTOR mines are stealthy threats to shipping and subs. SLMM is a Mark 48 torpedo modified for use as an undersea mine. It's currently the U.S. Navy's only self-propelled mine, with an electric motor giving it a range of about 9 miles. It has an acoustic system to detect approaching ships and can be fitted with either a magnetic-seismic or a magnetic-seismic-pressure firing mechanism.

When a SLMM is launched from a submarine, an onboard inertial navigation system guides it to a preprogrammed location where it will bury its head in the sea bottom. At this point our bashful SLMM arms itself and lies patiently in wait for an enemy ship to pass within range of its 530-pound warhead. Its acoustic hydrophone sensors detect the presence of approaching vessels. As a ship passes overhead, SLMM's firing system determines whether the vessel fits the parameters for a target of opportunity. If it doesn't, SLMM stays shy and continues hiding its head in the sand. If it does, SLMM goes, as they say on 70th Street in Brooklyn, *ba-boom*. ISLMM (for improved SLMM) is a two-warhead upgrade of the mine system that would attack two separate targets; it would have greater range, course-change capabilities, and a lot more digital street smarts than its predecessor mine.

CAPTOR mines are deployed in deeper waters than SLMM and are primarily antisubmarine weapons. Like SLMM, they anchor themselves to the sea floor where their acoustic detection systems listen for the approach of enemy targets. Unlike SLMM they drop to the bottom as soon as they exit the mother sub's torpedo tube. Instead of exploding when the proper conditions for activation are met, CAPTOR mines launch a Mark 46 torpedo at the target that homes in using active sonar. Because the distance between them is very small, by the time the sub's crew hears the telltale ping of the incoming torpedo's sonar, they're already candidates for free harp lessons.

## MINE COUNTERMEASURES

With stealthy mines like SLMM and CAPTOR out there, mine countermeasures need to be stealthy, too. Demagnetizing the hulls of ships from time to time can help protect vessels from detection, but won't always work, especially when mines' firing systems have multiple sensors built into them. Traditional minesweeping systems are also increasingly ineffective since advanced mines can distinguish between decoys and real targets by matching acoustic signatures against an onboard database. High-tech mines will increasingly pose major threats in littoral and deep-water warfare. Enter the UUV.

# CHAPTER 18: REMOTE-CONTROLLED NAVAL WARFARE SYSTEMS

Unmanned underwater vehicles are in use and in development by the USN and other navies to fill the primary role of undersea minefield reconnaissance. They could prove useful in other missions, too, such as stealthily tracking enemy subs, but the need to develop a mine counter-measures capability is critical if the U.S. Navy is to play its projected role as spearhead of U.S. power projection "from the sea" onto distant shores in future regional conflicts.

Here is another version of Exocet versus the ship of the line, where a stealthy asymmetric threat can destroy a weapon many times its cost, size, and importance to friendly forces. UUVs, themselves small, stealthy, and far less costly than the submarines and ships they are protecting, are designed to fight fire with fire by pitting stealth against stealth.

There are many UUV programs in place throughout the navies of the world, and many more UUVs operated and in private development by commercial interests. Two complementary U.S. Navy UUV programs are illustrative of the general trend in UUV development and deployment. These are NMRS and LMRS, the near- and long-term mine reconnais-sance systems, respectively; the second is a follow-on program to the first and will replace NMRS once the system is perfected later in this decade.

These systems are essentially micro-submarines that, like SLMM and CAPTOR mines, can be launched from the torpedo tubes of attack subs. Actually, "launched" isn't precisely correct, since NMRS (as will be LMRS) is in fact loaded backward into a sub's torpedo tube (it's compati-ble with the Los Angeles–class SSN 688) and, when deployed, backs out under its own power. Once free of the sub, but still tethered to it by a steel cable and a drogue assembly that fits on top of the UUV, NMRS is towed to its mission zone.

There the UUV releases the drogue, paying out fiber-optic cable as it activates its forward- and side-looking sensor suite and begins to hunt the sea bottom for the presence of minefields. Imagery transmitted through the fiber-optic cable is viewed in real time; the UUV is controlled by a remote teleoperator crew aboard the SSN. Once the mission is over, the UUV mates up with the drogue and both are winched back into the sub via the torpedo tube.

The record of the UUV's sortie can be retrieved from the system for later analysis and action. Based on the intelligence gained from the mission the minefield can be marked on charts and bypassed by maritime forces in the vicinity.

There are several classified UUVs that have been operated by the United States, and several that are unclassified but that the Navy doesn't like to talk about because they're kind of secret. Among the classified projects are deep-ocean search and recovery devices that were used during the Cold War to retrieve various things the Soviets and ourselves ... shall we say ... dropped ... on the ocean floor—such as, for example, nuclear bombs.

One such secret incident involving a UUV recovery of a lost nuclear bomb took place after a U.S. B-52 on NATO maneuvers collided with the fuelbird it was tanking from 30,000 feet above the coast of Palomares, Spain, in January 1966. In the process its four-munition nuclear payload was lost. Three of the four weapons were recovered, but the fourth nuke had fallen into the drink. It was known to be somewhere at the bottom of the Med, but exactly where was anybody's guess.

The manned recovery minisub Alvin located the missing A-bomb but failed to retrieve it. Since James Bond was busy unhooking a bra somewhere in Bangkok, the Free World needed to try another approach. This was a secret experimental UUV called CURV for cable-controlled underwater recovery vehicle. CURV succeeded in latching onto the nuke, but just barely, as the UUV itself got tangled up in the pesky nuke's parachute and both had to be winched aboard the recovery ship, one hanging onto the other.

As usual the Soviets were even more hapless than Our Side was, and several covert missions using UUVs to recover miscellaneous objects lost on the sea bottom were successfully mounted. These included debris from Soviet missile tests, wreckage of Russian space probes that had plunged into the ocean, and the wreckage of lost Russian submarines. (An entire Soviet sub was also recovered intact by Howard Hughes's specially equipped manned vessel, Glomar Explorer, in a joint USN-CIA clandestine project in 1973 known as Project Jennifer.)

LMRS, which is being developed to see service by 2010, is to be a completely autonomous UUV, although similar in shape, size, and general operating principles to NMRS. The fully untethered UUV would be able to operate for more than 40 hours at considerably greater distances and depths from the mother sub than NMRS before returning.

It's worth noting that neither this UUV system nor LMRS is capable of mine neutralization. This capability awaits future technological advancement. UUVs that could launch submunitions or kinetic energy fléchettes at minefields to detonate them in place are at least still a decade away, if not more.

## NAVAL UAVS

Unmanned aerial vehicles are also in use by naval forces to stealthily collect airborne surveillance and reconnaissance intel. As already mentioned, the U.S. Navy fields maritime versions of various UAVs in use by other service branches. One such UAV is Predator. This UAV is a medium altitude vehicle with long range and high endurance.

Predator UAVs, which are equipped to collect imagery from synthetic aperture radar, video cameras, and forward-looking infrared (FLIR), have Ku-band satellite data links. This means they possess over-the-horizon capability—because the earth's curvature cuts off radio transmissions, Predators can bounce signals off satellites to ship-based command centers, AWACs aircraft, or even inland Marine expeditionary forces.

*(U.S. Navy)*

*A Predator unmanned aerial vehicle (UAV) flies above the aircraft carrier USS* Carl Vinson *(CVN 70) on a simulated Navy aerial reconnaissance flight off the coast of southern California on December 5, 1995. The UAV was launched from San Nicholas Island off the coast of southern California.*

One of the things wanted in a ship-deployable UAV is compactness; a UAV with a small footprint takes up less space on a crowded deck. Rotary wing design UAVs—small, helicopter-like vehicles—are therefore preferable to more conventional, plane-like designs such as Predator's. Rotary wing designs are also very stealthy. This is why microhelicopters are being developed for future naval UAV programs.

One design already tested is Sentinel, a peanut-shaped UAV mentioned in an earlier chapter. Newer designs, such as the Fire Scout VTUAV (vertical takeoff and landing tactical unmanned air vehicle) much more resemble tiny manned helos. As the T for "tactical" implies, Fire Scout would be used as stealthy spotter aircraft for precision fire support. It would be digitally linked by satellite to Marines in theater who could use it to gather intelligence on where enemy armor, artillery, or troops are located, so that ground units could engage those forces with counterfire or counterattack. Links from the VTUAV to F-35 JSF aircraft or Super Hornets operating in the vicinity, or to attack helicopters such as Apache or Super Cobra, could also be useful in helping to direct fire.

The VTUAV could also be used in place of manned aircraft to carry out battle damage assessment (BDA) missions, in which damage done by a bombing mission is analyzed to determine what's been hit, what's still standing, and what still needs to be targeted on the next inbound sorties. VTUAVs could also help reduce friendly fire casualties by augmenting targeting data from other combat platforms in the area. Fire Scout, which entered low-rate initial production (LRIP) for the USN in May 2001 has undergone shipboard trials; the VTUAV is under consideration for low-observable littoral combat ships that are planned to enter service circa 2007.

# PART 4

# LAND WARFARE OPERATIONS

The day in which mechanized armor could inspire fear because it was virtually impervious to attack is long gone. And with respect to peer aggressors, today it's armor that is an endangered species unless it changes radically. And change it will. As the ground attack phase of the War in Iraq demonstrated, the land battle has already been transformed by lighter, faster, and more mobile forces. It's been estimated that a modern infantry company packs the firepower of a World War II battalion. Land warfare forces will continue to shrink, and with a smaller force footprint, they will become stealthier—right down to the foot soldier, as we'll see.

# CHAPTER 19

# CAMOUFLAGE AND DECEPTION: THE ART OF *MASKIROVKA*

In warfare the reduction of discoverability increases survivability. Again, you can't kill what you can't see (at least not with any guarantee of success). The purpose of camouflage is to make invisible, or make unrecognizable, all aspects of friendly forces that might lead to discovery and recognition by the enemy. Its role includes the hiding of friendly troops, weapons, force positions, vehicles, and command and control facilities so the enemy will not be able to see, hear, or otherwise detect them through radar, thermal imaging, TEMPEST, or other exploitations of combat sensor systems.

As noted earlier, camouflage can also be viewed as a countermeasure to reconnaissance and surveillance. By this definition, deception operations, in which disinformation, secrecy, decoys, maneuver, and spoofing are used in an effort to make the enemy draw false conclusions about the size, nature, and disposition of friendly military forces, and to deceive him into taking actions unfavorable to his battle plans and in support of friendly plans, can also be considered as being directly linked to the tactical art of camouflage. Camouflage and deception also include the use of cover and natural and synthetic protection (field fortifications) that shield friendly forces from enemy view and from subsequent attack.

Russian strategists have in fact combined camouflage and deception in the single term *maskirovka*, which strikes me as a handier phrase-word for the subject at hand and somewhat less of a jawbreaker. So *maskirovka* will, for the purposes of this chapter, be used interchangeably with camouflage and deception.

According to the Soviet Military Encyclopedia of 1980, *maskirovka* is defined as "A means of securing the combat operations and daily activity of forces; a complex of measures designed to mislead the enemy as to the presence and disposition of forces and various military objects, their condition, combat readiness and operations, and also the plans of the commander.... *Maskirovka* contributes to the achievement of surprise for the actions of forces, the preservation of combat readiness and the increased survivability of objects." Soviet doctrine included three levels of *maskirovka*—strategic, tactical, and operational—as well as specific methodologies for its implementation, including concealment, creating false targets and creating diversions. The Soviets used *maskirovka* on a grand scale in World War II. During operation Bagration, begun in the Summer Offensive of June 1944, *maskirovka* was practiced to deceive, entrap, and destroy German Army Groups, severely weakening Hitler's forces by the time the fierce Russian winter set in.

Because there are no set procedures for *maskirovka*, and because it is a fluid art that changes with the nature of specific battlefields and armies (obviously *maskirovka* in the snows of Siberia will be very different from *maskirovka* in the burning sands of the Rub al Khali desert of Saudi Arabia), it will be discussed within the general context of its role as a countermeasure to reconnaissance and surveillance.

## NATURAL PROTECTION

The oldest optical sensor in the world is scanning this page right now: the human eye. Countermeasures against visual detection were probably the first ever invented (actually it was probably as important to deceive the *animal* eye as well, since hunting required camouflage as much as did war).

To add to our storehouse of stealth mythology, it's worth noting that the *Tarnkappe* won by Siegfried from the dwarf king Alberich in the Norse Nibelunglied saga rendered him invisible. Wearing the *Tarnkappe*, Siegfried was able to defeat Brunhilde, the Ice Queen, in battle.

*Tarnkappes* (or is that *Tarnkappen*?) not being available to the average Viking berserker, other methods of making military forces invisible to view were sought after by pretechnological warriors. These were easy enough to find in the natural environment; leaves, branches, mud, smoke, and many other materials ready to hand could all be pressed into service to help conceal the warrior band from its enemies or prey. Without a doubt nature itself suggested camouflage to early humans; patterns displayed on plumage, scales, and fur helped protect creatures that flew, crept, swam, or sprinted from predators by helping them blend into the scenery. Natural formations, such as boulders that seemed to have been sculpted by unseen giants to resemble human heads or faces, probably also suggested camouflage to early man.

Even with industrialized and high-tech warfare, natural camouflage continues to be useful in the field: They don't call practitioners of commando warfare "treeheads" for nothing, after all. For as long as soldiers have been marching through mud they've also covered themselves with some of it to afford concealment and added a few sprigs of the local flora for added effect. In hunting, pelts of the local fauna might have also come in handy; if you looked like a bison and smelled like a bison, you might be able to get up close enough to a bison to turn the bison into dinner (and that ain't no lie, son).

Soldiers have probably always dug holes as hide sites, and a good hide site should best be well camouflaged. During the Desert Shield buildup preceding the Gulf War, Delta Force forward observation teams were inserted into Iraq to collect prestrike intelligence. The teams constructed hide sites they called spider holes. The spider holes made use of sand, rocks, and pebbles to disguise their presence by making the covers of the hide sites hard to spot from a distance—much like the trapdoors that various species of desert arachnids are fond of weaving to conceal themselves from the insects they like to eat.

Some of those special forces teams learned the hard way what our cave-dwelling ancestors could probably have told them—visual camouflage is user friendly but doesn't always work. In one notorious incident the children of a local village quickly noticed a spider hole despite its camouflage. A large number of Iraqi troops soon arrived and the team barely escaped with its hides intact during an emergency helo extraction.

# CAMOUFLAGE NETTING

Using netting to conceal ground assets from detection began to evolve during World War I following the first consistent use of aircraft to conduct reconnaissance and surveillance by a modern military force. By World War II the use of netting had evolved to a highly refined art, using color and design schemes that were intended to make the netting seem to blend into the terrain when viewed from above.

Yet netting has traditionally had two main limitations. First, netting is stealthy only to visual camouflage; it affords little or no protection against infrared, thermal, radar, or other nonvisual reconnaissance and surveillance methods. Secondly, netting isn't useful for concealment of many military ground systems. Among these are systems with radar antennas that rapidly rotate, weapons that pivot, or those weapons that make frequent and quick changes in position.

Since high-tech weapon platforms increasingly fit these parameters, traditional camouflage netting is becoming obsolete on the battlefield. Where it continues to be used it's been replaced by equally high-tech netting that's not only visually stealthy but has good thermal, radar, and TEMPEST concealing properties as well.

New generation camouflage netting will make the hidden objects low-observable by decreasing heat or radar signatures by the use of computer-controlled weaving techniques and layers of radar-absorbent polymers to create a mesh that distributes heat and dissipates radar energies. To be effective, netting, like other camouflage methods and devices, must not only deflect and dissipate energies but also do so in a way that doesn't create a hot spot or "black hole" to enemy observers; this can be as bad as or worse than unfriendlies seeing through the net. The trick is to reduce the detection signatures in such a way that the hidden object blends in with the background and effectively vanishes to enemy sensors.

Finally, stealthy netting needs to do what traditional netting has always done but do it much better. It has to be good at defeating visual reconnaissance and surveillance. One method is to precision-tailor the netting color and pattern scheme to the terrain. This is done by first collecting overhead—aerial or satellite—imaging data of the operations area and then converting the data to a computer-generated camouflage pattern which is then spray painted by an automated process onto the netting. The result can be camouflage netting that seems to blend right into the scenery, and can conceal a multitude of unpleasant surprises for the other side.

## CAMOUFLAGE CLOTHING

The story of Siegfried's magical hat should have probably gone here, because the use of coverings to conceal the human body and make it appear to be something else is also as old as warfare. As noted, pelts were certainly worn by primitive hunters to steal up close to prey, but a set of skins probably came in handy during battles with other cave dwellers, too, especially when humans reached the agricultural stage and invaders clad in sheepskins could steal in amidst baah-ing herds.

I wouldn't be surprised if old Biblical passages about wolves in sheepfolds, and evil ones coming in the guise of lambs, had a lot to do with the sneak attack mode du jour at the dawn of history.

Come to think of it, the old sheepskin coat I bought on Bleecker Street and wore when I went to enlist in the Army long ago sure fooled the sergeant behind the desk at the enlistment center at Times Square. I guess that was one reason I didn't join up that particular day; I wasn't exactly Ulysses clad with regal stateliness in the Golden Fleece or anything. The NCO had the strange idea I was some kind of hippie trying to goof on him and he threw me out. (The damn coat smelled pretty bad, too.) So I didn't end up going to 'Nam. Instead I finished college and went to Someplace They Never Actually Told Me (it's kind of hard to tell where you're at while kicking boxes out of low-flying cargo planes, I've found).

But—not to waste another precious second of your time with accounts of my youthful caprices, and to get back to the subject of camo—what you wear is definitely more important when it comes to stealth than who you are underneath. Camouflage clothing began to replace the ODs (olive drabs) worn by GIs (dogfaces) in World War II only in specific theaters of war and only with specific forces. The time-honored OD combat fatigues were standard kit for U.S. forces in Korea and later in Southeast Asia.

Only with the advent of the Gulf War did the hoary olive drab attire of the U.S. infantry soldier give way to battle dress designed with a pattern and color scheme intended to blend into the desert landscape—the so-called chocolate chips camo pattern (though had the Cold War turned hot in central Europe, U.S. troops would have certainly been fielded wearing woodland camo battle dress proposed as a common NATO standard by that time).

As warfare grows increasingly digitized, the battle dress of the soldier will grow increasingly adept at camouflage and resistant to multispectral imaging methods. Patterns that change like those of the chameleon's skin, to blend into the background, even invisibility, are some of the methods at concealment for the future infantry soldier. But more on this in a little while.

## OF PAINT, FOAM, AND SMOKE

A good paint job can work wonders for your stealthiness, compadre. During the Cold War NATO forces tried but failed to agree on a common standard for vehicle camouflage paint schemes. Like traditional camouflage netting, camouflage paint schemes are effective almost only within the optical range. In order for paint schemes to remain effective, paint needs to gain greater stealth properties, absorbing and dissipating thermal and radar energies being two important considerations. In addition to paint, foams began to make their appearance during the Cold War that had similar properties to paint but had the advantage of being able to be applied much more quickly and treat a wider variety of surfaces and textures with camouflage coatings.

Foams have been developed that have good radar- and thermal-absorbency properties. Other types of camouflage foam are formulated to be good absorbers of sound, and these can contribute to reduction of the acoustic signature of the protected field assets.

Smoke, like forms of body cover, is possibly among the oldest forms of camouflage. Like the wolf in the sheepfold, devils and demons of old frequently appeared out of smoke, and I suspect this belief might have had an origin in early stealth warfare, too.

Nevertheless, conventional smoke was last effective in shaking the bad guys when it spewed out of 007's lethally detailed Aston-Martin DB5. Conventional smoke screens have little or no value against imaging methods beyond the visual, such as thermal or radar. To my knowledge there is little development under way on developing smoke as an effective tool of stealth, although there was a flurry of interest in "super smoke" with multispectral properties a decade ago.

## ACTIVE CAMOUFLAGE

Until recently all camouflage-based countermeasures to reconnaissance and surveillance were passive—that is, they generated no electrical, electronic, or plasma energies of their own and merely absorbed, reflected, or dissipated energy probes directed at them. One reason for this was the absence of technological innovations to make active camouflage measures possible on the battlefield. In recent years the situation has changed and several active camouflage methods have been developed. In time it's likely that some or all will find their way into battlefield-ready systems.

Some of these involve plasma fields. The Russians have been working on active camouflage involving plasma fields for decades (although some believe this is disinformation). In this they have apparently evinced a radical departure from Western stealth research. This research has been kept highly secret, but reports have leaked out from time to time indicating they have developed functional prototypes of such active stealth systems. (They have reportedly also developed tank defense systems utilizing active shielding, possibly by a cloud of steel pellets, to destroy incoming projectiles before they can strike the armor.)

Another active camouflage approach is one that bends or displaces visible light striking an object in such a way as to make it flow around the object. This high-tech variation in visual camouflage would effectively make the subject of the *maskirovka* invisible to view. One prototype system, in the form of a stealth suit, has been developed in Japan. Although the system is still extremely crude it does work. When sufficiently advanced it could result in the achievement of something once only possible in the realm of myths, such as that of Siegfried's magic hat—cloaking soldiers with invisibility.

## DECEPTION OPERATIONS

As mentioned, *maskirovka* enshrines deception operations. These too, as we've noted in the introduction to this book, are as old as warfare itself. As we've also seen, deception operations were developed to an adroitly choreographed state-of-the art during World War II in Operation Bodyguard. Of more recent fame in the annals of deception is the famous "Hail Mary Play" developed by CENTCOM as part of the plan for the ground war phase of the Gulf War.

One thing I haven't talked about much, anent deception, is the use of decoys. Decoys are important to deception methods, and sophisticated decoys have been developed for aircraft and for submarine warfare deployment. These decoys are frequently constructed to use radar—or in the case of submersibles, sonar—countermeasures to deceive enemy forces with false target signatures. The object of the decoys is to draw enemy fire away from the real target.

Less well known are other types of decoys, especially those used in land warfare. These range from the crude thermal decoys constructed by Iraqi forces in the Gulf War in attempts to fool coalition strike aircraft into believing they had struck armor when in fact they had bombed wooden mockups propped against burning smudge pots, to sophisticated decoys used by more inventive and technically proficient military forces.

For example, bridge decoys and attendant mock preparations for river crossing can deceive the enemy as to the actual movements of friendly troops. In the Falklands War, Argentinean camouflage specialists constructed mock bomb craters that were so realistic-looking that they threw off RAF battle damage assessments and prevented follow-up strikes by the British.

Possibly the most ambitious piece of decoy deception in the annals of *maskirovka* was the development of a rail-mobile ICBM-basing strategy by the Soviets during the latter stages of the Cold War. The rail-mobile strategy used the "shell game" approach by constantly moving a mixture of real and decoy ballistic nuclear missiles around the vast spaces of the Russian heartland in such a way as to make detection of the real from the phony nukes extremely hard, if not impossible.

The United States countered by beginning development of its own variation on this strategy, the MX missile system, but also instituted an even more ambitious deception operation, one that might justly be called one of the most ambitious in all history—Star Wars.

The Strategic Defense Initiative of the Reagan years, better known by its acronym SDI, and known still better by the title of a movie of the same name, was a scheme to place what was described as a defensive space-based shield against nuclear missile attack in orbit around the earth. To those in-the-know, it didn't have a prayer of success—the technology, to say nothing of the money, to make it feasible just wasn't available. Nevertheless the Soviets bought the scam, or bought enough of it to expend more of their dwindling national energies and treasure to build an SDI capability of their own, hastening the USSR's collapse.

Fortunately for everybody, the Cold War drew to a close before these last superpower contests of nerve and will became an endgame played out across the Fulda Gap (a prominent invasion corridor from the east), and the plains of central Germany that lay beyond, into the heart of western Europe, after a Soviet surprise attack.

## THE NUCLEAR SHELL GAME

By the early 1980s the U.S. nuclear triad of land-, air-, and sea-based forces capable of successfully launching a counterstrike against the Soviet Union had become increasingly vulnerable to preemptive attack. While stealth aircraft were being secretly developed to solve the problem, steps were contemplated to make the U.S. land-based nuclear arsenal less vulnerable to preemptive attack by making it more stealthy. In December of 1982, an initiative known as the "densepack" system was proposed as a variation on mobile missile basing. The densepack strategy called for deploying Minuteman silos in closely spaced fields. This would theoretically require the Soviets to attack U.S. land-based nukes in salvos—so-called barrage attacks—which increased the chances of at least some of the U.S. nukes surviving to counterlaunch. The plan proposed by the Scowcroft Commission, a panel appointed by Ronald Reagan in 1983, was a variation on the venerable shell game in which bettors have to guess which shell hides a pea after a skilled sharper deftly moves the shells around on a table. Mobile basing was the nuclear version of the old shell game. Only the Russians would be trying to guess where American nukes were hidden instead of peas. Congress rejected these, and similar later plans, such as the mobile MX missile system, as unworkable.

# CHAPTER 20

# STEALTH AND THE TWENTY-FIRST CENTURY SOLDIER

Since World War II, the prototype of the foot soldier, at least in the United States, has been the type of GI depicted in Bill Mauldin's famous comic strip and his hilarious but sage and insightful book *Up Front*. Mauldin's two sad-sack grunts, Willie and Joe, are the epitome of the infantry soldiers who slogged across Europe through mud, rain, and enemy shelling to win the war for the Allies.

Unshaven, cocky, wary of authority, they have the thousand-yard stare of the combat veteran and the devil-may-care of those who've been to hell and back. Their best friends were their steel pot helmets and their ability to duck the incoming by hitting the dirt or diving into a nearby shell hole.

At first glance Willie and Joe don't seem to have much if anything to do with stealth, and yet a closer inspection reveals that these two universal American GIs did indeed have concerns regarding stealth warfare. In one cartoon two dogfaces report to base, "Able Fox Five to Able Fox. I got a target but ya gotta be patient." They're calling from a shell hole directly beneath a German Panzer tank, unseen by the enemy directly above their heads. In another, Willie's cracked to Joe about how good the tankers have it. Joe retorts, "I'd ruther dig. A movin' foxhole attracks th' eye." Another cartoon shows the pair hitting the dirt to avoid a shell burst, bullet tracks crisscrossing over their helmets. The caption reads, "I can't git no lower, Willie. Me buttons is in th' way."

It's obvious that the infantry soldier, as represented by these two icons of the U.S. GI, literally had a ground-level education in the concept of battlefield stealth. Their motto, if distilled from the captions, might be: "Maintain a small visual signature at all times" (or "when in doubt, hit the dirt"). It's also obvious that the foot soldiers of yesterday could have benefited from applied stealth technology to make them harder to see and aim at by the enemy.

## NIGHT VISION AS A TOOL OF STEALTH

Infantry forces have already become stealthier and, given the increasing need for battlefield countermeasures against reconnaissance and surveillance, will need to become stealthier yet in tomorrow's warfare. Passive night-vision technology combined with advances in miniaturization that resulted in compact, lightweight night-observation goggles (NOD) that could be worn on the helmet allowed the infantry soldier to fight at night with considerably greater effectiveness than ever before.

Night-vision technology for combat soldiers began with the first experimental infrared night scopes built at the end of World War II. These were active IR devices, relying on the illumination of the target by the same invisible IR beams that we fire at our TVs from handheld remotes. Because IR light is invisible only to the human eye, and can be detected by enemy sensors, the use of active IR devices quickly became what they took to calling a "suicide light" in the field. Image intensification (II) presented the next innovation. This was a passive system that relied on amplification of the small amount of ambient light present even in pitch darkness to enable forces to operate in the dark. Thermal imaging (TI) provided sharper imagery and other benefits, such as greater mobility due to compactness of systems.

Although there were and still are many drawbacks to wearable night-seeing devices for the infantry soldier (including bloom-out, an effect that smeared the visual field of last-generation NODs during flashes of light, completely screwing them up until reset, and post-mission visual impairment as a result of prolonged wear), these were outweighed by the benefits they bestowed. Their value in night operations was proven during the Gulf War, the first major regional conflict in which NODs were part of standard kit for special operations forces.

In fact the effectiveness of SOF in the Gulf was in large part made possible by the availability of new, portable, and lightweight night-vision gear. The anti-Scud war that U.S. Delta and UK SAS troopers waged in the Iraqi desert was a largely covert campaign and arguably the shining hour of special forces during the conflict.

Joint U.S.–UK fusion cells dropped by Pave Low helos operated largely by night, getting around on motorcycles (many of the Brit teams preferred these) and low-slung, weapon-bristling fast attack vehicles (FAVs) for U.S. commandos. These night operations would not have been possible without advanced NOD gear.

In desert warfare the skill that the Israelis call "reading Braille" is a must-have. To read Braille in the desert means developing a fingertip-feel for the subtle cues that make navigating the flat expanse of the desert possible. Part of the desert warrior's job is also to find hiding places on the desert for the purposes of ambush, staging an attack, or sheltering when not on the move.

Deserts appear to be flat but really aren't. Actually the arid landscape undulates, and there are always rises and declivities available for offensive tactical use. The converse is also true: Infantry forces operating on the open desert need to be wary of ambush by their opponents. Nocturnal operations in this environment can therefore pose unacceptable risks without the aid of night vision, making night vision the key to stealth.

Nevertheless there's another side to the night vision coin: Deserts are excellent thermal-imaging environments. The desert landscape, which radiates the heat absorbed during the day at a fairly constant and regular rate, provides the perfect null thermal background for humans and man-made objects of all kinds that reveal their own unique thermal signatures.

Those who've seen the opening scenes of the movie *Patriot Games*, in which a team of mercenary assassins is viewed through mock-thermal

imaging from an overhead angle as they silently infiltrate a terrorist training camp in the Libyan desert, have a good picture of what this means. In
other words, in modern warfare even the tip of your nose can become a
suicide light under the right set of circumstances.

While otherwise stealthy-as-spit troops can stick out like sore thumbs
under desert warfare conditions, this risk isn't limited only to the arid
places of the world or even to night operations per se. To greater or lesser
degrees it's a threat to stealth soldiering at any place and at any time.

## THE INFANTRY SOLDIER AS STEALTH WEAPON

Keeping in view the definition of stealth as a countermeasure to surveillance and reconnaissance, many of the same stealth applications that have
made aircraft like the F-117A hard to detect can serve the same purpose
when applied to GI Joes and Janes. Just as the biological weapon platform
that is the soldier can use the man-portable equivalent of a stealth aircraft's night-seeing FLIR, other stealth features of war machinery can be
tailored to the soldier-in-the-loop.

Some of these features are prosaic, such as the use of *maskirovka* discussed in the preceding chapter. As already noted, camouflage field uniforms, including helmets and gloves, are already standard kit for coalition
forces. Personal and man-portable weapons too can be camouflaged by the
use of paints or special add-ons, such as those that fit around combat
rifles, enclosing barrel, receiver, and stock in a camouflage pattern that can
be changed to match new combat environments. Maneuver tactics tailored
to the theater of operations, such as reading Braille in the desert, are as
old as soldiering, but will probably always be necessary to stealthy warcraft
for the infantry soldier.

Other stealth advancements have already come about through the digitization of the battlefield. The grunt on the ground is increasingly becoming a high-tech weapon platform meshed into a network of forces on land,
sea, air, and space. Willie and Joe might have had little more than their
helmets and BAR rifles to protect them, and a field telephone to link them
to HQ, but this isn't the case anymore. The U.S. Army's Objective Force
of tomorrow will benefit from digitized and network-centric communications and intelligence.

## OBJECTIVE FORCE WARRIOR

Objective Force Warrior (OFW) is to be a major upgrade of the Land Warrior future soldier system. The OFW system is to include a family of lightweight weapons with advanced fire control, optimized for urban combat and synchronized with other shooters in theater. Sensors will allow the stealth-suited soldier of tomorrow to collect tactical intelligence and be linked to ground, air, sea, and space assets in the battle space including UAVs and satellites. If you're tired of being called a wuss, trade in your bodhidarma for some high-tech body armor. The Scorpion IPA combat ensemble has been designed by the U.S. Army's Natick Soldier Center to demonstrate how OFW might actually look in action. The Scorpion is made of advanced lightweight ballistic protective materials that protect the soldier inside an armored shell complete with its own interior microclimate and sensor-to-shooter links that show targeting and tactical data on the integrated head-mounted display. The Scorpion is designed to provide good "signature management," meaning that the armored shell is also visually and thermally stealthy.

*(Natick Soldier Center. Photo: Sara Underhill, U.S. Army Soldier System Center)*

*The Scorpion IPA Combat Ensemble. Designed for the Objective Force Warrior, the new combat "shell" is to provide lightweight body armor that is also an effective camouflage system.*

Advanced warfighting experiments (AWE) conducted since the end of the Gulf War in support of the U.S. Army's Force XXI and Army After Next initiatives have fielded ground forces linked by C⁴IFTW—C⁴I for the warfighter—technologies in which advanced sensor-to-shooter networks afforded a shared situational awareness and real-time battle space synchronization with troops in the field, commanders in the rear, overhead assets such as helicopters, AWACS, and JSTARS surveillance and reconnaissance aircraft, and mechanized armor, such as main battle tanks, in the theater.

The Pentagon's Land Warrior 2000, the British MOD's Infantryman 2000, the French ECAD Advanced Combat Soldier System (*équipement du Combattant Débarqué*), the NATO-sponsored CRISAT (collaborative research into small arms technology) and biannual Kernel Blitz exercises for joint U.S. Navy and Marine amphibious operations, are all examples of efforts to study and perfect techniques to link ground forces via a combat information superhighway that have been geared up to study battlefield C² at the brigade and below level.

This networking of forces by digitization helps make them stealthier because it enables the fielding of smaller, faster, and more mobile ground attack elements, giving forces a "leaner footprint" in Pentagonese. At the same time these forces are equipped with smarter, lighter, and more lethal weapons than ground-combat units of previous eras. They can also quickly call in close air support (CAS) from attack helos, F-22 Raptors, and UCAVs; launch their own remote-piloted aircraft for reconnaissance or attack; or even direct artillery fire from distant batteries from their positions in the field. Being linked to these big-footprint forces gives twenty-first century infantry units an almost virtual link to powerful force multipliers that can be almost pulled out of a hat on very short notice.

Not to present too rosy a picture of CAS, one of the reasons it *hasn't* been practiced as a component of infantry combat doctrine in decades until quite recently is that the risks it entails often outweigh the benefits it promises. Had coalition forces fighting in Iraq engaged a peer competitor with a functional military, the helicopters and planes that provide CAS would have been exposed to threats from air and ground, such as SAMs and fighter aircraft, that have long vexed warplanners. Ground forces

> have been leery, with good reason, of calling in air power to do what they might better do themselves.

Appearing small on radar scopes is very much like being physically small in unit disposition on the ground; whether based on illusion or physical reality, smallness helps make forces harder to see and therefore (daring to repeat myself endlessly) harder to kill. The creation of a leaner force footprint coupled with higher mobility and digitized communications networks for the warfighter have been cornerstones of Pentagon force transformation strategy since the Gulf War. In fact it's been a preoccupation of both Clinton and Bush Defense Departments alike, regardless of Dick Cheney's statements in the 2000 vice-presidential debate.

The proof in the pudding was the ground war phase of the War in Iraq in which the AWEs of past years resulted in a real-world force embodying many, if not most, of the innovations developed in the course of the prior 12 years. Future infantry forces will be even more digitized, but it's also possible that stealth innovations will go far beyond even today's cutting edge applications in tomorrow's combat theaters.

## STEALTHING THE SOLDIER

Siegfried put on an invisible hat, Frodo had his enchanted cape, and many other mythical heroes have donned costumes that made them low-observable. In reality the stealthing of the soldier will probably result in uniforms and other wearable and portable combat gear that lower the visual, thermal, radar, TEMPEST, and even the olfactory signatures of the straight-leg infantry grunt.

At the same time miniaturized sensor equipment linked to small arms, including portable missile launchers, would be necessary to maintain tactical surprise against unfriendly stealth forces on the ground, whether they were mechanized armor formations or enemy infantry units.

Just as RAM skins, radar-absorbing composite materials, and IR countermeasures have helped to stealth-up aircraft, similar measures would result in wearable combat gear with stealth properties to turn the foot soldier into the supertrooper of tomorrow. Programs like Land Warrior and ECAD have already produced and tested prototypes of such stealth suiting.

A suit, based on the results of several programs, might be made of fabric that has good radar-absorbent and thermal-reflective properties. It might be "custom-tailored" to a specific operational environment by using computer-aided design and manufacturing techniques (CAD-CAM) in the same way as high-tech camo netting discussed in the preceding chapter. Another proposed technique would be to spray the suit with biodegradable colors that could change shade and patterning chameleonically. Yet another proposal involves designing advanced, microprocessor-controlled liquid crystal displays into the fabric to produce patterns that shift and change against the background, matching woodland, desert, or jungle environments according to a preprogrammed database of camouflage patterns stored in the suit's onboard computer.

This modular exterior, one that could be removed and replaced by a new outer shell to meet changing operational requirements, would fit over an underlayer that provides an entirely self-contained environment for the soldier. Breathable air would be filtered from battlefield contaminants, and cooled or heated to provide an internal microclimate. The suit itself would be made of lightweight ballistic armored material, with extra ballistic protection built into the lower leg area to protect against land mines.

If all of this sounds a little far fetched, consider this: A professor at the University of Tokyo's School of Engineering, Susuma Tachi, has recently developed a crude but workable suit of invisibility which he demonstrated in the spring of 2003. Wearers of the suit appear semitransparent, with objects in the background, such as mailboxes and passersby, visible through their bodies. Tachi claims that a commercially viable version of the suit could be available within a few years, and given the accelerating pace of technological advancement, it's not that much of a conceptual leap to envision actual invisibility for military forces by the year 2020. If so, it would represent taking stealth to an entirely new level.

# CHAPTER 21

# STEALTH IN MOBILE WARFARE

Agile, mobile, lethal—those three words sum up the underlying premise behind defense transformation. They apply to all sectors of warfare, but especially to the transformation of land warfighting forces into a twenty-first–century army under Pentagon plans like Force XXI, Land Warrior, Army After Next, and other ongoing and future initiatives under the Defense Transformation for the 21st Century Act of 2003. While a great deal has already changed, the tactics, strategy, and equipment for the land battle have in some regards only recently begun to transform from Cold War models.

After the dust clears and the position papers have been written, after the hyperbole and bureaucratic saber-rattling fades away, it all boils down to an attempt to create a military force that is smaller, faster on its feet, networked with theater and strategic forces, and crams more destructive power into a smaller package than ever before with greater accuracy in putting that destructive power on target.

And, of course, you also need stealth. To murder an old refrain, for transformation to work, you gotta have stealth, miles and miles and miles of stealth. All of these other attributes of a twenty-first–century military force listed won't amount, as Bogey once said, to a hill of beans if the enemy sees you coming. A land warfare force for the twenty-first century must be a stealth force or it doesn't stand a chance against the threats it has to face, for land forces, as nowhere else in the spectrum of warfare, will face not only conventional force on force threats, such as other troops and other tanks, but also asymmetric threats. These are harder to define, but they would include everything from the crude tank-killing guerilla tactics practiced by the former Afghan *mujahideen* against Soviet armor, to super mortar rounds that hunt armor like hawks hunt armadillos (okay, maybe hawks don't hunt armadillos, but you get the picture).

Beyond this, and possibly more to the point, is that these smaller, faster, lighter forces need to do all the things that larger forces requiring longer logistics chains did in the past, do them better and faster, and get it all over with sooner. To achieve these objectives, twenty-first–century land forces will work more closely with air power in a relationship that harks back to tactics not used since World War II. Close air support, or CAS, for ground warfare units, would increasingly fill the role traditionally played by artillery and mortars in putting fire on targets prior to assaults or in supporting troops in counterattacks. CAS played just this role during the 2003 ground war in Iraq and was one of the reasons that coalition forces made such rapid progress.

Despite expanding Pentagon budgets (the latest, at this writing, marking the sixth straight annual increase since post-Cold War budgets bottomed in 1998 after 13 years of decline), transformational processes will mainly represent reapportionment of forces and the adoption of new concepts rather than the wholesale fielding of exotic new hardware.

One reason for this is that after all is said and done, there's still not enough money for the Pentagon to invest in as many new weapons systems as it would like to buy. On the contrary, the transformational strategy so far has meant cutting some major programs, such as Crusader, a super-accurate self-propelled howitzer, and foregoing upgrades to existing systems, such as the M1A1 Abrams and the M2 Bradley fighting vehicle, in favor of investing in newer, lighter, and cheaper systems more in tune with the reshaping of the force footprint into a leaner, meaner package.

## STEALTH THROUGH MOBILITY

There is an ancient holy trinity of warfare—move, communicate, and shoot. It is held as an article of faith by all elements of the land battle. Mastering these three principles can spell success while failing to respect them can lead to defeat. As we've seen, smaller footprints for forces give them stealth attributes. They're harder to detect by enemy reconnaissance and surveillance. They can hit and then run, quickly repositioning to strike again at another target before enemy ranging and targeting systems, such as antimortar radar, can establish their location.

As the ancient Chinese military strategist, Sun Tzu, enjoined military commanders who would be successful in war,

> At first be like a modest maiden,
> And the enemy will open his door;
> Afterward be as swift as a scurrying rabbit,
> And the enemy will be too late to resist you.

Small yet lethal formations that can move quickly across terrain, that can be rapidly inserted into and extracted from combat areas by helicopter, that are linked by global-mobile digital communication networks to other forces in theater, and are armed with compact, yet lethal weapons, such as man-portable antiarmor missile launchers, present a modern confirmation of the honorable General Sun's advice.

### THE SHADOW STEALTH RECONNAISSANCE VEHICLE

The U.S. Marine Corps and Special Operations Command are closely monitoring a new deep strike, deep reconnaissance vehicle program called Shadow. The Shadow is a reconnaissance, surveillance, targeting vehicle (RST-V), developed by General Dynamics Land Systems. The Shadow RST-V was developed for the Marine Corps Warfighting Laboratory, sponsored by the Defense Advanced Research Projects Agency (DARPA) and the Office of Naval Research (ONR). The Shadow RST-V is a 4×4 hybrid electric drive vehicle with reconnaissance, surveillance, targeting, and C3I (command, control, communications, and intelligence) capability coupled with integrated stealth and survivability features. The vehicle can be equipped in a range of mission variants including forward observer, forward air control, reconnaissance, light strike, battlefield ambulance, air defense, logistics, personnel carrier, antiarmor, and mortar weapons carrier. The roof of the Shadow can be extended to transform the vehicle into a mobile command post. When running in stealth mode, the Shadow can be powered by battery only, reducing the RST-V's acoustic and thermal signatures.

Tactics notwithstanding, a stealthy twenty-first–century land force should be equipped with vehicles that are as low-observable as possible. Combat vehicles of all types should be difficult to detect and hard for the enemy to recognize. This is one of the reasons for the development of the Stryker interim armored vehicle (IAV) and also behind the decision to fund the FFV's development at the expense of upgrades to existing armor. The Stryker is lighter, faster to build and service, and faster to deploy than an Abrams main battle tank, which is so ponderous that the heavy haulers of the airlift force, C-5s and C-17 transport planes, are necessary to transport the M1A1 to its destination, one tank at a time.

By contrast the Stryker is C-130 Hercules deployable, meaning it can be carried (one at a time) on the more numerous Hercules aircraft which can also take off and land on a wider range of airfields than larger planes; if carried onboard a C-5 or C-17, Strykers can be airlifted in groups of four and three, respectively. Once in theater, ground combat formations built around the Stryker would be capable of moving rapidly across rugged terrain in daylight, darkness, and all weather conditions thanks to its mobility and sensor systems.

Stealth is one of the factors in accepting the trade-off in mobility for firepower represented by changing the makeup of conventional armored forces. Again, the theory is that all the armed might in the world means very little if the weapon platform is vulnerable to reconnaissance, surveillance, and target acquisition (RSTA). Instead of using tanks or artillery to destroy an enemy force, next-generation forces would rely more heavily on close air support from air cover assets like Comanche or F-35 and lightweight vehicle-mounted or shoulder-launched missile systems such as LOSAT to attack with digitally enhanced smart weaponry.

*The Stryker Interim Fighting Vehicle is air-transportable to rapidly go wherever troops are needed.*

LOSAT, which stands for line of sight antitank, would replace the existing main infantry armament against tanks and other heavy armor, such as the M-901 TOW missile. Other weapons that would be used in this role would be so-called top-attack weapons such as the U.S. SADARM, the French STRYX, and other similar munitions. These are launch missiles or mortar rounds that, once over the battlefield, use nose-mounted seekers to detect enemy armor on the ground below. Once detected, and confirmed as an actual target rather than a decoy or countermeasure, the munition plunges downward to kill the armor via its most vulnerable points, which are located at the top of the vehicle. The most sophisticated of these projectiles can be programmed to aim themselves not just at the general vicinity of the top of the target vehicle, but at specific soft points identified through earlier intelligence and programmed into the round.

Because current and future potential antagonists have or will have lightweight, lethal and relatively inexpensive antiarmor weapon systems like the aforementioned, they will pose a growing asymmetric threat to friendly ground combat formations. It's likely that in future conflicts current-generation MBTs such as Abrams would be retained for force-on-force engagements with enemy main battle tanks, or kept in reserve until stealthier and more mobile forces reduced the danger of asymmetric threats to armor down to levels deemed acceptable to theater CINCs.

This will probably be the case, because one of the lessons of the Desert Wind air campaign phase of the Gulf War was that stealth forces were at their most valuable when used as "silver bullet" forces to spearhead the main assault. Once enemy forces and communications were degraded to the point where the opposition had been effectively decapitated and de-fanged, nonstealthy assets could productively enter the fray. In the Gulf War these nonstealthy forces were B-52s and other conventional aircraft. In future conflicts the BUFs (big, ugly f***ers) may be tanks.

## SENSOR TO SHOOTER

A lack of night combat capability means a hit probability of zero in dark-ness. During the Yom Kippur War of 1973–1974, Israel was bitterly con-fronted with this truth in combat against Syrian forces on the Golan Heights. It was only at dawn, after suffering heavy losses against the night-combat-capable Syrians in T-54 tanks, that Israeli armor was able to bring up reserves and, at the eleventh hour, prevent a Syrian break-through.

Stealth in night fighting for ground combat forces is based on the abil-ity to see in the dark while making detection of friendly forces difficult for the enemy. Without night vision capability a ground force is robbed of its most important stealth asset. To reframe the issue, the precision engage-ment capabilities of these more compact forces—the ability to place accu-rate fires on targets with high precision—is highly sensor-dependent. Mobile armor of every kind from tanks to APCs relies on a sensor-to-shooter loop in order to attack and counterattack and for surveillance and reconnaissance. During both Gulf wars, for example, TOW missile crews used the weapon's thermal aiming sights not only for target acquisition but also to perform recce operations at night or to resolve questionable objects behind cover or in bad weather.

Tank commanders refer to their "top vision" much like the way sub skippers think about periscope recces, except in tank warfare this vision is the actual human eyeball scanning the area outside the confines of the tank hull as the commander takes a quick look around through binoculars, and then ducks back inside. At all other times the crew receives all its in-formation concerning the outside world, including all-important tactical input about the whereabouts of enemy forces, via their sensor-to-shooter linkages, be these thermal, image-intensification, low-light TV, infrared, or what-have-you.

If those sensors run into trouble the outcome is something like what resulted from the ancient confrontation between the wily Ulysses and the Cyclops. Blind the steel monster and it can only flail helplessly around in impotent fury or try to run away, both of which are as suicidal options in today's and tomorrow's warfare as they were to the nemesis of the Greek soldiers shipwrecked while sailing homeward from Troy.

Such an asymmetric threat doesn't even need sophisticated technology to work, in fact. I recently bought a pocket-size laser projector for two bucks that shoots a pinpoint of ruby light at the press of a button. Were I to shine it at an MBT's sensors I could very likely paralyze them—and it. The fact that it's highly dangerous to go around shining laser lights on battlefields today notwithstanding, and the fact that I personally wouldn't be dumb enough to try this, doesn't mean that some fanatic true-believer wouldn't risk being cut down in order to give his buddies a chance to kill the tank. Anyway, I cite the story of my personal pocket laser only to illustrate a point, this being that blinding laser technology is both a threat to friendly armor and an attack capability against enemy armor that is important to considerations of stealth in the land battle of the future. Far more sophisticated blinding lasers are in development that can attack this Achilles' heel of armored vehicles. Once blinded they can then be acquired by standoff weaponry, such as missiles, and quickly destroyed or put out of commission.

One way to guard against this threat to stealth in mobile land forces is to have alternative or complementary sources of the reconnaissance and targeting data normally available through the local sensor-to-shooter grid. JSTARS and AWACS as well as other airborne assets such as the F-35 JSF can perform this function. Another platform that can do the job would be a space-based radar (SBR) system.

An SBR, presumably using a network of satellites equipped with high-resolution synthetic aperture radar (SAR) that could be accessed by ground forces as easily as a conventional GPS system, is one of the few new programs currently (and, of course, officially as opposed to covertly) funded by the Pentagon. The SBR would provide real-time intelligence of moving ground targets anywhere in the world, complementing and eventually replacing airborne platforms such as JSTARS.

Until this system is available, tactical UAVs could augment or replace the local sensor-to-shooter grid. In the interim—or possibly in the long-run, as SBR and tactical UAVs that could do this are still decades away—making sensors as survivable as possible is the best answer to preserving the combat-worthiness of mobile, agile and lethal land forces ... and keeping them as stealthy as possible.

## LOGISTICS FOOTPRINT

A lean logistics footprint is also important to keeping twenty-first–century forces mobile and stealthy. Logistics means not just supply lines, but also the coordination of other ground forces in the theater. When an operation is under way, the theater CINC establishes a precise timetable for the arrival of all forces at specific points in the battle space. These points are generally designated by phase lines, which can be actual physical demarcations on the landscape, or representations on a map grid, to indicate where forces need to stop before proceeding. If forces bypass their phase lines, they risk throwing the entire plan out of kilter. Commanders of divisional and smaller formations who've liked to lead from the front have sometimes ignored phase lines, with mixed results. During World War II Patton flouted Bradley's directive to stay put and made spectacular territorial gains whereas Monty, flouting Ike's wrath, pushed forward and in so doing courted disaster.

My point about stealth and logistics is that, at least in large-scale engagements, logistics have a very close connection to the stealthiness of deployed forces in theater. The more coordinated the logistical footprint of those forces, the stealthier they are; the less so, the more like sore thumbs they become to the ever-watchful enemy.

CHAPTER 22

# STEALTH IN TANK WARFARE AND NEW TANK DESIGNS

The Belt is what they called it during the Cold War. It zigzagged down the length of central Germany from the Baltic to the Federal Republic's southernmost frontiers. Officially it was the Central Region Missile Belt (CR Belt), a kind of Maginot Line that was supposed to keep the Soviets out of West Germany if they started World War III. Unlike the original Maginot Line in France, this barrier possessed scant, if any, physical fortifications. In place of concrete obstacles were batteries of surface-to-air missiles, conventional in peacetime but capable of rapid conversion to nuclear weapons in the event of an invasion from the Communist East.

Unlike the Maginot Line, the CR Belt was put in place not to defend against ground attack but to thwart Soviet tactical air. Waves of Russian fighter and bomber aircraft would have dashed toward industrial and urban targets in the industrialized Ruhr valley and major cities in the West. Other Soviet and Warsaw Pact aircraft would have provided top cover for mechanized armor and troop formations that would have swept across the plains of central Germany in a rush to seize and hold strategic centers of gravity. In accordance with Soviet military doctrine the invasion force would have struck swiftly, relying on speed, surprise, and overwhelming mass to roll back defensive lines and crush opposition.

Spearheading the advance would be armored formations with the fastest Russian tanks forming the point of the spearhead. When Field Marshal Heinz Guderian drove west through the Ardennes in 1940, it was the Maginot Line that stood in the way of the armored blitzkrieg of Panzers below and Stukas above. Had the Soviets attacked West Germany in the Cold War, they would have met USAF and German Luftwaffe resistance in the air and an opposing steel lance of mobile armor on the ground.

The Kremlin, Washington, and NATO knew that the opening hours of World War III would see the most massive tank battles in history, and they all made preparations. The lesson that defensive lines didn't work had been well learned in the previous world war; modern tactics called for mobile, force-on-force warfare, a clash of steel titans belching flame and hurling death at one another.

The tanks that would fight this battle, if it ever happened, were the most up-gunned ever built and the fleetest and most agile ever conceived. A primary design concern for all of them, regardless of country of origin, was the concept of tank-on-tank—or duel—capability. The main battle tanks of the Cold War were designed, first and foremost, to fight the tank duels that would open, and perhaps quickly decide, the outcome of the Third World War.

In corps level exercises such as REFORGER (Return of Forces to Germany), United States Abrams main battle tanks and German Leopard MBTs were pitted against mock Soviet forces that in actual combat would be opposing them in the latest Russian MBTs. Apart from their abilities to rapidly and accurately engage enemy armor and deliver high rates of fire, all tanks were easily as fast and virtually as maneuverable as a commercial SUV.

Fortunately for the world, these battles never took place, and after a decade and a half, regional conflict and asymmetric warfare have replaced superpower confrontation as the likeliest scenarios with which the United States and its allies will contend through the next several decades. As we've seen in the preceding chapter, the Pentagon has shelved plans to even upgrade the Abrams let alone produce a next-generation tank.

Stealth over speed, *maskirovka* over firepower, is the operative concept behind defense transformation. When the tank is sent into battle it will most generally be only after stealthier and more agile elements of the attack force have destroyed potential peer or asymmetric threats, or where threats to tank operations weren't significant in the first place, rarely if ever in the tank duel scenarios that were a hallmark in the design of current-era MBTs.

Because regional conflicts are the types of war scenarios the United States and its allies are likely to encounter throughout the next few decades, and these conflicts are unlikely to see armored clashes of the type envisaged during the Cold War, it's certain that today's MBTs will continue to be around for a long time to come, even if deployed differently than in the past.

## STEALTH AND THE SINGLE TANK

Nevertheless a time will come when the tank will finally change. Had the Cold War lasted another decade, it's intriguing to speculate whether the next generation of main battle tanks would have already been built. Considering that the next generation of howitzer, in the form of Crusader, was indeed produced, and that speculation began to run high concerning the obsolescent fleet of MBTs fielded by the U.S. Army and NATO allies, it's likely a new generation tank would certainly have been manufactured.

In the long run, a new generation of main battle tank, incorporating radical new technologies including stealth, will almost certainly become reality. Either that or the main battle tank will become obsolete, replaced by future armored vehicles along the lines of Stryker. Should the MBT continue to be fielded in its present role it will have to change eventually for a number of sound tactical reasons.

One is that the growth potential for the lethality of projectiles fired by chemical propellants was largely exhausted by the early 1990s. Advances in the protection of armored vehicles from kinetic energy projectiles, such as the depleted uranium darts fired by many advanced MBTs including the Abrams, and from the blast effect of conventional munitions, were such that the striking power of tank ammunition needed to increase by several orders of magnitude in order to keep pace with new development. It's axiomatic among tank researchers that in order for a new main battle tank to justify its development for the approximate 30 years of its service life, it needs to be at least one generation in striking power ahead of the best contender it's likely to encounter in battle.

By the end of the Cold War British, European, and Soviet advances in both gunnery and tank protection were such that this would no longer hold true for the Abrams given a continuation of the Cold War beyond around 1995. U.S. tankers in Vietnam felt reasonably well protected from enemy fires by wrapping discarded tank track links around the turrets of their M48 Pattons. By 1989, tanks and other armored vehicles were protected by various types of direct, or ballistic, protection and reactive armor, such as the Chobham system developed by the British.

Taking the form of explosive bricks draped around vulnerable areas of the tank or APC, such as turret or flanks, reactive armor exploded an instant before an enemy round would have struck the hull, dissipating its kinetic force and destroying the incoming projectile. Active protection measures, such as those being developed by the Russians at the end of the Cold War (and still under development), went beyond reactive armor by firing clouds of fléchettes or, by some (perhaps dubious) accounts, using fields of high-energy plasma, to form a protective shield around the vehicle.

The end result of these measures was to greatly reduce the lethality of tanks, since upgrades to chemical-based projectiles were limited by the laws of physics—if one side upgraded to a more powerful main gun, the other side could counter with better armor protection or slightly more powerful main armament. To break the stalemate an entirely new gun technology became necessary.

Even this wouldn't be enough to maintain parity let alone achieve dominance in the tank battle for any one side. New asymmetric threats to armored warfare began to grow in lethality and sophistication. TOW and SADARM are types of this threat we've already covered in preceding chapters, as well as the danger from blinding laser weapons. More conventional threats to armor will also come from airborne hunters such as Comanche and the Joint Strike Fighter used in the CAS role.

As we've already seen, tanks have gotten stealthier by an evolutionary process as they've had to cope with better means of being detected and targeted on the battlefield. Ultimately, new tanks would need to grow stealthier still, incorporating new hull geometries and other attributes into their design that would make them harder to see. Tanks would also need to be more self-sufficient, since current MBTs can't effectively operate unless supported by their MICVs for sustained operations. In short, a radical bottom-up redesign of the tank has been in the cards.

## A HYPERTANK EMERGES

A next-generation main battle tank could be thought of as a hypertank. This is what some have already dubbed it, and for want of a better term, that's what I'll call it here. The hypertank would still be designed to come out top dog in a tank duel but also share some of the attributes of the mobile light armored vehicles that are filling some traditional roles played by tanks in the interim. Apart from this, the nature of the tank duel will have changed considerably from Cold War definitions, as it had between World War II and the Cold War, by which time tank duels would be fought at standoff ranges with success usually going to the tank that detected its opponent first and launched the first salvo.

In short, by the DDEE (dramatic developments in Eastern Europe) era the tank duel had gone the way of the aerial dogfight—it had become not a duel at close quarters but a contest of sensor-to-shooter speed and accuracy at beyond visual ranges. Tank battles along precisely these lines were fought in the Gulf War between U.S. tankers and Iraqi Republican Guard armored divisions. With developments in long-range surveillance and reconnaissance, such as those discussed earlier, the trend will continue and new-generation tanks would need to evolve that could on the one hand detect enemy armor at greater and greater ranges while remaining stealthy to detection themselves.

Smaller, harder to see, harder to detect, mobile, agile, lethal, with a small logistics footprint, linked to other elements of the air-land battle by advanced digital communications—in short the hypertank, in order to remain a survivable warfare asset, would need all the attributes of other stealth systems, plus one more that none of the others possessed: a new main gun, one that was far deadlier than anything ever built before (more on this in a moment).

The hypertank would be built largely of composite materials, such as are stealth warplanes. These materials not only would be lightweight, but would be designed to offer good ballistic protection against blast and projectile strikes. Like present-day ballistic armor, these new polylaminate hulls would absorb the kinetic energies of the strike by being constructed in a way that dissipates the energy of the attack.

Current ballistic armors are designed to flake away where struck by a tank round; new tank hulls might be designed for even greater endurance using nanomaterials, such as "Buckyballs" to achieve the same result albeit with less trauma to the hull. The composite materials would also be highly resistant to radar, ladar, thermal, and other battlefield imaging to enhance the tank's stealthiness; so too the hull geometries would be computer-designed to be as resistant as possible to enemy RSTA.

The hypertank would be an all-electric tank. Its power train and drive system, including steering, braking, and transmission, would be controlled and powered electrically. This approach would reduce its weight and eliminate design constraints on its interior configuration and crew carriage requirements by doing away with the bulky electromechanical drive and control mechanisms of its diesel-powered ancestor. It would contribute to the tank's stealth by reducing its acoustic signature, much in the way that electric power trains reduce that of submarines.

Advanced vetronics, a vehicle control interface, would allow the tank driver to maneuver using real-time video information coupled with computer-generated graphic overlays indicating position, threat analysis, and weapons management data, displayed on a lightweight head-mounted display. Networked, global-mobile communications would transmit this data to battle managers at distant command centers. These personnel could assist in targeting and even assume direct control of the hypertank in emergencies.

The hypertank's main gun would need to be stealthy as well as lethal. Its design would need to complement the tank's low-observable attributes. The hull-penetrating turret of conventional tanks would be discarded as unstealthy. The hypertank's main gun would potentially be wholly or partially retractable into the top of the hull. Its movements would be controlled by advanced robotic servo technology. Instead of projectiles fired by chemical propellants, the hypertank's main gun would operate using an electrothermal or an electrothermal-chemical hybrid principle to propel rods of superdense metals at hyperkinetic velocities far in excess of today's gunnery capability.

The main gun would be not only faster and deadlier than conventional tank gunnery, but virtually silent, too. Computer-targeted and automatically loaded, these hyperweapons would have the standoff range, speed and agility necessary to engage fast-moving, multiple targets at long distances, such as aircraft, UAVs, and terminally guided missiles. Laser weapons might afford the hypertank with a second-line offensive capability against ground or smaller airborne targets, such as armored personnel carriers, other tanks, and helicopters or robotic UAVs.

The laser weapons could also play defensive roles. As part of the tank's active defense system, they might dazzle the seeker heads of incoming smart projectiles or destroy them while in flight. Other elements of the hypertank's active defense system would use ultrahigh-frequency sound to defeat the acoustic sensors of top-attack rounds and alter the hypertank's thermal signature to defeat FLIR seekers.

All of this admittedly sounds like pie-in-the-sky, and, for the moment, it most definitely is. I'm running out of space for this entry, so I'll skip the developmental problems that such an advanced-design tank poses. Suffice it to say that today, and for the foreseeable future, the hypertank is not going to happen. Still, something based on the concept will eventually evolve. Driven by the increasing pace of technological development and the rapid stealthing of the global battlefield, the emergence of the hypertank will become an eventual reality.

# CHAPTER 23

# STEALTHY BATTLEFIELD ROBOTS

Military robotics have been around in low-tech forms for a long time. Remote-controlled pocket tanks and primitive cruise missiles, such as the V-1, played their parts in combat during World War II. UAVs played a high-profile role in both wars in the Persian Gulf and also in KFOR peacekeeping operations in Bosnia. UCAVs have been used in the Gulf and in Afghanistan, as well as in Yemen, where an armed Predator drone recently blasted a vehicle, said to be carrying al Qaeda members, with a Hellfire missile.

Robotic systems are attractive to war planners because they're low-cost, low-risk, and high-payoff platforms. In an era in which Western societies (and increasingly that of the former Soviet Union) are unwilling to tolerate either prolonged commitment of forces or high mortality rates for troops, robotic systems are seen more and more as a way to perform extremely hazardous missions at minimal cost in national treasure and lost lives. They can also function with greater precision and reliability than human operators under dangerous circumstances, and can be tailored to the mission. Finally, robotic systems can operate with considerably more stealth than can personnel.

Robotic systems for land-warfare operations have been in the planning and development stages for some years. DARPA, the Defense Advanced Research Projects Agency, has been developing several types of robotic systems for the U.S. Army for reconnaissance and surveillance and combat. These range from autonomous to semiautonomous recce and fighting vehicles, to miniature probes intended to be launched toward suspected deep underground facilities and send reconnaissance data back to units in the field, or to a local command post, or the regional CINC headquarters.

At least some of these battlefield robots should be operational by the year 2012 if current development efforts are successful, although right now, and for the near term, remote-controlled vehicles for explosive ordnance disposal (EOD) and RSTA are all that are likely to be fielded. It will be at least a decade until the U.S. Army's plans for battlefield robots amount to more than white papers and DARPA Grand Challenges. For all of this the robotization of the battlefield is a trend that will one day probably lead to many if not most weapons platforms becoming unmanned and could potentially even lead to a totally unmanned, robotized battlefield.

## TACTICAL MOBILE ROBOTS

No one really knows what to call them yet, these robot soldiers of future battlefields, but one term in use today is tactical mobile robots (TMRs), and also tactical unmanned vehicles (TUVs). The main warhorses of this new combat theater will be ground robotic vehicles of various kinds. The first-generation systems of this type of robot have been the subject of DARPA and commercial development since the DDEE era and the subsequent Gulf War. These are remote-operated or teleoperated wheeled or tracked vehicles that carry sensors for RSTA operations. They're sometimes generically referred to as ground robotic vehicles (GRV) and also as UVs, for unmanned vehicles.

Systems of this type are the most likely to be encountered in combat in a decade or so. At this time they will carry weapons as well as sensors and be used in combat in place of armored vehicles. The next phase of development would be to build GRVs that are semiautonomous and could operate with minimal human oversight for extended periods.

These second-generation GRVs could function on the battlefield as outrider systems to main battle tanks or other manned armored vehicles of the future or they could be helo-delivered to their op zone and patrol by themselves, either individually or in swarms reminiscent of the TACIT RAINBOW concept. Small, with all-electric power trains, and built with acoustic, radar, visual, and other stealth attributes, as well as being agile and mobile, GRVs would present stealthy targets to enemy ground and airborne patrols. Later systems might graduate from wheeled mobility and use other, more exotic, forms of locomotion to negotiate rugged terrain or paths otherwise difficult to traverse.

GRVs could attack their targets by firing missiles from standoff range, or they could function as something like rolling Tomahawk missiles to destroy high-value targets such as underground or deeply buried command posts. To assault these targets, specific classes of GRVs could be developed that first penetrated the interior of the targeted installation, and then went into terminal mode and detonated, released an electromagnetic pulse to incapacitate electronic systems, ejected submunitions, or expelled an incapacitating nonlethal gas. Warheads such as the fuel-air explosive types used against al Qaeda and Taliban cave and underground outposts in Afghanistan could be another weapon of choice for future GRV armament.

## THE FINAL STAGE

When TMR technology has come of age, it's likely that GRVs and other types of TMRs would take the place of many manned combat systems in use today in the land war, at least in the opening phases of warfare in which the greatest danger from enemy forces exist to friendly troops. These future TMRs would essentially be robot tanks and other mechanized armor as well as mobile artillery and rocketry.

The TMRs could be air-deployed to forward areas and be controlled from command centers situated well in the rear, from ships or subs in littoral regions, from AWACs aircraft orbiting hundreds of miles away, or even from out of theater locations. In place of a battalion of human soldiers a robot battalion might one day be transported to a future battlefield. At first these robots would fight manned combat systems, but as time progressed, they might find that the opposition would be robots just like themselves.

## THE ULTIMATE KILLING SYSTEM

There seems no avoiding a few words on the endgame of battlefield robot development—the robot soldier. Technically speaking, there is no good reason why a fighting robot with humanoid attributes in locomotion, appearance, and behavior could not eventually be built. Granted, combat robots could in theory be designed more practically in other physical configurations. Nevertheless, there are powerful forces in the human psyche that suggest that anthropomorphic military robots will be developed and, perhaps, one day fielded in place of human troops.

These robots could be cyborgs—part biological entity, part machine— possibly constructed from clones of humans genetically engineered for strong combat skills. The clones could then be equipped with various internal sensor and weapon systems and production-lined as various model types. Years ago DARPA tried to develop the Dave Droid but this model immediately dunked its creators' heads in a nearby toilet and took off to party in Ibiza. Seriously, and to veer this chapter back to stealth for a moment, such cyborg supersoldiers could be stealthy warriors indeed. Created with internal versions of the same or similar stealth attributes discussed in connection with stealth suiting for the twenty-first–century infantry soldier, humanoid robots or cyborgs could be the ultimate stealth weapon, especially effective in urban operations because of their resemblance to human beings.

Among the downsides, possibly the ultimate downside, of anthropomorphic robots is what might be termed the Pandora's Box effect. Once they were numerous enough (and since we're speculating, why not add that they could manufacture more of themselves in clandestine factories) and advanced enough (they could upgrade themselves too without paying royalties to Microsoft) what would there be to stop them from taking over?

Humans have fallen victim to the cat-up-a-tree syndrome, especially with regard to their technological creations, which once developed, have sometimes threatened to destroy them. There's a danger in pursuing the development of fully autonomous combat robots. It's a danger with a fruition probably 50–100 years in the future, given the rate of technological advancement, but that's still too close for comfort for me.

# ROBOTIC DEVELOPMENT PROGRAMS

Development of battlefield robots continues with the Defense Department committed to spending hundreds of millions of dollars through the end of the decade to develop, test, and field battlefield robotics in the United States and similar programs in the United Kingdom, the European Union, the Commonwealth of Independent States, and Asian nations, including China and India, the last of which, as we've noted, are strongly committed to high-technology force developments and stealth warfare to modernize their militaries.

## Tactical Unmanned Vehicles

The Future Medium Light and Heavy Combat Vehicles would take the form of a robotic scout element of a modular vehicle from which it could disengage to conduct autonomous operations and then return and link back up with the parent vehicle. The concept is also referred to a "marsupial" system because of its obvious reference to the way marsupials carry their young. The scout vehicle could also be remote-operated.

A tactical unmanned vehicle (TUV) system capable of conducting remote reconnaissance, surveillance, and target acquisition (RSTA) and carrying out chemical warfare agent detection missions has been part of a joint Army-Marines development program. The TUV would be controlled by a robotic operator control unit (OCU) and would have a modular design, capable of being quickly changed or upgraded to accept new technologies and payloads, including weapons payloads.

A related DARPA project is the reconnaissance, surveillance, and targeting (RST) vehicle. The RST concept differs from the TUV principally in that unlike the TUV an RST would also be capable of carrying special forces personnel when configured for human carriage. The RST would be a hybrid electric vehicle, incorporating a mixture of electric and internal combustion motor technologies and using a beefed-up suspension system enabling it to move quickly across difficult terrain or bad roads. It would also be low-observable.

Another DARPA program is the advanced fire support system (AFS), which is to develop robotic missile and gun systems that can automatically deploy themselves, arm themselves, acquire their targets, and autonomously and stealthily attack those targets according to preprogrammed rules of engagement.

## Distant Portrait (DP)

Distant Portrait (DP) is the code name for a DARPA program to "develop and demonstrate advanced technologies for the accurate characterization of Deep Underground Facilities (DUF) for precision strike or counterproliferation." DP would develop an array of tactical mobile robots tailored specifically to conduct warfare against DUFs and buried installations. The TMRs would also be used against cave fortifications such as al Qaeda hideouts in Afghanistan and bunker complexes like the one beneath Saddam Hussein's presidential palace in Baghdad that was hit on the first night of the War in Iraq.

Among the TMRs proposed for Distant Portrait are Micro Air Vehicles (MAVs). These are defined by DARPA as "airborne vehicles no larger than fifteen centimeters in length, width or height, capable of performing a useful military mission at an affordable cost." These could be airdropped or launched from GRVs or by SOF units in the vicinity of the target. MAVs could perform a variety of missions; they could fly down narrow air shafts to conduct RSTA ops in underground bases, or function as tiny communications satellites and radar decoys. Some types could be deployed in clouds of small, smart antiarmor or antipersonnel mines that could penetrate DUFS, sight their targets, and explode, singly or in swarms.

MAV types of still smaller size have been proposed. One type called Smart Dust (SD) foresees the creation of robots of one millimeter or less to be used for surveillance and reconnaissance, for example as antipersonnel mine swarms, and communications transmitters. Prototypes of one inch have already been developed. Future development of even tinier SD may give an entirely new meaning to the phrase "Up your nose."

# PART 5

# OUR ALLIES' AND ADVERSARIES' QUEST FOR STEALTH AND COUNTERSTEALTH

Stealth technology is proliferating throughout the world at an ever-increasing rate. In the near term, it poses the risk of stealth weaponry falling into the wrong hands; in the long-run, the end of a veritable U.S. stealth monopoly. Like other nations, rogue states that support terrorism are also interested in acquiring stealth and have begun stealth programs of their own. Stealth is also high on the wish lists of terrorist groups. As a potent tool of asymmetric warfare, stealth weaponry could afford such groups with a way of striking at Western societies with devastating effect.

The race to build up stealth forces has also sparked a race to develop strategies and technologies that can penetrate the cloak of stealth's invisibility and detect the presence of stealth systems. Even as they rush to place stealth into their order of battle, many countries are at the same time attempting to develop counter-measures to their adversaries' stealth.

The proliferation of stealth will ultimately go even farther than its use as a tool of warfare between nation states. Stealth has already begun to leak through into civilian societies both as a technology and as a mode of *maskirovka*.

# CHAPTER 24

# COUNTERSTEALTH TECHNOLOGIES

In the early morning hours of March 27, 1999, an F-117A stealth fighter took off on a routine mission over Kosovo. Its target was a Serb military position that was threatening KFOR efforts to consolidate control of Kosovo. The NATO effort to roll back the Serbs in Yugoslavia had been late in coming, and when it finally did materialize, it took the form of a strategic bombing campaign almost exclusively using tactical air in place of ground troops.

Precision-guided missiles like Tomahawk and JDAM freefall bombs, dropped from F-117A Nighthawks and capable of being guided with almost unerring accuracy to ground targets by satellite, were the primary weapons of this war. The Serbs, a second-wave military force armed with the weaponry of a past era of warfare, were facing a third-wave military titan armed with digitized weaponry, cloaked by stealth, and able to strike from afar under cover of darkness with blinding speed and surgical precision.

The results were predictable. Although the Serbs were tenacious in their determination to maintain control of Kosovo and repel NATO forces, and although they successfully used *maskirovka* to conceal many of their tanks, armored carriers, heavy weaponry, and arms caches from destruction by coalition bombing sorties, the endgame was never in doubt. Day by day, hour by hour, the Serbs' military capability was being degraded by the unceasing punishment meted out by superior forces that were rarely seen until they struck. The outcome was predictable. The Serbian military was being rolled back from Kosovo and there wasn't a damn thing it could do about it. The Serbs' leader, Slobodan Milosevic, would hold on to power in Belgrade a while longer, but his ouster was also assured.

Yet in the early morning hours of March 27, something happened that has never been officially explained by the Pentagon. An F-117A Night-hawk did not return to base as expected. Reports began filtering in that the unthinkable had happened. In fact the stealth fighter had crashed. It was possible, members of the president's National Security Council admitted as they manned the polished hardwood table in the NSC crisis room in the White House basement, that the Serbs had actually shot the invisible plane down.

## THE POOR MAN'S ANSWER TO STEALTH

As time has passed it's become highly probable that the F-117A was in fact downed over Bojanovici by a Serbian missile. Probably this was one of the batteries of SA-3 surface-to-air missiles that Serb ground forces were known to be operating in the area as antiaircraft weapons.

The SA-3 is not a very sophisticated SAM. In fact it's considered junk as SAMs go. The missile system, christened GOA by NATO, and called the S-125 NEVA-M by the Soviets who first put it into service in 1961, relies on the P-15M SQUAT EYE radar, which is an x-band or tracking type, to detect and acquire aircraft. The SA-3 was once deemed a serious threat to U.S. military aviation, but that was back in 1964 when new Model 1 versions of the weapon were seen cropping up in batteries located in the bristling belts of defensive missiles that girdled the Soviet heartland.

These versions, their ground radars capable of tracking six targets at a time, the missiles being solid-fueled for quick turnaround times between firing (unlike liquid-fueled rockets which required fueling before firing), posed a chilling threat to U.S. strategic bombing missions into the Soviet

Union in any coming hot war. But that was then, and, as they say, this is now: By the spring of 1999 when NATO, under U.S. leadership, was prosecuting its air war against the Serbs in Kosovo, the SA-3 was just another museum piece that the Russians had sold at cut-rate prices—still highly useful back in the early days when the opposition was the Croatian air force, but a joke when the world's only military superpower was running the show. Even Saddam Hussein's army in the Gulf War didn't bother with the SA-3: The lowest missile on Baghdad's SAM totem pole was the SA-4 GANEF. Even the Iraqis wouldn't dirty their hands with outdated SA-3s.

Obviously the SA-3 system was deemed no match for the F-117A Nighthawk. The stealth fighter had proved its mettle during Desert Wind, the air-war phase of Desert Storm, against far more formidable Iraqi radars, and had come away unscathed, save for one or two random shrapnel holes that were discovered on planes by inspection crews at secret bases such as the one at Khamis Mushait in the Asir Mountain range of southwestern Saudi Arabia completed by the U.S. Army Corps of Engineers in 1980. (Shoot, I wasn't supposed to tell you that!)

True, there was heavy SEAD by other coalition aircraft and helicraft to pave the way for the black planes, but even so, there were SAM radars trying to track them over Baghdad on the initial nights of the air war that would have lit up less stealthy planes like movie marquees. Gun camera video footage, such as that of the now famous Paveway-augmented PGM strike on the "AT&T Building" downtown, left no doubt that stealth delivered as promised. The Nighthawks were as low-observable as advertised, and the F-117As were later used to strike targets inside Iraq during the joint U.S.–UK Desert Fox air campaign in 1998, and other actions previous and subsequent.

Over the darkened skies of Kosovo in 1999, there was no reason to doubt that the F-117A owned the night, just as it had over Baghdad under far more formidable SAM coverage. Yet something had brought the stealthy aircraft down, shattering its lightweight composite hull to pieces and strewing the wreckage across the rolling Yugoslavian pastureland. There it awaited the growing light of the new dawn to be found by villagers who had come out to see what had happened after hearing an explosion and seeing a flash in the night skies.

In a post-downing press briefing, USAF Maj. Gen. Bruce Carlson would neither confirm nor deny what specifically was believed to have been the cause of the downing of the stealth, nor was the identity of the pilot, who had been rescued soon afterward by Delta Force operators, then or subsequently released. There was no way to be certain why the plane had crashed, but there was speculation.

I have my own theories about why the F-117A had crashed. For a year I had been writing a novel that posed the threat of counterstealth radar to low-observable aircraft like the Nighthawk. It was based on fact, but I'd had a hard time finding a publisher. For years, publishers rejected the premise on which the book was based as being too far-fetched. It could never happen, they'd told me. Not in real life anyway.

## THE WRECKAGE

As it became clearer that no convenient explanation for the crash was available, speculation turned to the possibility that the F-117A had been shot down by an SA-3. Could it have been a lucky shot? Literally a shot in the dark that just happened to strike the stealth fighter or explode close enough to the aircraft to bring it down?

Officials, such as the USAF's Carlson, weren't prepared to comment, but on one point they were in nearly unanimous agreement: The loss of the stealth fighter wasn't all that important to the military capability of the United States. The wreckage of the plane, which was being picked up and carted away by happy Serbs even as these statements were being made, would be of little value to potential enemies interested in learning the secrets of U.S. stealth technology by reverse-engineering or other efforts to study the recovered debris.

The F-117A was a second-generation stealth aircraft, approaching the end of its service life, and enough was known about its construction by then for it to yield few secrets to anyone. As if to demonstrate this lack of concern there wasn't even an attempt made to destroy the wreckage on the ground.

The official denials were in part true, for by this time enough technical intelligence on the F-117A had either leaked or been independently arrived at by third parties for the main operating principles to be well understood. Other countries could even manufacture some, but by no means all, of the key components of the stealth airframe. It's been suggested that the key features of the F-117A were in fact blown up by the pilot on ejection. But this can't be confirmed: The USAF isn't saying and the pilot's identity will probably never be known.

## CELL-PHONE RADAR

But what exactly was responsible for the crash of the F-117A? The answer is that it was most likely downed by a hit or near-miss from an SA-3 surface-to-air missile. It's also highly probable that the SA-3 strike was no mere lucky shot in the dark.

Despite the Pentagon's strange after-action downplaying of the stealth characteristics of the Nighthawk—the plane's stealthy attributes had never before been spoken of with anything but the highest praise by officialdom—the F-117A should never have been brought down by any SAM the Serbs had in their arsenal. Nor, it should be added, were pilot error, mechanical failure, or other accidental causes likely to have caused the crash, by the Pentagon's own admission.

This leaves counterstealth radar as the most probable cause of the incident—let's call it the shootdown. It was known for some time that form stealth, relying on angular surface features to deflect and dissipate radar energies of which the Nighthawk was constructed, was vulnerable to detection by certain types of radar systems.

A sophisticated type of counterstealth radar might have relied on computer augmentation. Such a system could use sophisticated signal processing to comb the backscatter of radar echoes returning to the antenna for specific frequencies known to indicate the presence of a stealth aircraft. Computer processing would assemble all the scattered returns in order to track the otherwise stealthy plane. Optimally such as system would be a passive radar system, one that uses a low-frequency transmitter or, better still, a network of low-frequency transmitters that are resistant to interception, in order to work. This was the type of counterstealth radar that figured in the plot of my novel *Shadow Down*.

But the Serbs, with their East Bloc surplus weapons, were not likely to possess such high-tech stealth countermeasures, which require sophisticated software and extremely fast and powerful computer hardware to work. Since their army did everything on a budget, it would figure that counterstealth would be done that way, too. A relatively low-tech and low-cost counterstealth radar system, commonly known as cell-phone radar, is a strong candidate for what the Serbs might have used.

Cell-phone radar is a passive radar technology that uses the discovery, credited to the Czechs, that the same ground-based network of cellular repeaters used to retransmit third-generation (3G) cellular phone signals across a network can also detect the presence of stealth aircraft. Although the F-117A was tested against a wide range of SAM and tracking radars known to be in use by adversarial military forces, commercial cellular phone transmission systems were not considered at the time. (Similar low-frequency radar was known to be good at detecting stealth but worthless because it was unreliable at tracking stealth.)

Unlike the case with x-band tracking radar and other radar types that the stealth fighter is very good at deceiving, the F-117A is not as low-observable to cell-phone radar. Used in tandem with commercial GPS systems and commercial software running on microcomputers, as well as acoustic detection sensors that are situated near the antenna elements of the ground detection array, the system is said to be capable of spotting stealth aircraft where more conventional radars would fail.

The existence of cell-phone radar is not in dispute. A British engineering firm, Roke Manor Research Limited, which is a division of Siemens, markets a cell-phone radar under the trademarked name CELLDAR. As already mentioned, a Czech firm has developed a similar system marketed as TAMARA. There are other players in the counterstealth radar game as well. As we'll see in the following chapter, the Russians, finding themselves without the funds to compete with the United States in first-line stealth systems, have devoted their efforts to developing counterstealth radars with which they've equipped their latest SAM systems.

Even though the United States has already been fielding prototypes of third-wave stealth aircraft, and despite the devil-may-care attitude with which the news of the downed stealth fighter's wreckage in Serb hands was greeted at the Pentagon, the U.S. defense establishment views counter-stealth with great concern.

As mentioned at the start of this chapter, counterstealth was a concern for CENTCOM during the initial air war phase of the War in Iraq. It was known that the Hussein regime had been actively pursuing the acquisition of the TAMARA system. As we've noted, such cell-phone radar systems operate best with extended networks of cellular retransmission antennas that funnel reflected signals back to a central computer processing system that collects and analyses the signals to track stealth aircraft.

Seen in this light, it becomes clearer as to possible clandestine objectives of the joint U.S.–UK air strikes of December 1998 during Desert Fox, subsequent actions in 2002, and the Shock and Awe phase of the air campaign in March 2003. The Pentagon stated that the goal of Desert Fox was "to strike military and security targets in Iraq that contribute to Iraq's ability to produce, store, maintain and deliver weapons of mass destruction."

In August 2002, coalition smart munitions again struck the major Iraqi C2 node at al-Nukhaib that had been hit in 1998 using PGMs tailored to the destruction of fiber-optic nodes. Again, in the 2003 Shock and Awe campaign, one of the first targets was Iraq's fiber-optic infrastructure and transmission nodes. Since it's now fairly certain that the United States and United Kingdom had no direct knowledge of Iraqi weapons of mass destruction in 1998, 2002, or 2003, we can plausibly conjecture that the true object of the strikes was to destroy Iraqi capability of another kind—a low-tech but still dangerous TAMARA network that was intended to give Saddam Hussein the ability to detect one of the prime symbols of America's much-hated "long technological arm." If nothing else, the downing of a stealth fighter over Baghdad would have given Saddam a propaganda bonanza. No matter what the outcome of the fighting, if Saddam had managed to parade captured stealth fighter pilots before CNN cameras, or better still, display wreckage like the Serbs did in Kosovo, he would have been seen as a folk hero to the Arab street.

*One of the leaflets dropped by coalition aircraft during the Shock and Awe campaign warning Iraqis to stay away from fiber-optic cable networks. Could these have been targeted because they were key to a counterstealth radar system?*

In that case, the U.S.–UK coalition might have come away winning some battles yet, in a certain sense, losing the war. Clearly such an outcome might have likely been determined by warplanners in Washington and London to be forestalled using any means possible. Stealth is as much a symbol of power as it is a weapon of war, and for defeat to be lasting in twenty-first century warfare, it must be as much a mental construct as it is a physical reality. The die had been cast in preliminary attacks between 1998 and 2003 for an all-out blitz that might have had the suppression of Saddam's counterstealth weapon as its secret primary target.

# CHAPTER 25

# RUSSIA'S QUEST FOR STEALTH AND COUNTERSTEALTH

As this book was being written, the *Moscow Times* reported on MAKS 2003, otherwise known as the Moscow Air Show. There were some firsts this year, the major one being military aircraft exhibits from the United States, thanks to improved relations between the Kremlin and the White House. The downside was that the United States sent only F-15 and F-16 fighters and a B-52 strategic bomber, all relics of the Cold War, as exhibits. Conspicuous by their absence were first-line American fighter aircraft such as the F-22 or the F-35.

As the *Times* noted, although many countries around the world will get variants of the F-35 Joint Strike Fighter, the United States obviously wasn't interested in selling its most advanced stealth aircraft to the Commonwealth of Independent States (CIS). Despite the end of the Cold War and new cooperation between the two former superpower adversaries, lingering vestiges of Cold War power dynamics still prevail.

One of these dynamics is the determination of the Kremlin to return its military to a state-of-the-art force rivaling or surpassing that of the United States. For well over a decade Russia has been engaged in crash programs to upgrade its order of battle with high-technology weapon systems of all kinds. These programs have been funded in large part by hard currency generated from global sales of Russian arms large and small and nuclear technology transfers, such as those to India and Iran, which could result in nuclear weapon manufacturing capability. Another source of funding has been the diversion of American nonlethal monetary aid to the former Soviet Union.

Stealth technology is high on the Kremlin's military wish list because of its vital necessity to the transformation of Russia's military forces. Among the lessons learned from the Gulf War was that stealth, coupled with precision strike capabilities, brought about a revolution in the way wars could be fought.

Russia's predicament today is that it can't afford to compete with the United States in development programs in key areas, especially in stealth. At the same time it's clear to the Kremlin that the United States won't sell it advanced stealth technology under any circumstances. The CIS has therefore taken a double-ended approach to stealth. It has invested in the production of advanced technology test beds for stealthy fighter planes and bomber aircraft while at the same time establishing programs to develop countermeasures to the stealth systems in use by the United States and other nations.

Under different circumstances there would probably now be a new arms race between the former Soviet Union and the United States, one based on stealth and battlefield automation and digitization instead of megatonnage, throw weights, and the other factors in the old nuclear calculus of the Cold War. Actually there is an ongoing arms race but it's as yet undeclared and still extremely one-sided, with the CIS lagging far behind the United States and struggling desperately to catch up.

If the history of the Cold War is any guide, the U.S. lead could erode before very long. Immediately after World War II the U.S. lead in nuclear weaponry was also unassailable, but by the start of the DDEE era the Soviets had not only caught up but were dangerously ahead in many regards.

Ominously, part of today's stealth research and development in the CIS is to build a new breed of nuclear warheads that are stealthy enough to counter any American nuclear missile defense such as the NMD program currently underway. Russia's SS-27 ICBM (Topol-M) is equipped with a maneuvering warhead system that is both agile and stealthy. The CIS might argue that, since the United States unilaterally broke existing treaties with Russia in building NMD, it has the right to build systems that could penetrate NMD defenses for purely defensive purposes—if the United States possesses a missile shield that makes it safe from nuclear attack, it could theoretically launch a nuclear strike on Russia some day that could not be countered.

## STEALTH SECRETS THROUGH ESPIONAGE

In the past the Russians have resorted to espionage and purchases of American technology from third parties to obtain the essential building blocks of advanced weapon systems it did not have the resources to produce on its own. These include the precision lathe machinery used to cut stealthy anticavitation propellers for Russian nuclear subs, and naval intelligence on U.S. submarine warfare, as discussed in a previous chapter. Among other acquisitions were critical systems and design elements of the U.S. B-1 Lancer strategic bomber, resulting in the Russian Blackjack bomber that so closely resembles the B-1 it was quickly dubbed the "B-1sky."

Stealth technology was also covertly acquired by similar means during the Cold War and afterward. By 2001 there were open admissions from U.S. and Russian officials that the wreckage from the F-117A that had been shot down over Yugoslavia in 1999 had in fact been bought from the Serbs and had undergone analysis and testing in Russian battle labs.

According to reports, the wreckage was used in experiments whose primary purpose was to help Russia's military design bureaus, such as the Almaz Central Design Bureau, which had acquired F-117A crash debris for analysis, develop indigenous stealth aircraft technology. Reports and statements concerning the usefulness of the aircraft wreckage to CIS counterstealth programs are unclear and contradictory.

Official disavowals from the Pentagon and the U.S. defense sector, such as those voiced by Maj. Gen. Bruce Carlson in his April 20, 1999, DOD news brief on the shootdown, seem to follow the line that the acquisition of stealth wreckage by the CIS poses little risk of countermeasures to U.S. stealth hardware. According to Carlson, and others, the greatest threat from the acquisition would be to help the Russians design stealthier aircraft somewhere down the line, essentially because knowing how stealth works is worthless without the precision tools and equipment necessary to manufacture combat-worthy weapon systems based on that knowledge.

In short, the Serbs ostensibly shot down an F-117A using what appears to be primitive technology and weaponry, and the Russians bought the wreckage of a plane considered so valuable that its operating characteristics have only been publicly revealed in the vaguest terms to this day. Additionally, this plane has been shown under armed military guard in numerous photographs, from those taken at military hangars, to those taken at public exhibits at air shows. Even considering all this, the Russians really didn't get diddly-squat when they got the F-117A.

Some accounts—there are few but they do exist—have it that a second F-117A was damaged in another attempted shootdown during the air campaign in Yugoslavia but was able to return to base. There are also reports that one F-117A was brought down during the Gulf War but the crash was hushed up. This may be a distortion of the known fact that F-117As did not always return unscathed after sorties in the Gulf War. The fact that many returned with superficial damage from triple-A or SAM shrapnel has been openly acknowledged. Then again, there may have been an F-117A downing in the Gulf that was never revealed. Who knows? Another version of the 1999 stealth fighter shootdown has it that the downing was due to faulty IFF (interrogation friend or foe) on the part of the U.S. warplane that mistakenly reported a Serbian MiG-21 flying CAP (combat air patrol) in the vicinity as a friendly aircraft. IFF works by electronically interrogating planes and other combat systems in the vicinity. When the F-117A emerged from a cloud bank, according to the 1999 report in the Russian newspaper *Novaya Gazeta,* the MiG made visual contact and opened up with its nose cannon, blowing the U.S. plane out of the air. Given that IFF, which didn't work right in the Gulf War, wasn't all that better in 1999, this explanation might be plausible as an alternative to the counterstealth detection theory.

Although I grant that critical systems might have been destroyed by the pilot once he knew the plane had been irrevocably damaged, and while there is also the possibility that the Russians might have even deliberately intended to acquire the F-117A wreckage as a kind of high-tech Judas goat to lead them down the bridle path in stealth development, and while the official statements might just be plain right on the money, I still think on balance that it's plausible to assume that the CIS did in fact get its money's worth from the acquisition, and that the wreckage proved useful in Russian stealth and counterstealth development efforts.

One reason for surmising this is Russia's track record: The Russians have always gotten their money's worth before in acquisitions of Western defense technology. Another reason is that in the years following the shootdown over Yugoslavia a number of innovations and enhancements to Russia's stealth and counterstealth programs began to appear. Among these were improved versions of the SA-10 Grumble surface-to-air missile system resulting in the S-300 ZRK upgrade for indigenous use and the scaled-back S-300 MU-2 export version.

Both of these SAM types—and other Russian SAMs as well—were advertised as being able to track, acquire, and kill stealth targets at long range. Indeed, while continuing to insist that the Russians really didn't learn much from the F-117A debris, the U.S. Defense Department quietly made arrangements to purchase specimens of the advanced, not-for-export ZRK version of the S-300 SAM in order to study the efficiency of its reputed stealth countermeasures. This sale, when made public in Russia, raised a furor—*Pravda* dubbed the sale "one of the greatest American espionage coups" of all time. Possibly it was right.

Russians were particularly incensed because, according to other accounts in *Pravda*, it was Russia and not the United States that actually invented stealth in the first place. According to *Pravda*, Russia first developed visual stealth—stealth that could make aircraft virtually invisible to the human eye—prior to 1938 but the advent of radar made this form of stealth irrelevant during the ensuing Second World War.

Later, it's avowed that Russian technical innovation led to the further development of stealthiness to radar in the mid-1960s, but the ever-opportunistic Americans stole the secrets from the Motherland by ferreting out nuggets of technical wisdom from published accounts in Soviet technical journals. According to Russian reports, Lockheed Skunk Works's Ben Rich acknowledged the United States's debt to Russian scientist Pyotr Ufimtsev, whose 1966 article on stealth was pounced on in particular for its revolutionary insights into Soviet stealth advances.

Finally, Russian conspiracy theorists have another slant on what it was that really crashed near Roswell, New Mexico, in 1946. This wasn't a UFO or a weather balloon, they claim, but a top-secret American stealth aircraft built, in large part, using purloined Russian stealth technology.

## RUSSIA'S STEALTH AND COUNTERSTEALTH INITIATIVES

We've already discussed counterstealth radar in the preceding chapter and have noted that there are commercially available versions of this detection system. It's been charged by some that these don't and can't work, mainly because they're based on low-frequency radar detection principles. The reason for this charge is that while low-frequency radars are capable of tracking stealth aircraft (which will, under certain conditions, reflect radar beams regardless of stealthy shaping) they're not effective at maintaining the track. Tracking, or x-band, radars are good at this, which is why stealth is designed to evade them.

In point of fact, low-frequency radar systems based on a wide area network of ground antenna elements can be effective at tracking and maintaining the track of stealth aircraft. When coupled with acoustic sensors, other forms of radar, TEMPEST detection, and multispectral data fusion—programs run on powerful computers that can blend or paste together many radar returns from separate receivers and create a representation of the object being tracked on video display screens—low-frequency counterstealth radars can indeed work. Multispectral data fusion can also be useful in screening out the backdrop of thermal, radio, and acoustic noise during battle that helps stealthy aircraft remain hidden to enemy detection.

A primitive system based on this technology is thought to be responsible for the F-117A downing of 1999. CIS researchers are developing more sophisticated applications of this same technology into indigenous counterstealth radar for Russia's military forces as well as for export.

To briefly return to espionage, the acquisition of a closely held U.S. computer program used in rapid prototyping of stealth systems called MM3D (Method of Moments in Three Dimensions), may have aided Russian design bureaus in developing stealth and counterstealth applications along with the captured wreckage and other technical data on stealth gained through espionage over the years. The program was purloined from computers at the Lockheed Skunk Works in the late 1990s. MM3D's "optimizer," can, at a mouse-click, quickly simulate how changes to an existing aircraft design stored on disk can affect the plane's stealth attributes. If you're working on stealth, it's damn sure a handy thing to have.

## NUTS AND BOLTS APPLICATIONS

Regardless of how the Russians got their low-observable know-how, they've been hard at work designing, testing, and in some cases marketing, new stealth and counterstealth systems of many kinds. Reports about precisely what avenues of research and development they're pursuing have often been sketchy. Enough, however, has filtered through to indicate that, in addition to more conventional passive stealth approaches, such as forms stealth, shared apertures (for low probability of intercept radars and communications), RAM skins, and the use of composite materials in fuselage construction, many exotic and active approaches to masking combat aircraft and other weapon systems from detection have also been attempted. It should be understood that most, if not all, of these are known to Western stealth developers, and that it's also possible that some or many of them have been at least tried in stealth systems developed by the United States. Nevertheless, the Russians are pursuing these approaches in a dynamic way in their indigenous stealth programs.

Among the exotic Russian approaches to stealth is a technique known as active cancellation (AC). This works by transmitting a false radar return when hostile radar is detected. The false return matches the original echo closely enough in wavelength and power to cancel it out, making it appear that no radar contact was ever made. There are various approaches to making AC work. One is to apply coatings to the airframe, such as advanced RAM appliqués, that enable electrical currents to be conducted from one part of the fuselage to another, so they bend or wrap around the hull.

Another Russian stealth application is active plasma (AP). AP uses plasma generators, such as electron guns or arc dischargers, to cloak the airframe, or vulnerable parts thereof, in a stream of ionized gas. Stealth protection based on AP works on the principle that this ionized gas, or plasma, produces virtually no reflections to search and track radar and could alone, without any other form of stealth technology, reduce an air-craft's RCS to a size comparable with the reductions produced by the best conventional stealth shaping methods.

Plasma is also weightless, and so could mean lighter airframes, and it doesn't have to be periodically replaced like RAM skins. Critics claim that AP is disinformation, unworkable, or both. Reasons given include the facts that cocooning a warplane in plasma can make it glow at night (something you obviously don't want in a stealth aircraft) and that its very invisibility to radar produces a sort of moving hole in enemy radar coverage that's a dead giveaway. All this being true doesn't necessarily rule out functional AP systems. If not available today, there is no theoretical reason that by using the right approach to applying the technology an AP system couldn't be made workable in the not-too-distant future.

## ATF-Skis

Just as the Backfire was dubbed the B-1sky back in the 1980s, advanced technology fighter concept demonstrator aircraft—test beds for a new generation of stealthy Russian fighters to replace aging MiG and Sukhoi models currently in the RUSAF inventory—have been dubbed "ATF-skis." The nickname implies that Western aircraft technology has been used in the design of these planes as it has been in past weapon systems produced indigenously in Russia.

The issue aside of whether Russian warplanes have used copycat, reverse-engineering design approaches, few would deny that planes like the MiG-29 Fulcrum or SU-27 Flanker are justifications of Russian design philosophy based on the need to meet and exceed the performance of Western peer competitor aircraft. The same design philosophy has been applied to the two ATF demonstrators for fifth-generation Russian fighter planes that are intended to compete with advanced western aircraft like the F-22 and F-35 in performance, precision engagement capability and stealth.

The SU-47 Berkut (Golden Eagle) is the Sukhoi Design Bureau's entry into the CIS advanced tactical fighter program. An earlier prototype, the S-37, was first flown in September 1997. After redesign, to include features such as a thrust-vectoring engine, the ATF again underwent flight trials in December 2001. The Berkut's forward-swept midwings and all-moving forward canard wings give the SU-47 a unique appearance; its tailplanes and canted vertical stabilizers are reminiscent of U.S. ATF designs like the YF-23 and F-22.

The S-37 Berkut (Golden Eagle) stealth fighter.

While the forward-swept wings are efficient in high-speed maneuvers, they make the fighter unwieldy under varying operating conditions. The Berkut was designed to use a computerized fly-by-wire system like the F-117A and B-2 to maintain stability. Over 13 percent of its airframe consists of radar-absorbent composite materials, and it shares other western stealth attributes to limit its RCS including internal weapons carriage and shared sensor apertures. In May 2002, RUSAF selected Sukhoi as the prime contractor for the future PAK FA fighter program. The PAK FA is to be based on the SU-47 but without the Berkut's forward-swept wings.

The other Russian ATF contender is the MiG 1.42 MFI Multirole Frontline Fighter (*Mnogofunktsionalny Frontovoi Istrebitel*). The MFI is intended, as MAPO (the MiG design bureau) puts it, as the "direct Russian equivalent of the USAF F-22." Like the F-22 and the other Russian

ATF contender, the SU-47, the MFI is capable of supersonic cruise (the attainment of supersonic speeds without using afterburner thrust), uses fly-by-wire controls, and has an advanced digital cockpit.

The MFI also uses a high percentage of composite materials in the construction of the airframe and incorporates stealth design attributes to make the plane low-observable. More conventional in appearance than the Berkut, the MFI also features forward-mounted canard wings and thrust-vectoring engines. The MFI is said to be both an air-dominance fighter like the F-22 but also capable of long-range strike engagements like the F-35, so it could carry weapons internally or externally depending on the mission.

Other Russian stealth aircraft programs include the T-60S stealth bomber, also being developed by the Sukhoi Design Bureau and said to include "extensive stealth design features" that make it comparable to the B-2 stealth bomber.

Still, whether any of these Russian stealth aircraft ever go into production is debatable. Aerospace experts in the United States, the NATO countries, and the CIS itself all agree that the huge budgetary expenditures needed to fund full development of these advanced tactical aircraft programs are not presently available (although Russia can earn dollars by selling stealth technology to other nations). This doesn't mean that Russian stealth aircraft that can compete with the West's most advanced warplanes, including stealth fighter aircraft, won't be available in the foreseeable future.

On the contrary, given the Kremlin's determination to upgrade Russia's military forces to achieve parity with the United States, and given the fact that stealth and precision engagement capability is critical to having any chance at prevailing in twenty-first–century warfare, Russia will either have to build advanced stealth warplanes or accept the fact that it's permanently vulnerable to attack by those modernized forces that do possess such capabilities. This clearly means that while the United States might continue to hold the lead in these key military sectors, the CIS is poised to become a near-peer competitor in stealth warfare sometime in the coming decades. Whether we like it or not, this development seems to be in the cards.

# CHAPTER 26

# EURO STEALTH

Adversaries and allies alike were startled by the speed and precision of the coalition campaign against Iraq during the Gulf War. Third-wave military forces using digital sensor-to-shooter networks, employing combined arms air-land battle tactics and shrouded by stealth, were able to overcome the world's fourth largest standing army with never-before-seen speed and precision. The world learned that a second-wave military such as Iraq's could not prevail in battle when faced with an advanced combat force leveraging high-technology, jointness, and low-observable aircraft and missiles.

Also dealt a crippling blow was the prestige of the CIS's military arsenal. From T-72 main battle tanks, to advanced SAM anti-aircraft systems, to MiG air superiority fighters, the Russian arms that had largely made up the weapons inventory of Saddam's armies were outperformed, outmaneuvered, and in the end destroyed. In many cases these Soviet-supplied offensive and defensive weapons were blown to smithereens before they could loose a first shot. Battle damage assessment imagery depicting row upon row of dug-in Soviet tanks blasted by precision-guided weapons offered mute testament to the fate of Russian armor when faced by advanced Western forces. When not trying in vain to track the fleeting radar contacts of stealth fighters, Iraq's MiG squadrons were sent to find sanctuary in neighboring Iran. Those MiGs that saw action did so largely by accident while trying to flee, as they ran afoul of U.S. warplanes flying combat air patrols.

It was not only Russian arms that were tried in the balance and found wanting. Iraq hadn't just equipped its armed forces with Russian weaponry; its order of battle and combat doctrine were also structured along classic Soviet lines of force integration and battlefield deployment. Saddam's generals had been trained to use their Soviet weapons within the framework of Soviet methods of waging war.

From the Kalashnikov rifles carried by the Iraqi foot soldier, to the fighter aircraft flown by Saddam's top guns, the weapons systems used by his military were all integrated into a force that was fielded according to Soviet principles. Soviet advisors had trained Saddam's elite Republican Guard tank units in the tactics of armored warfare, for example. Just as Russian-made T-72 main battle tanks proved no match for M1A2 Abrams MBTs in combat, the tactics used by Iraqi tank commanders proved inferior to the principles of warfare in which coalition tankers were proficient.

Nations like China, which had built its armed forces along the lines of the Soviet order of battle, including indigenously produced copycat weaponry, and Egypt, whose armed forces were still undergoing a years-long process of slow transition from a Soviet-trained and equipped military to a force employing U.S. doctrine and water matériel, were all shocked into immediate reexaminations of their military futures by the revolution in military affairs brought about in Desert Storm.

Beijing, for one, was shocked into the realization that China's second-wave forces, though numerically strong—indeed of gargantuan proportions—comprised what's known in Pentagonese as a "hollow force" when compared with a numerically small but technologically advanced third-wave military like that of the United States. As a result China embarked almost overnight on a transformation of its ground, air, and naval forces intended to upgrade these into a twenty-first–century military, one of whose cornerstones was that "all future warfare will be a combat between stealth and detection" according to a Chinese doctrinal paper.

Nearer to the fray, athwart the western edge of the Arabian Peninsula, warplanners in the Egyptian capital, Cairo, were also sparked to accelerate their force transformation from its past all-Soviet model to its future integration along U.S. lines. Unlike the Chinese, and others, whose transformative plans could afford to wait for the moment, the Egyptians were sweating it out.

Their discomfiture was attributable to the presence of a neighboring country to the east of the Sinai desert which, if not a third-wave power already, was far closer to attaining the goal than they themselves were. Twice they had gone to war with the state of Israel and failed to win. Should a fifth Arab-Israeli conflict break out before their transformation was complete, the Egyptian military had every reason to expect defeat yet again at the hands of the IDF. Many other countries around the world were struggling with the same set of realizations and dilemmas as the Gulf War progressed.

But not all of them were past Soviet clients or potential future adversaries of the United States: Many were also America's friends and allies in the North Atlantic Treaty Organization, NATO.

## THE SECRET U.S.–UK STEALTH PARTNERSHIP

The NATO nations, including the closest global partner of the United States, the United Kingdom, were also stunned by the revolution in military affairs displayed in the Persian Gulf in 1991. Britain, for example, was chagrined by a high shootdown rate for Tornado GR.1 fighters by Iraqi SAMs and triple-A. The high rate of attrition for those planes was later explainable through their being used in extremely low-level bombing missions—Tornados were well suited to airfield area denial operations because they carried bomblet dispensers such as the MW-1 and JP.233; in the course of these runway cratering missions they were more heavily exposed to enemy fire than U.S. warplanes.

Nevertheless, Britain, too, got a wake-up call concerning the value of stealth aircraft as a result of these and other experiences in the Persian Gulf. Within covert organs of Her Majesty's government, secret plans had long been afoot to develop an indigenous stealth aircraft. In the inner circles of the British Ministry of Defence (MOD), moreover, a great deal was known concerning the technology and operational principles of U.S. low-observable warfare.

British personnel, including RAF pilots on exchange programs, had been secretly involved in the stealth fighter programs run by the United States for a long time. Unknown to the public in both the United States and UK, a secret protocol between Ronald Reagan and Margaret Thatcher had led to a handful of key officials within the MOD gaining unprecedented access to the F-177A stealth fighter since the early 1980s.

The partnership in stealth between the two transatlantic allies dates back to the Second World War where, as we've seen, the secrets of Operation Bodyguard, including Ultra and Enigma, were shared and cooperatively developed as a secret weapon against the Third Reich. Afterward, during the Cold War, the clandestine partnership in stealth continued against the Soviets and their East Bloc allies.

The development of modern stealth as a technology to make aircraft and other weapon systems invisible to radar was a natural outgrowth of this long-standing partnership. It was also the outcome of the Anglo-American allies' acquisitions of early stealth prototypes and technical discoveries made by the Germans during the war. Much of this, and key German technical personnel, had been acquired by the United States in 1945, but not all. Britain, too, got its hands on a great deal of German stealth research product, including secret radar-absorbent materials developed by Nazi scientists during the war.

One of the most sensitive military secrets of the Cold War is that in the early 1960s the Macmillan government in the UK turned over to the Kennedy administration virtually everything that the British knew about stealth technology, and it was a considerable amount. The British didn't then have the material resources to develop this technology, but the United States, with its vast, virtually unlimited industrial capacity and bottomless money pit, very much did. The stealth relationship entered a new, clandestine phase: the UK would henceforward be an insider in U.S. stealth development.

By the time the F-117A stealth fighter was rolled out of a hangar at Nellis Air Force Base in Nevada for its first public showing on April 21, 1990, ending speculation concerning the existence of a secret invisible warplane developed by the United States, British RAF pilots had been training on the F-117A for at least a year, indeed since the earliest prototypes were available for flight trials in 1982. Beyond this, the F-117A was evaluated for possible purchase by the RAF but turned down by MOD; at 10 Downing Street there were other plans concerning future acquisitions of stealth aircraft.

The UK had built its own warplanes for generations. It would do the same thing with stealth aircraft.

## THE FOAS PROJECT

If you travel the roads in the vicinity of the British Northwest Midlands, you'll pass picturesque cottages adorned with the gracefully sloping roofs of the thatcher's traditional art. If you're like me, you'll stop at one of the many country inns along the way for a ploughman's lunch and a pint of bitters before going on. At some point in your peregrinations, you'll also hear the unforgettable scream of RAF jets speeding past only a few score feet above your head. The UK uses the Northwest Midlands as the site of secret military proving grounds, much like the United States does with its Nevada desert, and as with the United States, Britain, too, has its own equivalent of places like Area 51.

At Warton, Lancashire, amid a fenced-off section of the rolling countryside patrolled by armed troops and attack dogs, there is a secret projects facility. It has been in existence by this point for well over a decade. It is a black research facility devoted to the development of an advanced British stealth aircraft scheduled to be rolled out by 2020, some 10 years after the UK is slated to receive the first of its Joint Strike Fighters from the United States. This aircraft will complement the F-35s the way U.S. stealth aircraft have complemented less stealthy planes in air combat. It's called the Future Offensive Aircraft System or FOAS. The stealth aircraft development program is the result of the U.S.–UK stealth partnership dating back to the end of World War II, and the reason behind Britain's disinterest in acquiring the F-117A when it was given the chance.

FOAS is part of a larger British stealth warfare strategy that includes the Future Aircraft Carrier and the Future Joint Combat Aircraft (FJCA) initiatives, for which the STOVL variant of the F-35 was chosen in September 2002. FOAS doesn't pertain to a single aircraft type per se but to a family of low-observable manned and unmanned aviation strike systems that all use a single, modular set of stealth, precision strike, and information warfare elements. The FOAS Manned Aircraft is intended to be the crown jewel stealth asset of the future RAF. The Manned Aircraft is envisioned as a delta lifting body somewhat similar in shape to the canceled U.S. Navy AX project. It's to share the same innovations in stealth of next-generation U.S. stealth aircraft including visual stealth and possibly active stealth measures like those mentioned in connection with CIS projects.

Because visual stealth makes it possible for stealth aircraft to conduct deep penetration strike missions in daylight, the FOAS Manned Aircraft would be an all-weather, day-night stealth fighter plane that could fly an assortment of missions. It could penetrate deep into enemy airspace or launch a conventional air-launched cruise missile (CALCM) also under development under the FOAS umbrella. MOD has contracted with French MBDA, Lockheed Martin, and British BAE Systems to perform feasibility studies for FOAS-CALCM, such as system integration with JSTARS, military satellites, and other C⁴I platforms with which it might interact in combat. The studies are farmed out as "technology work packages" that compartmentalize development on a need-to-know basis, with the grand designs known only to British MOD.

Also integrated into the Manned Aircraft development initiative is a UAV that would be used in tandem with the aircraft to conduct remote reconnaissance or possibly, in a UCAV configuration, be deployed as a drone weapon. The FOAS UAV is also interesting from the standpoint that it harks back to earlier secret U.S. programs using drone outrider vehicles in tandem with manned aircraft, such as the SR-71/D-21 manned/unmanned vehicle combination.

This and other similar projects have long been shrouded in secrecy in the United States and it's interesting to consider that some or all of them involved clandestine UK cooperation as a possible quid-pro-quo for British data on Nazi drone projects such as those discussed earlier in this book.

# THE POSTWAR GERMAN STEALTH COVER-UP

Despite their special relationship with the United States and the long-standing and close secret cooperation in stealth development between the two countries, FOAS represents a parting of the ways in many respects. America, to the British, has always been like a best friend who can always be depended on, but who has a nasty habit of rolling up his sleeves and wading into brawls at the first opportunity. To the Americans the British have always seemed a little overcautious. This fundamental difference almost put a rift in the Anglo-American alliance in the Second World War. It's still very much in evidence today in the joint OIF operations in Iraq and in political turmoil for the Blair government in Parliament and in the press.

Beyond this, Joe America, good friend that he is, has a special toy that he wants to keep to himself. It's called stealth. He'll let the other kids on the block play with it—but they can't keep it. Tommy Brit remembers what happened to the German kid when Joe found out he had a toy that was almost like Joe's. It's not talked about much on the block called NATO, but the fact is that Joe made the German kid stop playing with it.

To stop with the dumb kid metaphors, the Germans found out in 1987 that it wasn't a very good idea to be too open about stealth research to the United States, not, anyway, if you wanted to build your own indigenous stealth aircraft. As we know, German aircraft designers stumbled onto the secret of making aircraft low-observable to radar during World War II.

The United States, Britain, and the Soviets (who apparently had made their own stealth discoveries at around the same time) ferreted out as much German stealth know-how as they could obtain. The Soviet threat changed Allied thinking about postwar Germany and the country was encouraged to reindustrialize and to build up its armed forces. Germany's military-industrial complex revived during the Cold War and its warfare technology base expanded.

Though kept out of the secret U.S.–UK postwar stealth development loop, the Germans were faced with an even greater sense of vulnerability to Soviet attack than any other European country. Reconnaissance by the Luftwaffe in the 1970s revealed that Warsaw Pact air defenses along German borders were so dense that conventional aircraft would be chewed up by SAMs if the Luftwaffe ever had to fight the Hot War in Europe. The sobering news was that conventional aircraft wouldn't stand a snowball's chance of getting through the interlocking SAM belts that stood between them and their targets.

The Germans, having discovered stealth, now independently began development of a stealth fighter of their own, without the knowledge of their chief ally, the United States. With the deliberate aim of building a plane that could penetrate Warsaw Pact air defenses, they set about putting a jet fighter into production that was low-observable to radar and other forms of electronic detection.

To achieve their goal they turned to the equations of James Clerk Maxwell, whose nineteenth century computations formed the basis of many subsequent advancements in electronics, including radar. The Germans surmised that if Maxwell's principles were able to demonstrate how to devise radar systems, then they could also be used to find ways to defeat it. The result was the prototype of a stealth aircraft years before the United States had announced that it had built one.

## THE LAMPYRIDAE

This aircraft was known as the Lampyridae, or Firefly, medium-range missile fighter. The Lampyridae project had been ongoing since 1981 by the Luftwaffe under conditions of the strictest possible secrecy. At a classified facility at the Messerschmitt-Bolkow-Blohm (MBB) plant at Ottobrunn in the heart of Bavaria, the Firefly project had been taking shape for close to a decade.

Completely on their own, the Germans had succeeded in discovering the main secret of form stealth. The concept demonstrator they had built revealed an aerodynamic shaping approach that used the faceting on the airframe to deflect oncoming radar signals upward and away from the aircraft. This, and the use of radar-absorbent materials in construction for the Firefly, was virtually the identical approach used in the design of the F-117A that was proceeding along a parallel track in the United States.

In 1987, a year prior to the revelation that the United States had built a stealth fighter, a USAF delegation on a fact-finding mission to Germany was ushered into a secret, curtained-off corner of MBB's Bavarian aerospace development complex. There the blue-suiters got the shock of their careers. Luftwaffe officials and MBB executives drew back the curtain to reveal a prototype so similar to America's best-kept secret, the F-117A Nighthawk, that it almost appeared to be its twin.

As the final surprise they also learned that unlike the U.S. stealth fighter, which was a fighter in name only, being developed as a subsonic ultra-light bomber whose main protection lay in its low-observable attributes, the Lampyridae was to be a true supersonic fighter plane. Although nothing has been confirmed, it is widely believed that on learning of the Firefly's existence, Washington put severe pressure on Bonn to shut the program down.

More than mere jealousy of its lead in stealth technology was behind the hammer-blow from the highest levels of U.S. government that fell on Bonn. Even at the birth of the stealth era, the United States knew that the early faceted stealth designs were an interim development only. In stealth technology it's axiomatic that "seeing a little is learning a lot."

This is why to this day most information concerning stealth is actually disinformation and why photographs of even supposedly "obsolescent" stealth planes like the F-117A are carefully screened to show the aircraft from certain angles only. Back in 1987, before the unveiling of the F-117A, the prospect of a stealth demonstrator in which all the important features of secret stealth research were exposed to plain view gave personnel on the fourth floor of the Pentagon's E-Ring instant cases of heartburn (possibly one reason why ice cream is said to be the most popular food at the Building). Bonn was told to squash the Firefly or else, and it complied, fearing the loss of vital U.S. economic aid if it didn't.

The British haven't forgotten what happened to Germany in the 1980s, and while they have been in the stealth development loop with their American cousins, they've elected to keep certain aspects of their stealth programs to themselves. Because the Brits are very good at keeping secrets it's possible that FOAS stealth projects, when revealed, will hold some surprises for allies and adversaries alike.

## EUROPE'S THIRD STEALTH POWER

The French are conscious of having been the dominant military power on the continent for quite a long time. Whether or not it was Gallic pride that underlay their refusal to join the NATO alliance, the French have often been a close working partner to NATO but never a participating member. Not only were the French never in the U.S. stealth development loop as were the British, but the ancient rivalry between the two cross-Channel neighbors has resulted in an icy curtain of secrecy being drawn between Paris and London as well, at least as far as stealth goes.

With the development of the Rafale, the French have fielded an advanced multirole strike fighter with a very small radar cross-section. Built of composite, radar-absorbent materials that make up approximately 50 percent of the aircraft's gross weight, the Rafale is considered to be only 30 percent less stealthy than the F-22 Raptor fighter aircraft built by the United States.

Although the "D" in the Rafale D air force version of the French plane does in fact stand for *Discret*, the French term for stealth, the Rafale can't be considered a true stealth warplane. The Rafale is a highly maneuverable air-dominance fighter that is a peer competitor with other first-line aircraft in its class, but not a stealth aircraft per se. The French are aware of this, and they, too, have plans to develop an indigenously produced next-generation stealth fighter aircraft.

It's known that despite major cutbacks in funding for new aircraft projects in recent years that Rafale design teams have been kept in place, working on new computer modeling studies, including simulations using stealth software similar to Lockheed's MM3D development program. The French MOD has established high-tech research and development facilities at Dassault, France's principal aerospace defense contractor, whose aim appears to be the development of next-generation stealth aircraft.

It's apparent that the French teams are making use of rapid computer prototyping to leverage modern computer-aided design and computer-aided manufacturing technology. This would enable them to build an aircraft concept demonstrator in a much shorter span of time than was previously possible for earlier stealth warplane development teams in the

United States. Whether they succeed or not, and how soon, are the main questions.

## THE FUTURE OF EUROPEAN STEALTH

The F-35 Joint Strike Fighter will probably be the stealthiest plane in the inventories of many if not all European nations until 2020 at the earliest. The Eurofighter Typhoon multirole fighter, an advanced long-range fighter aircraft that is now in full production, will also be a primary European fighter aircraft. The Typhoon is considered by aviation experts to be the most advanced fighter now in production, with the possible exception of the U.S.-produced F-22.

The Eurofighter (formerly known as the EFA 2000) program was begun in 1983 under joint agreement between France, Germany, Italy, Spain, and the UK to develop a common air superiority fighter for the twenty-first century. France left the consortium in the early 1990s, having decided to acquire the Rafale instead. The Eurofighter that entered service in 2002 was built by the consortium made up of British Aerospace, the German DASA, Spanish CASA, and Italian Alenia aerospace firms. Nevertheless, although the Eurofighter has been designed to have a very small radar cross section and other low-observable features, the single fact that, like Rafale, it does not carry its weapons internally alone disqualifies it as a true stealth aircraft.

As to true European stealth programs, as we've just noted, some details of the UK's FOAS project are known, and educated guesses can be made concerning French stealth aircraft programs as well. It's also believed that German stealth development continued even after the abrupt cancellation of the Lampyridae project in 1987, with DASA (Daimler-Chrysler Aerospace), Germany's principle aerospace contractor, developing a new stealth prototype called TDEFS, which stood for technology demonstrator for enhancement of future systems. Like Firefly, TDEFS also collapsed, ostensibly because of lack of funding and lack of European co-sponsors such as those that backed development of the EFA.

In the near term, the output of European stealth design teams will probably be channeled into many of the same types of military systems that the Russians are currently building, such as low-observable cruise missiles and counterstealth radars. This is a troubling development to U.S. warplanners.

Like the CIS, European countries will want to fund their long-range stealth development programs by sales of smaller, more easily manufactured stealth weapons to still smaller states that cannot indigenously build their own systems. These shrink-wrapped stealth missiles and turnkey radar systems could have a serious impact on U.S. stealth, especially if they were made available to terrorists. Stealth proliferation might well be on the brink of becoming one of the prime threats to global peace in the twenty-first century.

# CHAPTER 27

# STEALTH PROLIFERATION

Stealth has been a virtual United States monopoly for at least 15 years, dating from the Pentagon's official revelations about the existence of the stealth fighter in 1988. The Gulf War proved that stealth worked. Moreover, that stealth was central to a revolution in military affairs that had practically overnight had a profound transformational effect on twenty-first–century warfare. While there have been many pivotal battles throughout history, there are correspondingly few where a key technological innovation has had as profound an effect as stealth did in the Gulf War in 1991.

The Roman orator Cicero once declared that "Endless money is the sinews of war." Stealth development cost untold billions of dollars, a considerable portion in black defense spending whose specific dollar amounts might never be known. The justification for these vast expenditures on stealth development was that stealth, combined with precision weaponry and advanced battle-field information operations, could shorten the length of wars, limit their intensity, and greatly reduce friendly casualties.

Among the lessons learned from the Gulf War was that stealth delivered as promised. Nonetheless, certain caveats go with this declaration. Cicero's remark can stand as a case in point. He was, after all, addressing the fondness of another great military civilization for using technological innovations to do exactly what

America's breakthroughs in applied military science have accomplished in more recent times. The Romans too spared no expense when it came to developing war machinery to win their battles. Their siege engines were feared throughout the ancient world. They, too, prized enemy scientists and would try to recruit them whenever possible. After the Romans captured Syracuse, in Sicily, after an eight-month siege in 212 B.C.E., the Greek mathematician and military inventor Archimedes was sought by Rome for this very purpose.

Rome conquered the ancient world using superior technology and advanced battle tactics. Yet Rome's enemies could and did study its methods, ultimately using them against the Romans. The Carthaginian warlord Hannibal was one of these. Carefully studying the methods of the Romans, he devised clever countermeasures to Roman tactics. In other cases Hannibal duplicated Roman innovations, matching or exceeding his enemies' achievements. Before the Punic Wars ended Hannibal had brought Rome to its knees by such tactics and had come within an ace of defeating it.

This is what's today called a blowback effect. Innovations— technological, tactical, or any other—can be and often are appropriated by the opposition and turned against their originators or inventors. In fact, battlefield innovations—let's just call them secret weapons—have rarely remained any one side's intellectual property for very long. After a period of monopoly by the victor they tend to begin to proliferate. This happened with tanks after World War I and with nuclear weapons after World War II, to cite but two examples.

As we've seen, the same is happening today with stealth. National armies around the world have been scrambling to modernize their forces after the Gulf War. Recognizing stealth as critical to the success of such transformation efforts, they have striven to acquire it by any means fair or foul.

Although no other nation besides the United States has the "endless money" to forge the sinews of a modern stealth warfare capability matching America's, many do have resources sufficient to fund less-ambitious indigenous programs or buy stealth weaponry from outside suppliers.

Then, too, secrets stolen through espionage and reverse-engineering can open up a fast track to stealth development. Industry can also be a source of stealth technology as commercial applications of stealth become marketed in the private sector, often by defense contractors who have developed stealth weaponry for the Defense Department, European ministries of defense, or other similar government agencies. (An interesting example is Germany's Fraunhofer Institute which, to all us Napsterites, is known as the originator of the MP3 music algorithm, but is also a well-known manufacturer of military robotics.)

The upshot is that stealth technology, like any other kind of technical knowledge, begins to slowly filter out of classified research labs and closely-guarded aircraft hangars despite efforts to stop, control, or limit its spread.

The position of officialdom is pretty much the same as Cicero's: We'll always manage to stay several steps ahead of the opposition; the cost will be high but it's worth it. Stealth is a kind of insurance policy against defeat on the battlefield and attack at home. It's like what insurers call a "Cadillac" policy, which is one that comes with all the trimmings. If you want the best insurance protection, you need to buy our stealth policy, even if it pinches the pocket a little.

Yet it sometimes becomes hard to determine where arms control ends and spin control takes over. How much stealth expertise can the United States feel comfortable with in the hands of potential adversaries in war, such as China? How much stealth expertise is enough to warrant concern when it's being used to develop weapons by a would-be peer competitor such as the CIS? How much stealth weaponry can Washington even justify being found in the arsenals of U.S. allies? What can be done to contain the spread of stealth? And how long before stealth blowback sets in and formerly secret American stealth technology is turned against its originator?

## STEALTH BLOWBACK

As long as stealth remains a U.S. monopoly it leverages the American high-tech edge and helps make the United States a military juggernaut. But as stealth technology leaks out, like sand through the halves of an hourglass, the balance of power could begin to shift. A little stealth can go a long way as a tool of asymmetric warfare.

This may be precisely what we'll have to contend with in future conflicts. The Gulf era model was that of a coalition led by a stealth-enabled America pitting silver bullet forces against nonstealthy opponents. But stealth proliferation has already reached a point where this scenario may no longer be applicable in the next war.

Painfully aware that big-ticket stealth hardware like the F-117A, B-2 bomber, or F-22 is far beyond their reach, and that their political alignments exclude them from purchasing U.S.-made stealth weaponry, such as the F-35 Joint Strike Fighter, nations on the out-list have devoted their resources to building or acquiring missiles, radars, and other means of detecting and killing stealth-based weapon systems. Stealth-on-stealth warfare is likely to be an unpleasant aspect of the next major regional conflict in which the United States is engaged.

The downing of a stealth fighter over Yugoslavia in 1999 presented a chilling specter of the kind of damage that antagonists equipped with methods of detecting, tracking, and targeting stealth aircraft might do to stealth forces. Fortunately, even given the possibility that some form of counterstealth detection was responsible for the shootdown, such a capability is in itself not sufficient to cripple friendly stealth assets.

Missions that stealth aircraft undertake are carefully planned to minimize risk to the warplanes and maximize the potential for destruction of enemy forces and infrastructure. Prior to the mission, other weapons, stealthy and conventional, will have destroyed enemy radars and blasted SAM sites. ECM aircraft such as Rivet Joint will have gathered intelligence concerning the types of electronic detection systems that enemy defenses along the projected track of the sortie are likely to have deployed.

Other aircraft may prepare the mission area with offensive ECM, chaff clouds, or other measures designed to blind or spoof enemy radar, acoustic, or other battlefield sensors. A counterstealth radar network could be of use against U.S. stealth warplanes only if it were functional, but the odds are that it would have been destroyed well before stealth planes passed over its area of coverage.

A far greater stealth-on-stealth risk is posed to low-observable war-planes by stealth-seeking SAMs. If sufficiently advanced, well-enough concealed to evade detection, or mounted on mobile platforms for fast getaways after firing, SAMs with stealth-detecting radar could present a significant threat to coalition aircraft. Apparently the Defense Department believes this to be the case.

As we've already noted, the Pentagon recently purchased an advanced, not-for-export, ZRK version of the Russian S-300 (SA-10 Grumble) SAM system for analysis to determine the risk it posed to U.S. stealth aircraft, and that the ZRK's stealth-seeking attributes were developed partly on the basis of Russian analysis of captured F-117A wreckage bought from the Serbs in 1999. Although the MPU version of the missile system isn't as sophisticated, it's nevertheless marketed as a stealth-seeking SAM, and future export upgrades of this and other Russian SAMs will feature enhanced capabilities for detecting stealth aircraft.

Stealth aircraft also run the risk of being shot down by nonstealthy warplanes, given that these have the assistance of advanced early warning systems. Here too, affordable third-party technology, resistant to disori-enting strikes intended to clear the way for stealth planes to follow-on, can downgrade the effectiveness of low-observable silver bullet forces.

Such an early warning system is marketed by Israel Aircraft Industries (IAI) as Phalcon. Phalcon is an advanced AWACS system that uses an active phased array radar mounted in large rectangular apertures on the sides of a modified Boeing 707 and inside the bulbous radome projecting from below the cockpit windows that gives the plane the appearance of some bizarre winged clown when viewed frontally. Phalcon, which made its first appearance at the 1993 Paris Air Show, has been billed as the most advanced airborne early warning, command and control system in the world.

One of Phalcon's most innovative features is counterstealth-detection capability. Indigenous versions of Phalcon are said to incorporate radar technology capable of detecting and tracking even conventionally low-observable aircraft. It's unclear how much stealth recognition technology is available in export versions of the system, such as the one later sold to Chile and flown as "Condor."

What is known is that since 1998 various agreements of cooperation between Israeli, U.S., and European defense contractors have resulted in marketing AWACS based on Phalcon on a worldwide basis. U.S. involvement has meant that the Defense Department has been able to keep a close eye on who gets how much Phalcon technology and to what uses they put it. In October 2003, for example, the United States backed down on its prior approval of the sale of a Phalcon system to India after Pakistan, another regional ally, protested, citing that the sale would "destabilize the existing strategic balance with far-reaching security implications for the region."

Regardless of who does or doesn't get Phalcon in the near-term, the point is that Phalcon or AWACS systems like it could prove very unhealthy for stealth aircraft entering future aerial war zones. For one thing, an AWACS, unlike a ground-based radar, has an extremely large coverage envelope, hundreds of miles on the average. It can therefore detect, with the right radar set, the approach of stealth attack planes from a long way off and guide enemy interceptors to within visual range where the stealth attributes of friendly aircraft wouldn't conceal them. It could also be useful in coordinating SAM defenses equipped with counterstealth, such as the S-300, that might otherwise become targets of interdiction strikes in the initial phases of the air war.

The main threat to AWACS would be from stealthy, long-range cruise missiles, such as AMRAAM, that could be launched at it from large stand-off ranges and blow it out of the sky before it could detect friendly inbound aircraft and direct planes, SAMs, or other weapons toward their positions. China, in fact, has developed a cruise missile system that is designed primarily to do exactly this to U.S. AWACS aircraft, intending to use it in the event of war in the Straits of Taiwan.

# OTHER CONSEQUENCES OF STEALTH PROLIFERATION

There are other scenarios where stealth blowback caused by the proliferation of stealth technology could pose the threat of regional and even global destabilization. Neither the United States nor its allies would necessarily have to be directly involved for this to happen, in fact. Local regional conflicts with one or both sides using stealth weaponry could produce extremely destabilizing conditions.

Regional disputes could be intensified by stealth because stealth enhances the lethality of conventional warfare and greases the slide toward escalation of the conflict. Once the conflict escalates it can become a vortex that draws bystanders in toward the center. The former bystanders, who are inevitably bigger powers, would then take sides and fight with one another. If all or most were stealth-capable, stealth-on-stealth warfare could produce a stalemate that might progress to the use of weapons of mass destruction as the conflict worsened.

During the Cold War, the dynamic of conventional nuclear deterrence ensured that the penalty for starting large-scale nuclear conflict proved too high for either side to make the first move. But the dynamic has broken down. Today low-yield, low-radiation nuclear weapons that are stealthy, agile, and precision-targetable are available to the United States and CIS for tactical battlefield use. The availability of such weapons of mass destruction could more easily result in miscalculations with devastating consequences than past generations of tactical nuclear weapons.

Similar miscalculations have happened before, leading to global disaster. In World War I, generals on both sides were equally convinced that they alone held the edge in raw artillery power, considered the decisive battlefield enabler of the day. This blunder resulted in stalemate that was only broken when one side introduced yet a newer and more destructive technology, the modern tank, that proved decisive in winning the war. In the meantime a war whose level of destruction was many orders of magnitude higher than anything in history that had preceded it raged on for years.

A modern scenario involving Azerbaijan as a flashpoint for East-West confrontation could be triggered by a web of international treaties between neighboring small states, such as Bulgaria and Armenia, and larger powers, such as the United States and Russia, as well as European nations, such as France and Britain. Azerbaijan lies athwart an underground ocean of petroleum reserves beneath the Caspian Sea. As this is written, a pipeline is being constructed by an international consortium including the United States. Until now, Russia has held a monopoly on oil exports from the region. The pipeline, known as the Baku-Tbilisi-Ceyhan

(BTC) pipeline, would skirt Russian territory and thus bypass Russian control. The Russians are concerned and Bulgaria and Armenia, Azerbaijan's neighbors, have expressed territorial claims on those same oil reserves.

By providing an alternative energy source to Saudi Arabia, the BTC pipeline would also permit the United States to disengage itself from dependence on OPEC crude within the next two decades. It could also turn the Transcaucasus region, in which Azerbaijan is located, into a global tinderbox should anything happen that might prevent or restrict the flow of essential petroleum to the energy-hungry industry and populace of the United States.

Even without the direct involvement of major powers in a regional conflict, larger circles of destabilization could balloon outward in the event that one or both combatants were equipped for stealth warfare, and, worse yet, if even one of them were also equipped with nuclear weapons. Such a scenario looms in the form of a third Egypt-Israeli war, or fifth Arab-Israeli conflict, which the presence of Syria alone would make it.

Within a decade of the Camp David Accords that resulted in the 1979 peace treaty between Egypt and Israel, tensions, and the buildup of forces for war, have steadily increased. Should Israel again find itself facing numerically superior forces on multiple fronts, it will surely attempt to leverage its high-technology advantages to the maximum in order to prevail.

Along with stealth and counterstealth, Israel's undeclared nuclear weapons arsenal would likely figure into the outcome of the battle. Egyptian plans would potentially call for a preemptive strike on this nuclear capability early on to prevent its use. Unfortunately such an action might in itself trigger a stealthy nuclear strike by Israel against Egypt. Stealth, coupled with mobility and precision engagement, might result in a dangerous escalation of this regional conflict to the nuclear level before the United States, patron of both countries, could intervene.

## LIVING IN STEALTH MODE

I've left out the danger posed by terrorists and other nonstate actors getting their hands on stealth weaponry, such as low-observable cruise missiles, and using these against the United States or other targets of their pseudo-holy ire. I've done so in part because September 11, 2001, made the consequences of this scenario all too painfully clear. Given the fact that crashing two commercial jetliners into the World Trade Center towers on the morning of a business day and careening a third plane into the Pentagon could certainly qualify as a form of stealth warfare, I think I'd be covering ground that's far too familiar to us all.

According to the FBI, at least one new plot to use a surface-to-air missile to shoot down an airliner has already been discovered and stopped. Suffice it to say that international terrorism will be as intent on acquiring the means of waging asymmetric stealth warfare as any nation-state, and may present challenges far more difficult to meet than anything we've previously had to face.

Beyond this, stealth blowback has already begun to affect us on many day-to-day levels of which most of us may not even be aware. The radar detector unobtrusively clipped behind your car's sun visor, the software you've installed to prevent unauthorized parties—often your boss—from monitoring your Internet usage and e-mail, and the efforts of hackers (and your boss) to penetrate your computer's defenses, even the pocket lie detector that may soon be part of your cell phone's list of fun features, are all aspects of an increasing stealth mode in which we're living.

As time passes, stealth technologies continue to filter down to street level, and social conventions change as a consequence, our lives are almost destined to be lived increasingly in stealth mode. As with other aspects concerning stealth warfare, having stealth on your side is great if the other guy doesn't have the same, but it can become problematic once stealth blowback sets in. At that point stealth can potentially change from an asset into a liability ... before you even see it coming.

# MAKING STEALTH VISIBLE

I believe stealth will have a profound influence on society in years to come. As has been the case with other technological innovations in the past, including those originally developed for military purposes, stealth technology has already begun to find its way into everyday affairs. The full ramifications of stealth proliferation can't yet be predicted, but it's certain to have as transformational an impact on civilian life as it has had on military affairs. I hope the explanation of stealth I've presented in the *Alpha Bravo Delta Guide to Stealth Warfare* will help make stealth high-observable to all readers, regardless of their level of technical knowledge, walk of life, or prior familiarity with the subject.

I've tried throughout to avoid a breathless, gee-whiz approach to the narrative. One of my hardest tasks in writing this book has been to translate technical and insider jargon into plain English and simple terms that hopefully anyone can understand.

Because defense initiatives change all the time, I've also tried wherever possible to discuss ongoing trends instead of specific programs, and to focus on the essentials of how these relate to the overall picture of stealth warfare. I've also tried to keep the narrative balanced and unbiased.

I believe stealth warfare is becoming a part of everyone's lives, but few realize it yet. Hopefully this book will raise readers' awareness concerning what's taking place. Hopefully it will help change stealth from an abstraction into a concrete set of facts and realities—put it on your radar screen, so to speak.

If you're reading that stealthy blip a little clearer now, my mission is accomplished.

# SELECTED GLOSSARY OF TERMS

**advanced tactical fighters (ATF)**   Refers to a new generation of fighter planes that is currently being built and fielded by several nations, including the United States. All these planes share certain common design features, especially the requirement that they can fly at supersonic speeds in "dry" mode, that is, without going to afterburner. Advanced avionics (aviation electronics) or control interfaces between pilot and plane, such as head-mounted displays (HMD), are also integral to the ATF concept.

**air dominance fighters**   Fighter planes such as the F-22 that are designed to completely sweep the skies of enemy aircraft. Air superiority fighters, such as the F-16, are intended to suppress enemy aircraft activity but also perform a number of other roles, including tactical bombing.

***The Arthashastra***   An ancient textbook for the warrior, written by Kautilya, a prime minister under Emperor Chandragupta Maurya of India. Kautilya, who claimed that a ruler should use any means to win and that his actions required no moral sanction, wrote about how troops could become invisible, endow themselves with night vision by special dietary and yogic practices, and fight without eating for an entire month.

**ASDIC**   Early sonar (derived from Anti-submarine Detection and Investigation Committee). Once U-boats were located by ASDIC they could be damaged or sunk by depth charges or, if found on or brought to the surface, could be attacked by deck guns or even rammed.

**Aurora Project**   Believed to be a classified program to develop high-altitude transonic stealth aircraft. It is believed that the project had already built manned and unmanned space-capable planes capable of flying at better than Mach 5 by the early 1990s.

**AX**   The Navy's A-12 AX program was intended to produce a strike-attack aircraft to replace the aging F-111 swing-wing fighter. The General Dynamics/Lockheed design team that set to work on the project produced a technology demonstrator mock-up of the aircraft prior to the axing of AX in 1994. The mock-up is an all-delta wing shaped aircraft with a bubble cockpit and single-pilot cabin with conformal bays for weapons carriage. The asymmetric air-scoops, engine nacelles buried deep in the fuselage, blended control surfaces, pointed nose, and groove channels on the upper wing surface to deflect and diffuse radar energies point to an extremely stealthy aircraft design.

**Blumlein modulator**   A device that, among other things, helped produce a sharp, clear image on a radar scope at closer ranges than ever before. Developed in WWII by the British it was a vast improvement over the "smeller" technique previously used in aerial night-fighting.

**the Bomb**   Otherwise known as the Turing Engine or Turing Universal Machine, it was the key to continuous decipherment of Enigma transmissions throughout the Second World War. Without the Bomb there would have been no Ultra. The Turing Engine was a machine specifically built to duplicate the performance of the thousands of Enigma machines that would come into being during the war. *See* Enigma.

**boomer**   Nuclear-powered ballistic missile submarines (SSBN) are called "boomers." They're called this for good reason, but it has nothing to do with the sound they make as they ply the ocean's depths. On the contrary, silence is the watchword when it comes to submarines of all types today, be they boomers, attack subs, or non-nuclear diesel-electric boats. (Submarines are always called "boats," never ships, by the way). The term "boomer" refers to the effects of the nuclear missiles carried by the boats—their thermonuclear concussions, up to 5,000 miles from the point of launch, would produce some pretty loud booms indeed.

**C⁴I for the warrior (C⁴IFTW)**   A set of technologies intended to afford the dismounted infantry soldier with a command, control, communications, computing, and intelligence (C⁴I) "cocoon" that will enhance his ability to understand the combat environment, aim and fire his weapons, and communicate with both forces in the immediate zone of operations and distant command centers behind the front lines. C⁴IFTW technologies may combine to produce the "supertrooper" of twenty-first–century land warfare.

**CAPTOR mines**   Submarine-deployed deep water mines that drop to the bottom as soon as they exit the mother sub's torpedo tube. Instead of exploding when the proper conditions for activation are met, CAPTOR mines launch a Mark 46 torpedo at the target that homes in using active sonar. Since the distance between them is very small, by the time the sub's crew hears the telltale ping of the incoming torpedo's sonar, they're already candidates for free harp lessons.

**cell-phone radar**   A passive radar technology that uses the discovery, credited to the Czechs, that the same ground-based network of cellular repeaters used to retransmit third-generation (3G) cellular phone signals across a network can also detect the presence of stealth aircraft.

**Chain Home (CH) radars**   What are today known as low-pulse repetition frequency or PRF radars, a form of pulse-Doppler radar. Developed by the British early in World War II, these radars worked by transmitting short pulses of high-frequency radio energy at a suspected target, a quadrant of the sky, or another area in which targets might be expected to be found.

**CORONA**   Code name for the first U.S. spy satellite, whose superior overhead imaging spelled the end of the early U-2 surveillance overflights of sensitive Soviet territory. In February 1959, Ike told the CIA that U-2 flights should be "held to a minimum pending the availability of this new equipment," anticipating satellite intel that was finally available in August 1960.

**Daventry Experiment** Proved that an aircraft could be detected by a radio device, leading to a crash program in England to develop radar that could be used militarily.

**DD(X) multimission destroyer** Previously known as the DD-21 Zumwalt-class land-attack vessel—the first of a family of stealthy surface vessels designed for littoral warfare by the U.S. Navy that is to include the CG (X) cruiser and the smaller LCS. The DD(X) is to replace Oliver Hazard Perry class frigates (FFG 7) and Spruance class destroyers (DD 963) starting in 2012. The stealth ship's main mission would be to provide land attack support for ground forces and also carry out traditional destroyer missions of antiair, antisurface, and undersea warfare.

**digital battlefield** A concept relying on advanced digital information networks to rapidly bring "sensor-to-shooter" data to military forces as the shape of the battle develops. It is related to the concept of the combined arms battlefield, in which joint interaction between air, sea, and ground forces enables a multilayered, multidimensional approach to waging war.

**Doodlebug** Nickname for the Nazi V-1 "buzz bomb," an early un-manned aerial vehicle that reached its targets by means of preprogrammed guidance systems, and then nose-dived to deliver its high-explosive war-head to ground targets. It's reported that Hitler was intent on building up a strike force of 50,000 V-1s to be launched against England.

**Dramatic Developments in Eastern Europe (DDEE)** Refers to an otherwise hard-to-name period roughly between the fall of the Berlin Wall and the KFOR campaign in Yugoslavia.

**Enigma** A cipher machine developed in Germany in the early years of the Nazi regime and intended to be an absolutely secure encipherment system. The Nazis believed that it was impenetrable right to the end. It might have been all the Germans thought it to be, had the British not acquired an Enigma through covert channels a few years before war was declared. *See also* Ultra.

**fifth dimension of warfare** Vision statements by the three U.S. service arms refer to those intangibles such as operations in the electromagnetic realm that are critical to the prosecution of war.

**Future Offensive Aircraft System (FOAS)** Part of a larger British stealth warfare strategy that includes the Future Aircraft Carrier and the

Future Joint Combat Aircraft (FJCA) initiatives, for which the STOVL variant of the F-35 was chosen in September 2002. FOAS doesn't pertain to a single aircraft type per se but to a family of low-observable manned and unmanned aviation strike systems that all use a single, modular set of stealth, precision strike, and information warfare elements.

**Future Strike Aircraft (FSA)**   In the FSA concept, announced in 1999, the U.S. Air Force wants to build "stealthy, supersonic strike aircraft designed to penetrate heavily defended airspace in the initial phase of a conflict and deliver precision-guided munitions on time-sensitive and other high-value targets." Obviously low-observable characteristics, multimach velocities, and high maneuverability will be among the qualities necessary for such aircraft.

**Hannibal**   Considered the founding father of stealth warfare by many military historians. In the third century B.C.E. Hannibal effectively used deception tactics to shred a much larger and far better equipped Roman army at a decisive battle at Lake Trasimenus.

**Horton wings**   The HO series of advanced aircraft based on so-called "flying wing" design leading to the Horton Ho IX prototype of a fast, stealthy, long-range bomber intended to carry a nuclear weapon. It's rumored that members of Lockheed's Skunk Works studied an HO housed at the Smithsonian during the development of the F-117A stealth fighter.

**Huff-Duff**   High-frequency direction finders, a portable and highly accurate radio direction finder system that was secretly placed aboard the combat vessels that escorted the merchant ships in transatlantic supply convoys beginning in the summer of 1942.

**Kettering Bug**   A World War I biplane with a 12-foot wingspan powered by a 40-horsepower Ford engine, the Kettering Bug could carry a bomb load equivalent to its own 300-pound weight and drop it on distant targets by means of fold-up wings that sent the Bug into a vertical dive at a remote radio signal. Launched from a wheeled trolley, cheap to manufacture at around $400 each, hard to hit by the enemy in the trenches, the Bug was ordered in large quantities in the waning months of the Great War. The Armistice came before the first Bugs reached the front, though, and all but a few production models were produced before the project was canceled shortly thereafter.

**Lampyridae (Firefly)**   A secret stealth prototype independently built by the Luftwaffe in the 1980s. It was intended to serve as a medium-range missile fighter. The Lampyridae project had been ongoing since 1981 by the Luftwaffe under conditions of the strictest possible secrecy. At a classified facility at the Messerschmitt-Bolkow-Blohm (MBB) plant at Ottobrunn in the heart of Bavaria, the Firefly project had been taking shape for close to a decade. The project was reputedly killed under pressure from Washington, as the United States was developing its F-117A stealth fighter at the same time.

**low-observable (LO) technology**   Otherwise known as stealth, it is a combination of methods designed to defeat radar identification of combat aircraft by reducing that aircraft's RCS or radar cross section.

**low probability of intercept (LPI) radar**   Long range yet extremely hard to detect and jam. Advanced stealth aircraft such as the F-22 Raptor are equipped with this type of stealthy radar.

**magneto-hydrodynamic propulsion system (MHD)**   Designed to augment or replace the nuclear engine in submarines for spurts of ultrasilent running or during emergencies. An MHD system produces a powerful magnetic field in an outer sleeve containing a liquid electrolyte, which encircles an inner propulsion tube, causing the sleeve to pulsate. The pulsations make the inner tube undulate, drawing seawater in through the front and expelling it from the rear in a jet powerful enough to propel a submarine through the sea.

**MALD**   Miniature air-launched decoy. MALDs would be carried onboard fighter and other aircraft and released when enemy radars threatened to acquire friendly aircraft as targets. The MALDs would then use their onboard computer systems to jam and spoof the radars, creating false echoes and other effects, while the actual plane executed high-speed evasive maneuvers.

*Maskirovka*   All-encompassing Russian term for stealth and deception applications in military usage.

**MAVs or micro-air vehicles**   The extremely small size of MAVs will optimize them to perform military missions that larger drones could not accomplish because of stealth, maneuverability, or other issues associated with their size. Smaller than MALDs, MAVs the size of hummingbirds might be sent out to detect biochemical agents in contaminated areas, act as tiny communications satellites or radar decoys, be used as nasty little flying antipersonnel or antiarmor mines, and also fly down airshafts for peeks into buildings in urban warfare environments. Recently it was revealed that MAVs similar to dragonflies built by DARPA could not be controlled in flight; although their surveillance systems did work well, they couldn't go anywhere, and so couldn't spy on anything.

**N-EMP**   Nuclear electromagnetic pulse. A wave of high energy that affects electrical and electronic systems unless these are specially protected or hardened against the effects. Non-nuclear EMP can also be produced for offensive purposes using particle beam generators.

**New Attack Submarine (NSSN)**   Being built as a successor to the Los Angeles–class boats, as well as the three sole Seawolf (Centurion-class) submarines in service. It's to be equipped with a far more spacious and elaborate internal lock in/lock out system for swimmers. These new Virginia-class attack boats will be equipped with a range of facilities for covert and special warfare missions, including search and rescue, reconnaissance, sabotage and diversionary attacks, forward observation for fire direction, and direct strikes against enemy objectives.

**Ninjutsu**   The Japanese martial art of Ninjutsu literally means the fighting art of stealth, and the ninja warrior's mastery of his discipline is intended to enable him to move like a shadow and strike the enemy unseen.

**Operation Paperclip**   Known also by its disinformation-name, Blue Sky, was the code name U.S. intelligence used to refer to the appropriation of the former Nazi brain trust and technology by the U.S. government after World War II.

**order of battle**   Refers to the disposition of all military forces in the theater of war and defines all practical aspects of how these forces will be deployed and in what relation to one another during the course of their participation in the battle. The electronic order of battle (EOB) is the "this definition" translated to electronic warfare components of the battle-space.

**propeller cavitation**   The propensity for spinning submarine propeller blades to form bubbles at certain speeds and depths; as the bubbles pop it's as telltale a sound as seltzer fizzing in a glass to eavesdropping sonar.

**radar cross section (RCS)**   An RCS is produced whenever the beams of search radars come into contact with aerodynamic surfaces on an aircraft's body, reflect off (backscatter), and are in turn picked up by receivers located on the ground or in the air. When there is high backscatter of radar pulses, the aircraft shows up on radar scopes in high definition and is said to have a large RCS. When radar energy is absorbed and backscatter is dissipated, the RCS is correspondingly small and the plane is said to be low observable.

**radar war**   The "radar war" of World War II was fought in the realm of clandestine operations, but involved real and often bloody combat, too. It was imperative to preserve the secrecy of Allied radars and just as imperative on the part of the Axis powers to find countermeasures to them. Military operations were undertaken to attack enemy radar stations, and at least in one instance to actually steal an advanced radar set right from under the noses of the Nazis.

**Revolution in Military Affairs (RMA)**   A kind of military perestroika, a new thinking that began to take shape after the breakup of the Soviet Union changed the bipolar superpower relationships of the Cold War into the multipolar regional relationships of the New World Order. This thinking solidified into doctrine in the wake of the War in the Gulf. Prior to these revolutionary developments, a completely different set of suppositions about future war prevailed. Of more recent coinage is the term information-based RMA (info-RMA or IRMA), referring to a similar revolution in information operations as they relate to the electronic order of battle (EOB). As a December 2000 white paper by the Japan Defense Agency predicts, future warfare will be conducted by high-tech conventional attacks in concert with stealth and cyberattacks, in which the relative superiority of information awareness will give one side the decisive advantage in the battlespace.

***Rotterdamgerat* or R-gerat radar sets**   Developed by the Germans late in the war from captured British H2S radars based on the cavity magnetron. Only a few production models were in existence by the war's end.

*Schornsteinfeger*   Literally translated "chimney sweep," it was an experimental compound made up of graphite particles bonded with rubber, which when applied to the hulls of German submarines was found to substantially dissipate radar energy striking the hull and so weaken returning radar echoes.

**Senior Bowl**   Code name for a program to produce the D-21 drone by Lockheed's Skunk Works. The drones were to be piggybacked on A-12 (and later SR-71) spy planes and used as pilotless aerial reconnaissance and surveillance vehicles. Its delta-wing shape and chined fuselage incorporating blended curved surfaces gave it good low-observable characteristics from its flanks, underside, and top while the tapering nose that ended in the sharp spikes of the ramjet engine inlets made for good frontal stealth. Some reports say they were also to have carried armament. The program to fit the D-21 to spy planes was terminated after a fatal accident. Its specifics are still shrouded in secrecy.

**shaping-and-masking techniques**   One of the primary elements of a plane's stealthiness. But using shaping-and-masking approaches to stealth design places certain performance penalties on the airframe of any aircraft depending on modified aerodynamic and control surfaces to lower its observability.

**Shiva**   Ancient Hindu god whose third eye illuminated the universe. The story of Shiva can be read as a metaphor for stealth.

**Skunk Works**   Lockheed's secret research center for the development of high-concept aircraft, including the U-2, SR-71 Blackbird, and the F-117A, headed by aircraft designer Clarence "Kelly" Johnson. Ben Rich, who succeeded Johnson at the Skunk Works, wrote that "a low observable aircraft has to be good in six disciplines—radar, infrared, noise, smoke, contrails and visibility—otherwise you flunk the course." The Skunk Works is now known as Lockheed-Martin's Advanced Development Projects department (ADP).

**SLMM**   A Mark 48 torpedo modified for use as an undersea mine. It's currently the U.S. Navy's only self-propelled mine, with an electric motor giving it a range of about nine miles. It has an acoustic system to detect approaching ships and can be fitted with either a magnetic-seismic or a magnetic-seismic-pressure firing mechanism.

**Sun-tzu**   Ancient Chinese military strategist who is these days quoted by Western generals as often as they once quoted Clausewitz; he also devoted considerable philosophical bandwidth to discussing stealth warfare.

***Swartze Kapelle* or "Black Orchestra"**   The anti-Hitler underground in the German High Command which gave the British advance knowledge of the details of Hitler's war plans.

**TACIT RAINBOW**   The code name for the AGM-136 air-launched cruise missile that was developed in the early 1980s and was one of the main forerunners of the Tomahawk land attack missile that followed. TACIT RAINBOW was essentially an antiradar missile cruise capability that meant it could be fired at targets at long range. It was relatively cheap and could be produced in large numbers. The missile was intended to be fired in swarms, each vehicle's onboard guidance system having been pre-programmed to strike a designated target area. On launch, TACIT RAIN-BOW would fly a track to this designated target area and then go into loiter mode until it detected enemy radar emissions.

***Telemobilskop* or Remote Object Viewing Machine**   An early form of radar device developed at the dawn of the twentieth century by the German scientist and inventor Christian Hulsmeyer. Hulsmeyer received patents in Germany, the UK, and the United States for *Der Telemobilskop* in 1904. The device, which had a 300-meter range, was originally intended to prevent ship collisions. Like many another invention ahead of its time—including the digital computer invented by Charles Babbage in 1850—*Der Telemobilskop* was considered of no practical value and was forgotten for decades.

**TLAM**   Pronounced *tee-lam*, it stands for Tomahawk Land Attack Missile and is how the military generally refers to what the media call "Tomahawks" or "Tomahawk missiles." By any name the Tomahawk has become an icon of stealth warfare and surgically precise destruction. The Tomahawk has also gone through a series of upgrades, known as blocks, to add further improvements to the system, with Block IV Tomahawks used in the second Gulf War. The Tomahawk is not only stealthy in flight, being able to fly ground-hugging nap-of-the-earth vectors toward remote inland targets, but is also stealthy because it can be launched from stealthy weapon platforms, like submarines, which can steal up close to the shore of a target undetected, launch their missiles and quickly lose themselves under the waves right after launch. The missile is so accurate that it can strike a specific individual building—or even a particular floor of that building—after a flight of more than 1,500 miles.

**Trident submarines**   The largest and most powerful undersea warships ever built in the free world. At 560 feet and 18,750 tons, they are the nation's first line of defense. Each sub is powered by a nuclear reactor and carries 24 ballistic missiles. Trident submarines are noted for their long-range missile capability and extremely quick operations.

**Trojan Horse**   Semimythical stealth vehicle that enabled the Greeks to enter the city of Troy undetected.

**Ultra**   Code name for a form of military intelligence denoting intercepts of German (and later Japanese) coded messages encrypted on the Enigma cipher machine in WWII. *See also* Enigma.

*Vernichtungschlag*   A World War II German military term for a battle strategy geared to no less than total annihilation of the enemy.

**virtual reality (VR)**   A technology developed by the military as a command-and-control interface between the soldier-in-the-loop and increasingly sophisticated weapons systems.

**weapons of mass destruction (WMD)**   Weapons capable of maximum destruction of human lives and physical infrastructure over a wide area. Nuclear munitions, high-energy conventional munitions, and chemical-biological warfare agents are all examples of WMDs.

**Window**   The Allied code name in World War II for dipole chaff, which is tiny strips of aluminum foil or aluminized glass fiber one-half wavelength long by approximately two millimeters in diameter. These were found to be highly efficient microwave reflectors.

**zeppelin raids**   Used dirigibles heavily laden with bombs to invade the UK in an ominous prefiguring of the attacks launched by Hitler a generation later with V-1 and V-2 missiles. The Zeppelins were the perfect stealth platforms for the delivery of air-to-ground munitions—they would even be formidable today, with natural radar-scattering shapes, near-silent propeller-driven flight, and low trajectory flight paths.

# RECOMMENDED READING AND RESEARCH SOURCES

This list doesn't pretend to be inclusive, but it provides a starting point. Researching stealth requires drawing on a body of cross-discipline information. I believe the following selections reflect this fact.

## BOOKS

### Stealth and Deception:

Bamford, James. *Body of Secrets: Anatomy of the Ultra-Secret National Security Agency: From the Cold War Through the Dawn of a New Century.* New York: Doubleday, 2001.

Freedman, Maurice J. *Unravelling Enigma: Winning the Code War at Station X.* Barnsley, South Yorkshire: Leo Cooper, 2002.

Goodall, James C. *America's Stealth Fighters and Bombers.* Osceola, WI: Motorbooks International, 1992.

Hinsley, F. H., and Alan Stripp, eds. *Codebreakers: The Inside Story of Bletchley Park*. Oxford and New York: Oxford University Press, 1993.

Sontag, Sherry, Christopher Drew, and Annette Lawrence Drew. *Blind Man's Bluff: The Untold Story of American Submarine Espionage*. New York: Harper & Row, 1999.

**Military Technology:**

Drexler, K. Eric. *Nanosystems: Molecular Machinery, Manufacturing, and Computation*. New York: Wiley, 1992.

Nissen, Jack Maurice, and A. W. Cockerill. *Winning the Radar War: A Memoir*. London: Robert Hale, 1987.

Toffler, Alvin, and Heidi Toffler. *War and Anti-War: Survival at the Dawn of the 21st Century*. Boston: Little, Brown, 1993.

Zakheim, Dov S., *Flight of the Lavi: Inside a U.S-Israeli Crisis*. Washington: Brassey's, 1996.

**Military History:**

Anderson, Jon Lee, and Scott Anderson, comps. *War Zones*. New York: Dodd, Mead, 1988.

Atkinson, Rick. *Crusade: The Untold Story of the Persian Gulf War*. Boston: Houghton Mifflin, 1993.

Barnaby, Frank, ed. *Future War: Armed Conflict in the Next Decade*. New York: Facts on File, 1984.

Churchill, Winston S. *The Second World War*. Boston: Houghton Mifflin, 1951.

Friedman, George, and Meredith Friedman. *The Future of War: Power, Technology & American World Dominance in the 21st Century*. New York: Crown Publishers, 1996.

Keegan, John. *The Mask of Command*. New York: Viking, 1987.

MacArthur, John R. *Second Front: Censorship and Propaganda in the Gulf War*. New York: Hill and Wang, 1992.

O'Heffernan, Patrick, Amory B. Lovins, and L. Hunter Lovins. *The First Nuclear World War: A Strategy for Preventing Nuclear Wars and the Spread of Nuclear Weapons*. New York: Morrow, 1983.

Sciolino, Elaine. *The Outlaw State: Saddam Hussein's Quest for Power and the Gulf Crisis*. New York: Wiley, 1991.

Smith, James, ed. *Desert Storm*. New York. Time Warner Publishing, 1991.

Smith, Stanley E., ed. *The United States Navy in World War II*. New York: Ballantine, 1978.

Weinberg, Gerhard L. *A World at Arms: A Global History of World War II*. New York: Cambridge University Press, 1994.

Wheatcroft, Andrew. *The World Atlas of Revolutions*. New York: Simon and Schuster, 1983.

**Military Biography:**

De la Billiere, Peter. *Storm Command: A Personal Account of the Gulf War*. London: HarperCollins, 1992.

Eisenhower, Dwight D. *Crusade in Europe*. Garden City, NY: Doubleday, 1948.

Speer, Albert. *Inside the Third Reich*. Translated by Richard and Clara Winston. New York: Macmillan, 1970.

**Strategy and Tactics:**

Clausewitz, Carl von. *On War*. Edited and translated by Michael Howard and Peter Paret. Princeton, NJ: Princeton University Press, 1976.

Ellis, John. *Brute Force: Allied Strategy and Tactics in the Second World War.* New York: Viking, 1990.

Grove, Eric. *Fleet to Fleet Encounters: Tsushima, Jutland, Philippine Sea.* London: Arms and Armour Press, 1991.

Shaw, Robert L. *Fighter Combat: Tactics and Maneuvering.* Annapolis, MD: Naval Institute Press, 1985.

Sun-tzu: *The Art of Warfare.* Translated by Roger T. Ames. New York: Ballantine Books, 1993.

**Weapons and Soldiering:**

Eshel, David. *Elite Fighting Units.* New York: Arco Pub., 1984.

Green, William, and Gordon Swanborough. *The Complete Book of Fighters.* New York: Barnes & Noble Books, 1998.

Harris, Robert, and Jeremy Paxman. *A Higher Form of Killing.* New York: Hill and Wang, 1982.

Hogg, Ian V., and John Weeks. *Military Small Arms of the 20th Century: A Comprehensive Illustrated Encyclopedia of the World's Small-Calibre Firearms.* Northbrook, IL: DBI Books, 1998.

Pasztor, Andy. *When the Pentagon Was for Sale.* New York: Scribner.

Polmar, Norman. *The Naval Institute Guide to the Ships and Aircraft of the U.S. Fleet.* Annapolis, MD: Naval Institute Press, 1998.

Powell, Colin L. *My American Journey.* New York: Random House, 1995.

*Russia's Top Guns.* New York: Gallery Books, 1990.

Sampson, Anthony. *The Arms Bazaar: From Lebanon to Lockheed.* New York: Bantam, 1978.

Schwarzkopf, H. Norman. *It Doesn't Take a Hero: General H. Norman Schwarzkopf, the Autobiography.* New York: Bantam Books, 1992.

Waller, Douglas C. *The Commandos: The Inside Story of America's Secret Soldiers.* New York: Simon & Schuster, 1994.

**General Reference:**

Burton, Bob. *Top Secret: A Clandestine Operator's Glossary of Terms.* Boulder, CO: Paladin Press, 1986.

Dickson, Paul. *War Slang: Fighting Words and Phrases of Americans from the Civil War to the Gulf War.* New York: Pocket Books, 1994.

*International Defense Equipment Catalogue.* Bonn: Mönch, 1998.

Kayyali, Maher S. *Modern Military Dictionary.* New York: Hippocrene Books, 1991.

Semler, Eric, James Benjamin, and Adam Gross. *The Language of Nuclear War: An Intelligent Citizen's Dictionary.* New York: Perennial Library, 1987.

Smith, Perry M. *Assignment Pentagon: The Insider's Guide to the Potomac Puzzle Palace.* Washington: Pergamon-Brassey's International Defense Publishers, 1989.

# PERIODICALS

*Air Power International*
*Army Times*
*Aviation Week*
*Defense News*
*Military History*
*Military Technology*
*Modern Simulation and Training*

*Proceedings*
*Special Forces Magazine*

# WEBSITES
**Government:**
Central Intelligence Agency
www.odci.gov/cia

Israeli Foreign Ministry
www.israel-mfa.gov.il

Japan Defense Agency
www.jda.go.jp

Ministry of Defence, United Kingdom
www.mod.uk

National Security Agency
www.fas.org/irp/nsa

Russia on the Net
www.ru

U.S. Department of Defense
www.defenselink.mil

**Military:**
Air Force Association
www.afa.org

Defense Advanced Research Projects Agency (DARPA)
www.arpa.mil

The Israel Defense Forces (I.D.F.)
www.idf.il

Joint Chiefs of Staff
www.dtic.mil/jcs

Natick Soldier Center
www.natick.army.mil

NATO
www.nato.int

Naval Undersea Warfare Center
www.npt.nuwc.navy.mil

STRICOM (U.S. Army)
www.stricom.army.mil

U.S. Air Force
www.acc.af.mil

U.S. Navy
www.ncts.navy.mil

**International Defense Contractors:**
Aerospatiale
www.aerospatiale.fr

Boeing Phantom Works
www.boeing.com

British Aerospace
www.britishaerospace.com

Dassault (Groupe Dassault)
www.dassault.fr

Defense News Online
www.defensenews.com

Eurofighter
  www.eurofighter.com

Lockheed Martin Skunk Works
  www.lmco.com

Sukhoi Design Bureau
  www.sukhoi.ru

# APPENDIX C

# THE HISTORICAL EVOLUTION OF STEALTH: A SELECTED TIMELINE

**Prehuman**   Nature evolves what might be considered the oldest radar systems ever developed (and still in use today). Among these is the biological ultrasonic sensor system of the common garden-variety bat—bat-radar.

**Prehistory**   In an era of myth, the gods make war among themselves using stealth and counterstealth, illustrated by the tale of Shiva and Parvati, in which Shiva miraculously opens a third eye to detect the evil that has arisen in darkness after his all-seeing cosmic vision is blacked out.

**Thirteenth century B.C.E.**   The Biblical Gideon uses stealth warfare to destroy the Midianites. According to the Book of Judges in the Old Testament, Gideon ordered his troops to use a tactic that would be repeated by General Patton in World War II; he ordered a deception campaign to convince the enemy that he had an extra army waiting in the wings, ready to stage a flank attack when his main forces had engaged.

**Twelfth century B.C.E.** After a fruitless 10-year siege of Troy, the ancient Greeks hit upon the strategy of using stealth to conquer where force of arms had previously failed. The semimythical story of the Trojan Horse illustrates the first recorded use of a stealth weapon system as part of a tactical camouflage and deception campaign in warfare.

**Sixth century B.C.E.** Sun-tzu, the ancient Chinese "General Sun," and the Indian statesman Kautilya, lay down what may be the first recorded precepts of stealth warfare. *The Arthashastra*, a textbook for the warrior, is written by Kautilya, a prime minister under Emperor Chandragupta Maurya. Kautilya, who claimed that a ruler should use any means to win and that his actions required no moral sanction, wrote about how troops could become invisible, endow themselves with night vision by special dietary and yogic practices, and fight without eating for an entire month.

**Third century B.C.E.** Hannibal, considered the founding father of stealth warfare by many military historians, nearly vanquishes Rome after a series of decisive battles. Hannibal effectively uses deception tactics to destroy a much larger and far better equipped Roman army in a decisive battle at Lake Trasimenus.

**1571** At the Battle of Lepanto the Turks almost win a decisive sea battle for the fate of Europe by using stealthy naval tactics against Genoese admiral Andria Doria.

**1689–1783** In the New World, both the French and Indian War and the campaigns of the later Revolutionary War see the use of stealth warfare tactics, in the first instance in the fighting between continental powers and their allies in America, and later by the 13 colonies that were to become the United States to win independence from Great Britain. During the French and Indian War, early commandos called Rogers' Rangers use stealth, and Rogers' rules of irregular warfare lay down techniques of surprise and stealth in attack that form the basis of modern commando operations.

**1896** Dr. Samuel Pierpont Langley flies a pilotless, steam-powered plane across the Potomac River on an approximate one-minute flight.

**1903** Carl Jatho flies a small pilotless plane powered by a gasoline engine over a distance of 196 feet at a height of 11 feet; this is farther, faster, and earlier than the Wright brothers flew.

**1904**   German scientist and inventor Christian Hulsmeyer receives patents for inventing *Der Telemobilskop* or Remote Object Viewing Machine, an early radar set.

**1914–1918**   World War I marks the dawn of stealth warfare in its current applications to industrial warfare. Airborne photosurveillance makes deception and camouflage a necessary feature of all warfare from now on. The "Kettering Bug," a primitive UCAV, is developed toward the end of the war, though never flown in combat.

**1930**   Engineers from the U.S. Naval Research Lab stumble onto the rediscovery of radar's basic working principles during a routine test, leading to one of the most important technological developments of World War II.

**1939–1945**   World War II witnesses the birth of modern stealth warfare. Key stealth systems in use today are developed and first used in combat. These include stealth aircraft, radar, and sonar. The Chain Home (CH) radar network, the first modern radar system, is established in Britain. Hitler's invasion of Poland, which marks the commencement of war, opens with a stealth attack by commando forces at a Polish border town. The Allies' Project Option leads to the development of modern remote-piloted vehicles while German aerospace researchers develop the so-called Horton Wings, prototypes of latter-day stealth aircraft.

**1946–1960**   The early stages of the Cold War era witness the development of the precursors of modern stealth programs. These include the B-35 and B-49 "flying wing" bombers, the U-2, and the SR-71 Blackbird. Stealth technology is deemed key to surveillance and reconnaissance of Communist China and Soviet Union. In 1956, the CIA begins working with the Lockheed Skunk Works's Kelly Johnson on the aircraft that will eventually become the SR-71 Blackbird. In 1960, President Eisenhower signs an executive order for the first prototype SR-71, but later favors the CORONA program to place the first spy satellites in orbit. An undersea race between the United States and Soviet Union to develop the stealthiest and deadliest nuclear ballistic missile and attack submarines begins.

**1961–1985**   The middle to late stages of the Cold War see the further development and refinement of stealth technology. The first SR-72 Blackbirds become operational, complementing satellite intelligence with overflights. The ramjet-powered D-21 surveillance drone, one of the earliest UAVs, is developed. Projects Lighting Bug, Compass Arrow, and secret stealth research programs like Red Wagon and Lucy Lee, lead to additional stealth breakthroughs. The top secret Have Blue program begins development of the B-2 and F-117A aircraft. The undersea contest between U.S. and Soviet submarines enters its final phase as the Russians catch up with U.S. undersea silencing technology. Simultaneous with Western aerospace stealth research, Russia conducts indigenous stealth research and development.

**1988**  Both the F-117A Stealth Fighter and the B-2 Stealth Bomber are officially revealed to the public. During an action in the Gulf, two Iraqi Exocet missiles strike the USS *Stark* broadside, underscoring the vulnerability to stealthy cruise missiles of large naval vessels.

**1989**  With the fall of the Berlin Wall and the subsequent breakup of the Soviet Union, the DDEE era begins. If anything, the end of the Cold War has sped up the pace of Russia and other nations to develop stealth designs and counter those of the United States. The SR-71 Blackbird is retired (though not permanently). The F-117A stealth fighter flies its maiden mission in Panama.

**1990**  The U.S. Advanced Tactical Fighter (ATF) project commences, producing true stealth fighter plane prototypes that will eventually lead to the production of the F-22 Raptor.

**1991**  Stealth warfare inaugurates coalition attacks that commence the first Gulf War. F-117A Nighthawks prove that stealth works by penetrating central Baghdad's air defense network, including heavy SAM defenses, to stage surgical strikes on priority targets.

**1993**  The U.S. Navy's advanced stealth fighter program, the A-12 AX, is canceled, to be replaced by the Super Hornet as an interim stealth aircraft until the projected delivery of the F-35 circa 2010.

**1996**  The Darkstar UAV, officially known as Tier III Minus, is test-flown at Edwards Air Force Base in Northern California. The maiden flight signals the start of a new era in stealthy unmanned aerial vehicles.

**1998**   Joint U.S.-UK air and missile strikes against Iraq during Operation Desert Fox betoken an effort to destroy Saddam Hussein's nascent counterstealth network.

**1999**   An F-117A Nighthawk is downed over Bosnia under circumstances never fully explained. Theories persist that it was brought down by a crude but effective counterstealth system used by the Serbs, and that the remnants of the Nighthawk's airframe were salvaged and sold to Russia, where they were studied for reverse-engineering efforts in Russia's program to develop stealth aircraft of its own for national use and export.

**2000**   The Pentagon's Land Warrior 2000, the British MOD's Infantryman 2000, the French ECAD, and the NATO-sponsored CRISAT, begin the incorporation of stealth features previously used in aerospace development with the dismounted infantry soldier.

**2001**   Stealth morphing, a technology pioneered by NASA for advanced aircraft, is announced. The USAF Space Operations Directorate announces the creation of new units, the 76th Space Control Squadron and the 527th Space Aggressor Squadron. These harbinger an era of stealth operations in space in the next two decades.

**2002**   JASSM, an advanced stealth-enabled cruise missile, enters its final preproduction phase. The United States acquires a sample of a high-tech Russian counterstealth missile, the S-300 ZRK SAM system said to be able to accurately track and kill stealthy aircraft. Boeing unveils the ultrasecret Bird of Prey aircraft project. New coalition strikes on Iraq may further target Saddam's efforts to install a counterstealth radar system. In Russia, Sukhoi is selected as the prime contractor for the future PAK FA stealth fighter program.

**2003–2004**   India and China lead developing nations in securing advanced stealth technology for their militaries. India conducts military studies into the ancient writings of Kautilya toward developing twenty-first–century technologies based thereon. The second war in Iraq opens with a "shock and awe" campaign heavily dependent on stealth warfare. India receives its first Russian-built Talwar stealth frigate. The Future Strike Aircraft (FSA) proposal is announced. The U.S. Defense Transformation for the 21st Century Act mandates development of new stealth technologies for the U.S. military. Phase 1 contractors are selected for the

FALCON (Force Application and Launch from the Continental United States) long-range strike-reconnaissance aircraft program.

**2010–2020**   The Joint Strike Fighter will enter international service. Stealthy tactical mobile robots (TMRs) will increasingly conduct high-risk and high-priority missions. The U.S. infantry conducts operations as a twenty-first–century Objective Force, enabled by stealth and digital information networks. The Future Attack Submarine (FSSN) stealthily prowls the undersea depths. The United States and UK both field advanced stealth aircraft carriers to replace today's nuclear carriers, which have become obsolete and increasingly vulnerable to assault by stealth weaponry.

**2020–2030**   By about 2020 the first-line long-range strike and recce aircraft in today's U.S. fleet, such as the B-1, B-2, and F-117, will have reached the ends of their active service lives. The Future Strike Aircraft (FSA), a next generation subsonic, supersonic, and hypersonic strike-reconnaissance aircraft with global range, is to replace these. In land warfare operations, the stealthy hypertank, armed with hyperkinetic weapons, replaces today's main battle tanks, which have become obsolete.

**2030 and beyond**   Anybody's guess.

# APPENDIX D

# STEALTH FIGHTER DOWN

The 1999 downing of an F-117A over Yugoslavia presented some unique insights into the technical specifications and operational aspects of stealth aircraft. Stealth operations usually take place amid an information blackout that rivals the secrecy of military operations in the field, and so many of the remarks by the Pentagon were unprecedented because of the glimpses into the inner secrets of stealth that they offered to public scrutiny. Below are some of the unclassified documents in which stealth was discussed, both in general terms and in relation to the shoot down. The first is a prepared statement to the press by Maj. Gen. Bruce Carlson, USAF, on the incident over Bojanovici, Yugoslavia. Although the prepared statement included three slides, which we were not able to reproduce here, the presentation is illuminating. It's followed by a spirited, often candid, and occasionally humorous question-and-answer session with the press. All documents are courtesy of the U.S. Department of Defense, which is solely responsible for their content.

# DOD NEWS BRIEFING

**Tuesday, April 20, 1999**
**Presenter:** Maj. Gen. Bruce Carlson, USAF, Director of Operational Requirements
**Subject: Stealth Fighters**

Maj. Gen. Carlson: I understand there's been some interest in the loss of the F-117 that we've had in the area of operations and some interest in the capabilities of our stealth airplanes, the F-117 and the B-2. And some interest in general in employment concepts that we use for those airplanes. I'd be glad to talk about those. I've got about three slides here to run over with you.

The F-117 and the B-2 are still being employed and will be for some time to come. And because of operational security and the safety of our air crews, I won't discuss specific operational details or tactics or targets. But I'd like to spend just a couple of minutes with you and talk about stealth airplanes.

We started out a long time ago building airplanes that had low observable technology incorporated into their design. The SR-71 was an example of where we took the aerodynamic design and then added some radar absorbing material to the airplane to make it slightly stealthy. And I'll give you a representation of that graphically here in a minute. We went to the second generation of airplanes and you can see we designed that airplane, the F-117, essentially from the bottom up to be stealthy. It was crude technology. It was developed at a time when we didn't have the modeling and computer power we needed to make the kind of aerodynamic design that we would have liked, but we built one that we thought was very stealthy. And of course, the night that Desert Storm opened the quote from Col. Al Whitley still is famous in the Air Force: "Boy, I hope this stuff really works." And of course, you know that it did. That isn't exactly what he said.

Then we came to the third generation of stealth airplanes. We built the B-2. And of course, by that time, we had the modeling tools and the design tools and the computing power to make an aerodynamic design that was optimum. And this airplane is [a] much higher altitude, much better performing airplane than the F-117. We were able to eliminate a lot of the radar absorbing material from the structure. And by the time we got to the fourth generation, we were able to add supersonic speed, the agility of an F-15, F-16 class airplane and do that with no degradation to the stealth. In addition to that, we were able to add a number of apertures, in other words, openings in the airplane's surface for antennas, radars and other sensors. And in the F-22, as an example, there are over a hundred of those apertures on the airplane, where if we jump back a couple of generations to the F-117, there are essentially a couple of aperture openings and the rest of them we hide when we go into combat.

This next chart gives you a summary of the kind of capabilities that we expect from our airplanes. Now, if you were doing vision and each one of these diagrams a surface-to-air missile or a radar at the very center, and in this case, one sitting on the top of a hill given the perfect view of the area around it, that would be considered its envelope of operation, its lethal range if it were a surface-to-air missile. When we take a conventional airplane and run it at that surface-to-air missile an infinite number of times, we develop a pattern of its susceptibility to that radar or that surface-to-air missile. And so you see, because of the shape of the airplane and the radar interface with the airplane, that's the sort of pattern that we come up to.

Now, in our first generation stealth airplanes, we focused the low observable technology in the front quarter at certain frequencies on the radar spectrum, mostly in what we call the target tracking or X-band area. That's the area that SAMs normally do their target tracking in on airplanes like a MiG-29 or an F-15 have their air-to-air radar in. So that's where we focused our work. And you can see there's a slight degradation in the capability of that SAM as that airplane is coming toward it. You notice, however, in the back, it's about the same area. Now, when we get to an airplane such as the F-117 or B-2 where we design it from the bottom up and use shaping optimally to lower its signature, we get a significantly reduced signature. It's not invisible. It never has been invisible. We know radars that can track our stealthy airplanes. They can sometimes find us. The key is that that zone of detectability or lethality is shrunk by orders of magnitude, but it's still not invisible.

Now, what does all that lead to? Our goal is that on the first day, we can, because we've shrunk those zones of lethality, find our way into the target area using good, detailed mission planning without being susceptible to either enemy radars or their missiles or their airplanes.

So that's sort of my story. And I'd be glad to answer any questions that you might have.

**Q:** General, could I ask, number one, have you determined whether or not the F-117 was shot down? Number two, there was some talk about Yugoslavia shipping parts from the F-117 back to Russia to study. Are you worried about losing what amounts to 20-year-old technology there? And if so, why didn't you bomb the wreckage to pieces so they couldn't use it?

**A:** I think you had four questions there. I'll try to answer them in order. First, we have lost about seven F-117s over the course of the program, which is about 18 years. We consider this essentially the seventh loss. We have an investigation. We have completed the first phase of that investigation. The second phase is ongoing. We have not determined the cause of that loss. We have eliminated an act of God and loss of consciousness by the pilot, but we haven't determined the cause of that loss. So we are fairly confident that in this case, we do know what happened, but because of the fact that this is an ongoing operation and we do have these young men flying into harm's way each night, I don't think it would be appropriate for me to talk about the results of that investigation any further.

Now, I think your second question was if they shipped the parts to Russia, would that concern us. Sure, it concerns us. We don't like to give anything away. I think we're just as protective of our technological advances as anyone is. However, if you go back to that first slide, that was what we called second generation stealth. And we've put a lot of distance between second generation and the airplanes that we're building now. We think that the result of that material, should it have gone to Russian hands—and you'll have to ask Gen. Wald about that. I'm not sure what operations went on over there at that time. But if it went over there, we think that the loss is minimal.

And then third, why didn't we bomb it. This was one of the last sorties of the evening for the F-117s. It fell in a—the airplane was lost and crashed in a rather remote location. It takes time to find those things. And I'm not sure that the commander in the field felt it was worth the risk to go in there and try to bomb it. But again, that's probably a question for Gen. Wald.

**Q:** General, I'm confused by the answer to that first question. Are you saying you don't know if it was shot down, or are you saying that you're not prepared to tell us for security reasons if it was shot down?

**A:** What I am prepared to tell you is that we are fairly confident we know what happened that caused the loss of this airplane. But because of the fact that this is an ongoing operation—I'm concerned about the safety of the air crews—I'm not prepared to divulge it.

**Q:** Now, for the B-2, it has a small signature, but it has a signature. Now, in Kosovo and in Serbia, do the Serbians have the capability of tracking by radar the B-2? And a second question I was kind of curious about, all these planes are putting out heat and quite a bit of heat. Can they be tracked by infrared?

**A:** In answer to your first question, can the F-117 or B-2 be tracked by radar, the answer to that question is yes. All vehicles can be tracked by radar. However, the key here is to know when you're being tracked by radar, what radars are tracking you and what the fidelity of that track is. For instance, a very low frequency radar has very little ability whether it's tracking a conventional, first-generation or a third-generation stealth airplane, has very little capability to track it with precision. They know the general area that the airplane may be in, but they can't track it with precision needed to guide either another airplane to it or a SAM to it. So what you need then is the target-tracking radars, the higher frequency radars that are much more accurate, and that's where the stealth airplanes that are designed from the bottom up have their significant advantages.

Now, in terms of infrared signature, certainly they give out heat. We have minimized the signature, the infrared signature on both the F-117 and the B-2, so it's significantly less than, for instance, an F-16, which has a round tail pipe that sticks out the end. Each of the exhausts has been designed to minimize that signature. We fly them at altitudes and in conditions at night where infrared tracking has very, very remote chances of detecting them.

**Q:** General, how would you assess the performance of the B-2 in these operations?

**A:** I think the B-2 is performing superbly, but probably that's a question for Gen. Wald.

**Q:** General, can we just ask you about the—to what extent—I mean, you talked about any compromise in stealth technology being minimal, but to what to extent and what value is there, can any of these things be reverse engineered or are there still parts of this that are secret that could help countries, whether it's Russia or any other country, develop their own stealth technology? Or can they learn anything about it from the wreckage of the plane that helps them defeat stealth technology?

**A:** As I said, we don't like to give anything away. We think that the damage, if parts of the airplane made it Russia, is minimal. I would just tell you this: The science involved with making an airplane low observable is not a secret. It involves shaping and radar absorbing material. The technology needed to make radar-absorbing material is available in a number of places. However, the manufacturing capability and the art of putting one of these airplanes together demands exceptionally close tolerances and highly skilled people. It has been our experience from looking at the other airplanes that we've seen developed and produced and fielded throughout the world that we are probably the only ones right now that can field this kind of technology.

**Q:** Just to follow up, Russia recently, I believe it was either earlier this year, maybe it was late last year, unveiled a plane that they said was a prototype of a stealth aircraft. Later, many aviation experts said in fact it wasn't a stealthy aircraft at all. Does Russia have any (inaudible) capability and was this fighter plane that they unveiled, in fact, any kind of stealth aircraft?

**A:** Well, I'm not an aviation expert. I'm just a fighter pilot. I haven't seen the airplane. I've seen pictures of it, and it certainly doesn't look like a stealth airplane to me.

**Q:** General, why isn't the B-2 forward deployed? Is it a question of maintenance, fragility? And doesn't that cut down on its combat role?

**A:** I don't know specifically why the CINC has decided to keep the B-2 here and staged out of the United States. I know that we have flown a significant number of sorties, and the airplane has done very well. You'll have to ask Gen. Wald if he has a comment on that.

**Q:** General, on the 117, have you been able to rule out the possibility that the VJ forces received advance information about that aircraft's flight?

**A:** I don't think I should comment on any of that.

**Q:** General, where does the B-1 fall in this category? Is it a second generation or first?

**A:** The B-1 would be a first generation airplane.

**Q:** General, in a briefing about 10 years ago on stealth, we just want to see if it's still relevant to Kosovo and other Soviet designed defenses. The rationale was that with stealth, by the time air defense station number one spotted you, he didn't have the computerized air defenses so that he could warn station number two to zero in on the airplane as it penetrated. In other words, the penetration ability of stealth was especially advantageous because the Soviet-made air defenses didn't have the computerized technology they needed to zero in on you right after you went from station one to station two to station three. Is that still the case, or is the Soviet-made equipment in Kosovo and other places since been computerized, they got rid of the vacuum tubes and therefore, that penetration advantage is no longer relevant?

**A:** Well, I'm not specifically familiar with what kind of equipment that they've upgraded in Kosovo or the FRY. But I do know that they are very capable. They are highly trained. They work very hard. They're highly motivated. So they present a very credible threat.

**Q:** General, in a place like Kosovo where we understand SAMs are being moved around quite a lot, do you ever get the kind of battlefield awareness that I think was on an earlier slide you showed us where the pilot would know exactly how to maneuver around the sites and have some assurance that he wasn't being tracked? And if you don't have that, are these folks flying with Prowlers or F-16 CJs to keep them safe?

**A:** We routinely package these airplanes with the suppression of enemy air defenses, both in terms of electronics and kinetic. In other words, we have HARM shooters, people that shoot high-speed, anti-radiation missiles. We also employ a number of intelligence assets in the field in the air to make sure they have the situation awareness they need prior to executing into the target area. So we keep them as aware as we possibly can.

**Q:** General, I understand that you're not going to explain what brought down the F-117 that was lost, but you did rule out a couple of general things, act of God, loss of consciousness by the pilot. Can you tell us whether this was not a result, for instance, of mechanical malfunction or some accidental factor, but, however, it was brought down was part of the hostile environment it was flying in?

**A:** We haven't ruled out some mechanical, some particular mechanical things, but the investigation is still ongoing, so I don't think I should comment any more.

**Q:** Last year, it was reported that Iraq was covertly trying to purchase an electronic warfare system from the Czechs called Tamara. Apparently, this thing has a way of triangulating, and it's reputed to be able to detect stealth aircraft. Are you concerned that Serbs may have some of this equipment, or do you see this as a future potential for neutralizing the benefits of stealth aircraft?

**A:** First, in particular comment to your question about that specific equipment, I'm not aware that the Yugoslavians have that particular set of equipment. Second, I'm not aware that the Czechs have been able to demonstrate that theory. And third, as I've stated before, airplanes, whether they're first, second, third or fourth, can be tracked, can be detected. The question is with what specificity and to how much detail you can track them and whether you can maintain the track. So, certainly, if someone after 20 years of us having stealth is able to invent something that would degrade in any way, and we're concerned about it, and we keep our eye on those things. But I'm not concerned that that's going to change the direction we're moving.

**Q:** Do you have any operational sensitivity—do you not anticipate that when—will you ever tell us as long as this conflict is going on what happened to that F-117 or will you wait until after the operation?

**A:** I would imagine that we'll wait until our kids are out of harm's way. And then if we think that there's an operational advantage to not telling you, we probably won't tell you.

**Q:** One of the curious things about the loss of this aircraft, assuming that there's a high probability that it might have been shot down in some ways, why in this whole conflict with thousands of sorties, the only plane that apparently has been brought down is the stealthy F-117, which in theory, should be one of the hardest planes to bring down? Any thoughts on why that could be the case? Why hasn't any other plane been shot down?

**A:** Well, if we determine that it was shot down, we'll work that question awful hard. As I've said, we've lost seven airplanes in the past out of our fleet of—I think we built 64 of them. And we're concerned about all those losses. We've taken steps in each case to investigate those losses in a great deal of detail. And in those cases, in the past, we've made changes to the design, changes to the cockpit, changes in training. And we will continue to do that with this loss.

**Q:** Just to clarify, all the previous losses you're talking about were accidents, is that correct?

**A:** Yes.

**Q:** (Inaudible) you say changes have been made. Without compromising security, can you say anything about any operational changes that have made regarding the F-117 to prevent this from happening again?

**A:** For the accidents in the past?

**Q:** No, this one, during this operation.

**A:** No, I won't say anything about operational changes we've made.

**Q:** Excuse me, General, you did say that some particular mechanical things, you haven't ruled out some particular mechanical things. Have you ruled out whether it might be the type of accident that occurred at the air show with the parts just started coming off the plane, and it went into an uncontrolled spin? The Baltimore air show, have you ruled that out?

**A:** No, we haven't ruled that out.

**Q:** General, sir, you mentioned that the point of stealth is to make it less observable to X-band, but it could still be visible or detectable on low frequency radars. Is this the case where you ran into multiple low frequency radars, and they were able to get a reasonable fix on it? Is that what happened?

**A:** I don't think I should comment on that. I kind of stated that up front.

**Q:** Yes, sir.

**Q:** To what degree are radar absorbent materials used on the F-22, and are they of similar sorts that were used on the F-117?

**A:** Just by way of comparison, the F-117 is completely covered with radar-absorbing material, and this airplane has a very small percentage of its surface covered with radar-absorbing materials. And the materials are, if these are second generation, then these are fourth and fifth generation. In fact, as we are developing the airplane, we have made changes in the materials themselves, mostly due to reliability and maintainability considerations. We just want to make this as easy to maintain as an F-15 or F-16 is on the flight line.

**Q:** General, we were told during—that some aspects of the F-117's flight such as when the [bomb-bay] doors are open or when it's engaged in a banking maneuver or something, that its radar signature might be a little greater. Could you just explain why that is and how that works?

**A:** Sure. I've flown the airplane before quite a bit. Let me just first say that when the doors open, there's no doubt in your mind they're open. They're about twice as big as that door that you see coming in the room over there, and there are two of them. So if you're at .85 Mach and the doors open, it gets your attention right away. When they close, there's no doubt in your mind that they've closed. In addition to that, there's a series of indications within the cockpit that tell you that. Now, just as we designed the airplane to its shape to reflect radar energy away from the receiving antenna, as soon as you put out a couple of big, flat plates that are twice the size of that door, you invent instantly a radar reflector. So that explains, I think, how come the signature increases. What we've done after we begin to fly the airplane operationally is significantly decrease the time that it takes for the door to open, the bomb to come off and the door to close so that that time is very, very small now.

**Q:** How is the B-2 holding up? Most of us were with you August a year and a half ago watched you give it a bath. And I know that you have improved the coating on it. What has this operation taught you? What has it shown you about the maintainability of the B-2?

**A:** The B-2 continues to improve in its maintainability. In fact, two of them landed the other day at Whiteman in the driving rain, and they had flown 30 hours. And the LO [low observable] maintenance was essentially routine. In other words, there were no major LO write-ups or no hits on the airplane that would have kept it from flying immediately thereafter. So we think we're turning the corner on low observable maintenance on the B-2. And I think it has great potential in the future. It's doing superbly over there now.

**Q:** Thank you.

The Defense Department's press agency also commented on the shoot down. Presented below are two press releases concerning the event.

# STEALTH FIGHTER DOWN IN YUGOSLAVIA, PILOT RESCUED

**By Linda D. Kozaryn**

**American Forces Press Service**

WASHINGTON—A U.S. F-117 Stealth fighter went down outside of Belgrade, Yugoslavia, March 27. A U.S. combat search and rescue team picked up the pilot several hours after the crash, and all returned safely to an undisclosed allied base.

"We do not know what caused this plane to crash," spokesman Ken Bacon said at the Pentagon shortly after the rescue was announced. "That's one of the things we'll learn as we interview the pilot and we talk to the people who flew the mission with him."

The Stealth fighter was reported missing at about 3 P.M. EST, Bacon said. "From that time until the moment we learned the pilot was safe and out of Yugoslav air space, we have concentrated on nothing but rescuing that pilot," he said.

Saluting the pilot's bravery and the rescue team's heroism, Bacon said, "they performed in a way that should make all Americans proud." He said the Stealth fighter has successfully flown hundreds of missions over Iraq and Yugoslavia through dense air defenses. "It will continue to be a mainline plane in this operation," he said.

# APPENDIX D: STEALTH FIGHTER DOWN

Yugoslav officials claimed Serb air defenses shot down the Stealth fighter and Serb television aired video of the burning wreckage. The video was then rebroadcast on CNN. Bacon stressed that it was premature to make any judgment on why the plane crashed until NATO officials had talked to the pilot and others on the mission.

Bacon denied Yugoslav claims that they have shot down several other NATO aircraft since Operation Allied Force began March 24. "We have no other confirmation of missing aircraft," he said. NATO aircraft, on the other hand, have shot down a total of five Yugoslav fighters, he confirmed.

Bacon refrained from providing further details on the loss of the Stealth fighter or the rescue effort. "This is a perilous environment. The Serbs have a robust air defense system. ... There may well be other times when we have to rescue pilots and the less said about our techniques for rescuing pilots, the better for the safety of the pilots."

Bacon stressed that the crash would not affect NATO's continuing air operations. "Nothing that happened today over Yugoslavia has dampened our resolve to see this operation through to its military ends," he said.

"We are undeterred by this," Bacon added. "We knew we were flying into a risky environment, and we will continue to fly in a way that minimizes the risk to our pilots while increasing our ability to perform our mission."

Bacon noted that earlier in the day, NATO Secretary General Javier Solana had announced that NATO was moving into phase two of the operation. NATO forces primarily targeted Yugoslav air defenses during phase one. In phase, two NATO is expanding the target list to focus more on the Yugoslav army and special police forces now operating in Kosovo.

NATO air power can seriously degrade the Yugoslavia's military infrastructure and diminish Yugoslav army and special police forces, Bacon said. "We will turn increasingly to dealing with forces in the field and the infrastructure necessary to support them."

NATO's goal is to diminish Yugoslav President Slobodan Milosevic's ability to continue "his murderous ways in Kosovo," Bacon said. "Those ways are continuing today. In fact, they've been intensifying, and we will intensify our efforts to stop that."

# STEALTH PILOT OK, NATO MISSION INTENSIFIES

**By Linda D. Kozaryn**

**American Forces Press Service**

WASHINGTON—The American Stealth fighter pilot shot down over Yugoslavia is in good shape and in safe hands, NATO officials announced March 28.

He is "actively engaged in working through the events of last night and otherwise continuing his military duties," said SHAPE spokesman British Royal Air Force Air Commodore David Wilby. Wilby, along with NATO spokesman Jamie Shea, addressed reporters in Brussels the morning after the March 27 crash, but provided no further details on why the F-117 Stealth fighter went down.

A U.S. search and rescue team picked up the pilot several hours after the F-117 went down outside Belgrade. Shortly after the rescue, the White House released a statement saying President Clinton was pleased that the pilot was safe. "I'm tremendously proud of the skill and bravery of the pilot and of the courageous individuals who participated in this operation," the president said.

Wilby noted that the "complex, courageous and extremely professionally-orchestrated rescue serves as a wonderful example of our united capabilities. To effect such a swift rescue, deep in hostile territory, was something of which we are all justly proud."

In the opening phase of Allied Force, aimed primarily at Yugoslavia's integrated air defense system, NATO air forces conducted more than 400 sorties. During the first two night attacks, allied troops in the air and at sea struck 90 targets throughout Yugoslavia and in Kosovo. On day three, a 2,000-pound, sea-launched cruise missile struck Yugoslavia during daylight, and NATO aircraft flew 249 sorties throughout the night, attacking military targets in Belgrade suburbs and elsewhere.

More than 60 allied planes flew more than 250 sorties the fourth night. Wilby confirmed that, despite Yugoslav claims to the contrary, no other NATO aircraft or crews have been lost since the strikes first began March 24. NATO forces, on the other hand, have shot down a total of five aircraft, a third of Yugoslavia's "top of the line fighters," according to Pentagon spokesman Ken Bacon.

## APPENDIX D:  STEALTH FIGHTER DOWN

Two U.S. F-15s shot down two MiG-29s and a Dutch F-16 shot down a third over Yugoslavia March 24, during the first wave of air attacks aimed at ending the Kosovo crisis.

Two U.S. F-15C fighters shot down two MiG-29s over Bosnia at about 11:35 EST, March 26. NATO AWACs detected the Yugoslav fighters heading into Bosnia and U.S. aircraft patrolling as part of Operation Deny Flight shot down the intruders about five miles inside Bosnia. The fate of the MiG pilots was unknown.

The Yugoslav flights over Bosnia represented a serious challenge, Bacon said. "We don't know why they were flying into Bosnia," he said. "We can only speculate at this stage. One possible reason could be to attack SFOR forces in Bosnia." Although MiG fighters are primarily intended for air-to-air combat, he said, they do have a ground attack role. "We don't know what ordnance they were carrying. When we learn that, we may be able to deduce more about their mission."

American troops in Bosnia have taken measures to improve security in light of the on-going NATO air campaign, Bacon said. "Our troops have now returned to wearing body armor all the time," he said. "We have been aware for some time of the possibility that our troops might be attacked."

The day after the Stealth crash, Wilby repeat that NATO forces are dealing with strong Yugoslav air defense system. "Some people talk of a 'David and Goliath' fight," he said. "I can assure you it's not that case. We are up against a very hostile, very well trained, sophisticated environment.... We have, however, done much to degrade the system."

In the coming days, Wilby said, NATO will take advantage of its high-tech equipment and every other means available "to make sure that when we go in for an attack it is as safe as possible for our air crews." Adverse weather forecast for the next few days will not disrupt NATO air strikes, Wilby added. "We are well prepared to attack in bad weather," he said. "We have contingency plans. Please don't think that bad weather is going to be President Milosevic's friend."

Poor weather conditions did force some NATO aircraft to return to base March 26 without launching munitions, however. The next morning, Shea explained that NATO pilots will abort their mission, if necessary, to avoid endangering innocent civilians. "If bad weather means the pilots cannot be certain of hitting the target with accuracy, thereby avoiding collateral damage, then the pilots are instructed not even to attempt to do so," he said.

Following the Stealth crash, both spokesmen stressed that the NATO's resolve and determination to end the Kosovo crisis remains high. NATO authorities are intensifying the mission as human distress and hardship within Kosovo escalates. British officials have announced they will add more aircraft to the NATO air campaign. Details on Britain's contribution and that of any other allied nations would be available the next day, Wilby said.

The alliance is adapting "extremely well" to the changing situation on the ground, Wilby noted. "There are tremendous contingency plans going on, a tremendous amount of innovative thought," he said. "We will use all the technology and the experience at our hands to make sure we adapt well to the situation that we find ourselves in."

The air campaign is now moving into its second phase, aimed at cracking down on the Yugoslav tanks, artillery, and units in the field responsible for the suffering, Shea said. "They will feel the heat as quickly as we can apply it to them, believe me."

The NATO spokesman said the situation in Kosovo is now one of "organized anarchy," and human disaster is imminent. NATO initiated air strikes when it did, he said, because the they saw this 'scorched earth' policy getting underway."

Instead of attacking Kosovo Liberation Army elements, Serb forces are now systematically burning villages, looting property, separating families and committing "wanton acts of killing," Shea said. The "truly horrible" situation now unfolding, Shea said resembles the mass ethnic cleansing that occurred in Bosnia in 1992.

NATO strikes did not cause this systematic, pre-planned violence, Shea repeatedly stressed. It began even as peace talks were underway in France, and "has been rising up to a crescendo ever since." There is now a race against time to save as many lives as possible, Shea admitted. He strongly advised Yugoslav commanders and others involved in the offensive military action to take heed. Eventually, they would be held accountable; they will not be able to escape with impunity.

Nearly a half million people are reported to have been displaced by the Kosovo violence. International news sources note that refugees now leaving Kosovo are mainly women and children. The whereabouts of Kosovar Albanian men is unknown.

# INDEX